Collecting Old Books

This edition is dedicated to Judy Rich Lauder, Librarian and Book Collector.

Collecting Old Books

Percy Fitzgerald's
The Book Fancier

Edited and introduced by
Daniel Gutierrez

WESTPHALIA PRESS
An imprint of Policy Studies Organization

Collecting Old Books:
Percy Fitzgerald's
The Book Fancier

Westphalia Press
An imprint of Policy Studies Organization
dgutierrezs@ipsonet.org

For information:
Westphalia Press
1527 New Hampshire Ave., N.W.
Washington, D.C. 20036

ISBN-13: 978-0944285992
ISBN-10: 0944285996

Updated material and comments on this
edition can be found at the Policy Studies
Organization website:
http://www.ipsonet.org/

INTRODUCTION TO THE
NEW EDITION

PERCY Hetherington Fitzgerald (1834-1925) attended the Roman Catholic public school, Stonyhurst and Trinity College, Dublin, and became a crown prosecutor in Ireland. But he was influenced by meeting a bevy of writers, including Charles Dickens in 1856. Fitzgerald recalled that, "I was plodding on contentedly at the Bar without getting 'no forrarder,' with slender meagre prospects, but with a hankering after 'writing,' when I came to read [Forster's] *Life of Goldsmith* ... which filled me with admiration. The author was at the moment gathering materials for his *Life of Swift*, when it occurred to me that I might be useful to him in getting up all the local Swiftian relics, traditions, etc. I set to work, obtained them, made the sketches, and sent them to him in a batch. He was

E

supremely grateful, and never forgot the volunteered trifling service. To it I owe a host of literary friends and acquaintance with the 'great guns,' Dickens, Carlyle, and the rest; and when I ventured to try my prentice pen, it was Forster who took personal charge of the venture." (See Percy Hetherington. *John Forster, 1812-1876*, Chapman & Hall, London, 1903.) He was also a sculptor and executed statues of James Boswell in Lichfield and Dr. Johnson in the Strand. The bust of Dickens in the Pump Room at Bath is by him. Besides all that, he was the drama critic for the *Sunday Observer,* and wrote books on the theatre, including one on the operas of Gilbert and Sullivan. Unsurprisingly, he was a dedicated book collector, amassing a huge collection and prowling antiquarian shops. That enthusiasm shines on the pages of what is one of the most entertaining books handed down to us form the Victorian age about the challenges of being a bibliophile.

Daniel Gutierrez

F

THE BOOK FANCIER

OR THE

Romance of Book Collecting

BY

PERCY FITZGERALD

LONDON

SAMPSON LOW, MARSTON, SEARLE, & RIVINGTON

CROWN BUILDINGS, 188 FLEET STREET

1887

TO

GEORGE AUGUSTUS SALA,

CRITIC AND CONNOISSEUR,

𝕿𝖍𝖎𝖘 𝖁𝖔𝖑𝖚𝖒𝖊,

ON A

SUBJECT CONGENIAL TO HIS TASTES,

IS

INSCRIBED BY HIS FRIEND

THE AUTHOR.

PREFACE.

WITHIN the last few years there has been a revival
of the old and elegant taste of the book-fancier,
as well as of that passion or faith which is
described with such amiable enthusiasm in the
little tract of the worthy Bishop Richard of Bury.
The history and pedigree of books, of printers, &c.,
has always been a favourite study with the learned,
attested by the profound and scholarly treatises of
the Panzers, Hains, De Bures, Brunets, and our
own Lowndes. But this subject has its popular
graces also, and there is a sort of romantic interest
attached to all that is associated with books—the
rare old edition, the old printer, the blear-eyed
collector, the binder, the sale, and the stray survivor of a whole edition, by some miracle preserved
to our time. These topics seemed to kindle such
writers as the late Dr. Hill Burton—perhaps the
first in our time to deal popularly with such
matters; Mr. Andrew Lang being the latest to
illustrate this subject from his abundant stores

of knowledge. Having from the earliest date had a taste for this fascinating pursuit—and when a boy I formed a very respectable collection of Elzevirs, and looked on auction days as festivals— I have ventured to add my contribution to the rest. This little volume will be found to contain many curious and interesting things not readily accessible, and deals in some fashion with almost everything that is connected with "book." Due allowance must be made for the enthusiasm of the collector, who from the days of the excellent Dr. Frognall Dibdin has been good-naturedly allowed ever to see gold and silver and jewels in his mouldy treasures.

For some curious information concerning book-binding I am indebted to the papers of the late Mr. Sanders of Oxford. Other obligations I have acknowledged in the notes.

ATHENÆUM CLUB,
September 1886.

CONTENTS.

THE BOOK FANCIER.

—◆—

§ Of Book Collectors and Book Dealers.

MY darling books ! " exclaims an enthu-
siastic collector, Silvestre de Sacy ;
" a day will come when you will be
laid out on the saleroom table, and
others will buy and possess you —
persons, perhaps, less worthy of you than your old
master.   Yet how dear to me are they all ! for have
I not chosen them one by one, gathered them in
with the sweat of my brow ?   I do love you all !   It
seems as if, by long and sweet companionship, you
had become part of myself.   But in this world
nothing is secure."

Some such pang or foreboding as this has often
wrung the collector's heart as he surveys his treasures
ranged within their glass-bound tenements ; for he
knows that, whatever securities he may contrive, their
dispersion is almost inevitable.   The more precious
the collection, the more certain the temptation ; and

A

there is even a grim legend of one library carried to the saleroom, "by order of the relatives," on the very day after the interment of the owner. Yet here there is a righteous Nemesis; for too often, indeed, the "hobby" has been ridden at the sacrifice of family comforts, and even family embarrassment,— hence the pressing temptation to recover what is thought to have been unrighteously abstracted. Yet a cloud of pleasant romantic associations still envelops the amiable collector, often a man of simple manners and tastes, whose holiday is a prowl among the "old bookshops," and whose triumph is his return home with some mouldy but precious little duodecimo. He will exhibit to you with trembling glee his *Elzevir Rabelais*, secured out of a book-box at the door, "all at a shilling," or his rare *Jenson* in folio, purchased from a "country dealer" for the vast price of £10, but which "he knows is worth five times the money,"—as indeed it is. But alas! behind all this is the grim tragic idea of, as it were, "writing in water," of gathering for dispersion, of heaping up only for scattering, of that final, fatal day when all shall be sold and others buy again! He is but a bibliophilist Danaïd, vainly filling his pitcher—the water running out at bottom!

The book-collecting passion was alluded to long ago in Lucian, who asks: "Why do you buy so many books? You are blind, and you buy a grand mirror; you are deaf, and you purchase fine musical instruments; you have no hair, and you get yourself a comb." This is perhaps the most bitter stroke yet given to the bibliomaniac. More pleasantly sarcastic, too, are the lines of old Brandt in his "Ship of Fools," where our maniac is ever a conspicuous passenger:—

" Still am I busy bookes assembling,
For to have plentie it is a pleasaunt thing
In my conceyt, to have them ay at hand,
But what they meane do I not understande."

One might weep over the mad folly of old Magliabecchi—" the Glutton of Books "—who covered floor, bed, and every portion of his house with books. When he wished to sleep, he would throw an old rug over any books that were on the floor, and stretch himself upon them, or he would cast himself, completely dressed, into his unmade bed, which was filled full of books, taking a basin of coals with him. Often he thus, quite unintentionally, set himself and his bed on fire. Notwithstanding this confusion, he could lay his hand on any book at any moment, though buried under a load of disorderly volumes. But most "untidy" literary men and scholars can do this, to a great extent, in the case of their papers as well as of books. To the housemaid eye there is a hopeless confusion.

No " hobby " is so old, so enduring, or respectable as this. Almost from the first days of writing it declared itself, and down to this hour it has flourished. The very literature of the subject is enormous, and would fill a small library. There is a dictionary on the subject of books that deals with books — that is, things of paper and print. About printers and printing alone, its various styles and forms, there are treatises without end ; grand encyclopædic dictionaries written by the pundits— Hain, Panzer, De Bure, the greater Brunet, and many more. There can be no doubt, indeed, that a book falls within the domain of art, for it is a thing of arrangement and disposition, and with such elements it is obvious there must be one sort of arrangement or disposition that is more pleasing than another.

The ordinary book-hunter, stall-ranger, or "prowler" has a store of joys and delight, even in anticipating their fruition, which he can gratify to the full in this London of ours, as well as did old Monkbarns in the "wynds" and purlieus of Edinburgh. He becomes a character. "Of the old bookstall hunters," writes Mr. Sanders in his MS., *penes me*, "Richard Smyth, one of the Secondaries of the City of London from 1644 to 1655, was said to be so devoted to the pleasant toils of book collecting, that he resigned his office (and emoluments of £700 a year) expressly that he might take his rounds among the booksellers' shops, especially in Little Britain. Dr. John North delighted in the small editions of the classics by Seb. Gryphius. His biographer says : ' I have borne him company at a bookstall for many hours together, and minding him of the time he hath made a dozen offers before he would quit.' Sterne was fond of looking over bookstalls, and writes exultingly of a bargain made by Mr. Shandy, who had the good fortune to get Bruscambille's *Prologue on Noses* [12mo, Paris, 1612] almost for nothing, that is, for three half-crowns. ' There are not three Bruscambilles in Christendom [said the stall-man] except what are chained up in the libraries of the curious. My father flung down the money as quick as lightning, took Bruscambille into his bosom, hyed home from Piccadilly to Coleman Street with it, as he would have hyed home with a treasure, without taking his hand once off from Bruscambille all the way.' The Rev. Richard Farmer, D.D., was a great lover of bookstalls. His library sold in 1798 for £2210, his pictures for £500, all of which, it is believed, were purchased by the

Doctor for much under £500. The Rev. J. Brand,
F.A.S., whose compact library of 'unique, scarce,
rare, and curious works' was sold at the beginning
of the century for upwards of £6000, almost daily
visited the bookstalls between Piccadilly and Mile
End—a rather extensive range—and generally returned from these excursions with his deep and wide
pockets well laden, and it is said his volumes were
chiefly collected in this way, and for comparatively
small sums. The old Duke of Roxburghe wandered
industriously and zealously from bookshop to bookstall over the world, just as he wandered over the
moor stalking the deer. Madame D'Arblay mentions that Queen Charlotte, speaking of a book in her
library, said, 'I picked the book up on a stall.
Oh, it's amazing what good books there are on
stalls!' On which Mrs. Delany, fancying that her
Majesty was in the habit of exploring book stalls in
person, expressed her surprise. 'Why,' said the
Queen, 'I don't pick them up myself; but I have a
servant, very clever, and if they are not to be had at
the booksellers', they are not for me more than for
another.' Still Dr. Croly says that Queen Charlotte
was in the habit of paying visits, with a lady-in-
waiting, to Holywell Street and Ludgate Hill, where
second-hand books were offered for sale. 'In no
instance,' says he, 'was her Majesty recognised or
interfered with.' Her Majesty's taste went further,
and it is not generally known that she had a private
press of her own. This we learn from a volume,
' Miscellaneous Poems, printed in 1812 by E. Hardy
for her Majesty Queen Charlotte, at the Frogmore
Lodge Press.' Only thirty copies were printed as
presents for the Queen's select friends. Most of the
royal family had this taste for typography and books,

and the author possesses some verses printed in red
ink by George Prince of Wales (afterwards George
IV.) when a child.   George III. at one time pro-
posed setting up a press in the palace.

" ' How often,' says Sir Walter Scott, speaking with
the voice of the old antiquary, Monkbarns, ' have I
stood haggling on a penny, lest, by a too ready acqui-
escence in the dealer's first price, he should be led to
suspect the value I set upon the article !   How have
I trembled lest some passing stranger should chop in
between me and the prize ; and then, Mr. Lovel, the
sly satisfaction with which one pays the consideration
and pockets the article, affecting a cold indifference
while the hand is trembling with pleasure ! '   Southey
could not pass a stall without ' just running his eye
over for *one* minute,' even, we are told, if the coach
which was to take him to see Coleridge at Hampstead
was within that time of starting.   The great lawyer,
Francis Hargrave, is said to have formed his extensive library merely by ' picking up ' at bookstalls,
seldom, if ever, purchasing a volume at what is called
a ' regular ' bookseller's.   This library was purchased
for £8000 for the British Museum.   Charles Butler,
another lawyer of eminence, also ranged bookstalls,
and many a rare book he has secured for a few shillings, worth as many pounds.   This was his frequent
boast.   Lord Macaulay was peculiarly fond of rummaging the bookstalls, and scarcely a dusty old bookshop in any by-court or out-of-the-way corner in
London escaped his attention.   No one so ready to
mount a ladder and scour the top shelf for quarto
pamphlets or curious literary relics of a bygone age,
and come down after an hour's examination covered
with dust and cobwebs, sending for a bun to take the
place of his usual luncheon.   He was not ashamed

to act as his own porter, and, like most of the eminent
bookworms, ancient and modern, was not above carrying a shabby old folio through a fashionable thorough-
fare." The late Mark Pattison had a special fancy
for the little antique Latin pocket volumes published in myriads a couple of centuries ago. It is
curious to think of scholars "wise and old" issuing
their profoundest lucubrations in volumes about the
size of a small Prayer-Book or Pocket Testament;
but such was the fashion. Long histories, such as
Strada *On the Belgian War*, a work as long as
"Hume and Smollett," or even "Gibbon," were thus
squeezed into portable shape. Eyes in those days
must have been stouter and clearer.

The bookworm, bibliophilist, or book fancier is a
favourite and almost dramatic figure, with his dim
eyes, rusty clothing, and eccentric affection for his
treasures. We have a sympathetic tenderness for
his lone, solitary ways, his self-denial and privations,
his hungry ardour and prowlings after his "midnight
darlings." If the truth were known, this sympathy
would be found to be thrown away; for his greed,
akin to that of the miser, would make him sacrifice
all that is human to all that is of *paper*. He is likely
enough to be morose, snarling, grasping, and would
find the most exquisite pleasure in getting from some
poor but ignorant dealer for a shilling what was
worth guineas. This is the triumph of the *chasse à
livres*. The prospect of parting with his old friends
adds a new pang to death. Friends, relatives, he
can leave behind with indifference, but his dear books
"cannot bear him company." Here was the de-
parture of a late book lover thus quaintly portrayed :—" He had a quite human fondness for his
books ; nothing annoyed him so much *as to hear one*

of them fall; and dusting them, which he reduced to
a science, seemed to give him real pleasure.   In his
last illness the sight of any of his favourites depressed
him greatly.   'Ah!' he would say, 'I am to leave
my books;' and sometimes, 'They have been more to
me than my friends.'   He would ask for them one
after the other, *till he was literally covered almost
to his shoulders*, as he lay, and the floor around
him was strewn with them.   He used to say that
the sight of books was necessary to him at his
work; and once reading how Schiller always kept
'rotten apples' in his study because their scent
was beneficial to him, he pointed to some shelves
above his head, where he kept his oldest and most
prized editions, and said, 'There are my rotten
apples.'" *

In the last century there flourished—if the term
be not too extravagant—a book hunter named Wilson, better and more ungraciously known as "Snuffy
Davy," who once picked up on a stall in a Dutch
town a small black-letter quarto, for which he paid
twopence. This proved to be one of the first English-
printed books, Caxton's "Game of Chess." He sold
it to a London bookseller, Osborne, celebrated for
being knocked down by Dr. Johnson with one of his
own folios, for £20. Osborne disposed of it to Dr.

* Mr. Gladstone is a diligent searcher of the stalls.   The
book fancier often comes on his track, and has seen a little
parcel—a bit of old theology, a rare poet, a nice old edition
of Lamb—set aside to be sent home to Downing Street.   Sometimes, when he is cheapening a book in a more public place
than Holywell Street, a curious crowd will gather outside,
staring in unmeaningly, as the vulgar gaper knows how to do.
This "draws" the eminent virtuoso, who strides out impatiently,
the stall-man execrating the idlers, who, perhaps, have hindered
a bargain.   All catalogues are sent to him and read, and returned marked with orders.

Askew for £65 ; and on his death it was purchased for the Windsor library for £370. At the present time the original twopence would have multiplied into a thousand pounds. All your book hunters will tell us that such surprises are part of the joys of their calling. Yet I fancy the loyal heart would feel a twinge or scruple as he carries off from the humble and ignorant dealer, for a shilling or two, a volume that may be worth ten or twenty pounds. No sophistry will veil the sharpness of the transaction, in which profit is made of poverty and ignorance ; and it would not be difficult to make an equitable decision, the buyer, as discoverer, being entitled to perhaps the larger share, and the owner to the rest. Instances of *trouvailles* of this sort are within the experience of every book fancier.

A few lots that in 1807 were bought for £8, 1s., produced at Heber's in 1836, £238, 17s. At the same time the " Chronica Gulielmi Thom " sold for £85, having in 1807 changed hands for 12s. This famous library consisted of 105,000 volumes. " The Storye of Frederick of Jensen," Anwarpe, 1518, with that of " Mary of Nemegen " and the " Lyfe of Vergilius," bound in one volume, cost the Duke of Roxburghe also 12s., and produced at his sale in 1812, £186, 14s. Dr. Gosset had seen in his lifetime the first Psalter of 1481 sold at Wilcox's for 5s., resold to Dr. Askew for 5 guineas, at whose sale it fetched 16 guineas. He had seen Dr. Farmer give 5s. 9d. for Painter's " Palace of Pleasure," and the same resold for 20 guineas ; and at Brand's sale he saw a blackletter article, the original cost of which was 3s. 6d., rise in a second sale to £100 and upwards. Of the " Tragedy of Dido, Queen of Carthage," written by Marlowe and Nash, printed by the Widdowe Orwin,

B

quarto, London, 1594, only three copies are known to exist. The Duke of Devonshire's copy cost Henderson the actor *fourpence;* it sold at the Heber sale in 1834 for £39 ! Another was purchased by Malone at Dr. Wright's sale, 1787, for 16 guineas ; a third, purchased by Mr. Reed for *eighteenpence*, of Mr. Flackton, bookseller, Canterbury, and presented by him in exchange to Stevens, sold at the latter's sale in 1800 for £17. Again, Mr. Rodd, the eminent bookseller, bought in the early part of this century a volume of rare tracts for threepence three-farthings (being its fair weight when put in the scales), which he sold about 1830 to Mr. Heber for £50 ! And again, for the "Mirror of Magistrates" (by G. H.), quarto, 1618, a bookseller at Lancaster gave the sum of threepence and sold for 10 guineas. It produced at Sotheby's in 1857, £20, 10s.

Malone, the Shakesperean scholar, tells of a precious little collection bound in one volume, and which contained some ten tracts of poetry by Daniel and others, written circa 1590. "Its history," he says, "is a curious one. The volume is just fit for the waistcoat pocket—four and a half inches long by three broad—pretty thick, well printed, and in good condition. It was sold at the sale of Dr. Bernard's books in 1698 for *one shilling and threepence.* Afterwards, probably passing through many hands, it came into the possession of a broker at Salisbury, where, about thirty years ago, Mr. Warton found it among a parcel of old iron and other lumber, and I think purchased it for *sixpence.* Since his death, his brother, Dr. Joseph Warton, very kindly presented it to me ; and I have honoured it with a new cover, and have preserved above the name of my poor friend Mr. Thomas Warton, which was written at the inside of the old cover, as a memorial of that very elegant and ingenious writer."

This would now be priced at thirty or forty guineas. But a much more extraordinary illustration of the "ups and downs" of sales was exhibited at the Roxburghe sale, where there was offered no less than *ten* "Wynkyn de Wordes," with a "Pynson and a Wyer," which in all brought £538. Yet these rarities had actually formed a single volume when in Dr. Farmer's possession, and at his sale fetched but twenty guineas !

The system of "old book dealing" has been so perfected or methodised, that the days for the patient explorer going his rounds with the certainty of "picking up," as it was called, some treasure or rarity, seem to have departed. The value of everything really worth anything is known ; no hunting in "book-boxes" or on the outside shelves of the stall will discover a prize. The finding an old quarto Shakespeare bound up with a lot of tracts is a dream. Still the man of taste and judgment may make his rounds, and find pleasure in redeeming many a pretty and useful volume, worth much more to him than the shilling or two he pays.

The "old book" sellers of London and of portions of the country are an interesting class, many of them enthusiasts, all knowing their business thoroughly, and some with that pleasant quaintness which has often come from living retired in dark Rembrandtish shops, among their antique and musty volumes. The amount of bibliographic lore they acquire and spend over their catalogues is often surprising. They maintain a correspondence with half the literary men of the kingdom, and this adds a tone to their minds. The latter rely on their humble friends and assistants, who, when these patrons are in want of some special work, exert themselves and put certain "sleuth-hounds"—well known to the trade, with a strange faculty for "nosing" books—on the track. Most *littérateurs* will admit that they always find in good catalogues agreeable and piquant reading, and there are some —such as Ridler's of Booksellers' Row, Salkeld's, Georges's, Bennett's of Birmingham—which are really most entertaining as well as instructive. My worthy ally of Booksellers' Row has a style of his own, and I often envy his readiness of knowledge and resource. His bazaar has an antique look; the venerable boxes and shelves look into the street; within these are the darkened chambers where volumes are stored and stacked, and old monks might be at work. No enthusiast of printing could sing with more appropriateness the merits and charms of his tomes. Here is an honest bit of enthusiasm:— "ALDINE.—Hieronymi Opera, 2 vols. in 1, thick folio, rubricated throughout in red and blue (with the exception of a slight water-stain), a very fine large copy of this noble volume of early typography, new calf gilt, exceedingly rare, £2, 12s. 6d. Venet., A. de Torresano de Asola, 1488."

On which he comments:— "This interesting publication is connected with the early Aldine press, the printer being the father-in-law and afterwards partner of the elder Aldus. Dibdin says of this volume—'If the lover of fine and legible printing wishes for a specimen of one of the choicest productions of the XV. Century, let him lose no opportunity of obtaining the present impression when a reasonable hope of its possession is held out to him; nor is the work less intrinsically valuable than its exterior form is inviting. A nobler book cannot grace the shelves of any collection.' "

Or better still :—" MENTELIN'S PRESS, 1465.— Conradi de Alemania, Concordantiæ Bibliorum, thick roy. folio, first edition, black letter, the first page surrounded with a broad illuminated border in gold and colours, and illuminated throughout. A most superb copy of this early monument of typography in its infancy, printed by one of the secret workmen of Guttenberg, handsome copy, bound in hogskin, gold and blind tooling on back and sides, from the Syston Park Collection, of the greatest rarity, fourteen guineas. Strasburg, J. Mentelin, 1465. First edition and the first Bible Concordance ever printed. Cost Sir John Thorold £30, 10s., bought of Payne and Foss, 1829. See also his MS. note ; not in the Spencer Collection, ascribed by Panzer to the press of Mentelin. The birthplace of printing has been hotly disputed : there are partisans who have endeavoured to prove that Strasburg was the original seat of the invention, and assert Mentelin the real inventor of the art, and describe Guttenberg as the robber of his priceless secret, &c. See a long account of this famous printer in *Humphrey's History of Printing*. Any one wishing to possess a fine and beautiful specimen of early typography could not require a more desirable book than the above. In fact, a more noble volume could not grace the shelves of the finest collection."

Who would not be attracted by this glowing language? The praise of this book is like the taste of rich ripe fruit in the mouth. For this enticing treasure £24 was asked. Yet at a sale in 1827, Herbert's copy sold for £1, 13s.

Most of these men can tell us curious and interest-

ing incidents of their experience of buyers in the
olden days.   So Mr. Stibbs, on allusion to Charles
Lamb, will relate how he had many of his folios—
"huge armfuls"—the "midnight darlings" he be-
wailed, passing through his hands.   He noted what
ragged veterans they were, how soiled, thumbed, and
generally dirty.   His confrère, Wilson, has had
Cobbett, Leigh Hunt, and others of the time,
dropping in.   Many of these men have been writers
themselves, such as Hindley, who has worked on
Catnach literature—street cries, ballads, &c.   One
of the most interesting of this class was an old and
rather wizened man, who, when dealing, invariably
pointed his speech with a succession of short grunts,
increasing in intensity as he grew obdurate, disappearing wholly when the bargain was a very good
one for him.   He lived in a little den of books, and
was usually interrupted when pursuing "his literary
avocations."   He was easy to sell, but terrible to
the peripatetic vendor of a stray volume, whom he
greeted with a sort of ferocity.   Yet this man was
amiable, had a simplicity worthy of Goldsmith—
wrote in a charming, easy, unaffected style ; indeed,
he had once been a schoolmaster.   He collected
folk-lore, and at last made a collection of stories of
fairies, &c., which he had picked up himself, and
which was published with much success.   He signed
himself quaintly "Philomath."   He had never been
in London or the great cities, and once wrote to me
that he "could picture me sitting of some fine
summer's evening with a book under the trees in
Trafalgar Square."

Foremost among them is the now celebrated Mr.
Quaritch of London, the very Napoleon of booksellers.   His enterprise and daring has really had a

momentous influence in stimulating prices. He suggests one of those great financiers who rule the market with a nod. He has brought books, as it were, "within the range of practical politics." No one who passes his rather dark and unpretending place of business at No. 15 Piccadilly could guess at the vast character of his transactions; neither would any one who sees at some great sale his plain figure, somewhat of Jewish cast, with the ancient felt hat to which his friends attach a sort of mysterious and superstitious power, donned on great occasions, suppose that this was the careless bidder of hundreds and thousands of pounds. In that repository of his are stored away priceless volumes.* Lately inter-

* "Mr. Quaritch is by no means an easy man to get at, *unless* you wish to see him on business. He was in his sanctum, a small, dark room, almost filled with the table, a few chairs, and two or three bookcases, containing several thousand pounds' worth of rare volumes, protected from the dust by glass doors. He discoursed in a pessimistic strain of the decadence of the general buyer and collector, 'a sign of the materialistic age we live in.' Book buying and book collecting in its proper sense has gradually declined since 1830. It was before that time that the great libraries were formed. 'At the Hamilton sale I spent £40,000, and at the Sunderland sale £33,000; and most of my purchases are now in the house here. I have known well most of the collectors of my time; three Dukes of Hamilton, for instance; and there you see the portrait of one of my best customers—the late Earl of Crawford, whose body was stolen. But, as I have said, the fashion has changed now-a-days. Collectors go in for first editions of Keats, Shelley, Thackeray, Dickens, and for the engravings of Cruikshank and Phiz. Then sporting literature is greatly in demand. Another very good customer is the country gentleman, who generally aspires to have in his library the best books on his county history. But I cannot enumerate the demands and crazes. Show me a man's library, and I will tell you his character and his attainments.' He began business in Castle Street some forty years ago—never mind how old he is now. No one having talked five minutes to the Bismarck of the book trade could fail to see that he had to do with a keen trader, up to every move on the board, and to every trick of the trade. His hunting-grounds are all over the face of the

viewed by an agent of the *Pall Mall Gazette*, he
communicated some very interesting information.

The great book dealer added the careless remark,
" Most of my purchases "—made in the great sales
two and three years ago—" are in the house here ; "
these costly things lying there, as it were, at interest,
which the buyer may have to pay. But the market
for the greater books is scarcely in London. There
are the grand collectors abroad, such as the Duke of
Aumale and Rothschild, makers of grand and costly
libraries.

earth ; he gathers his harvest from the five continents, and stores
it up in Piccadilly. ' Now will you come with me, and I will
show you a few of the rooms here.' And as we went, my guide
pointed with pride to this pile and that, to this pile and that.
Here was a bundle of Eastern manuscripts worth thousands,
there a case full of Mexican manuscripts written at the time of
the conquest ; here was the ' pigsty,' as he calls one of the rooms,
full of musty tomes and books as yet uncatalogued.   Mr.
Quaritch proceeded to expatiate upon his morocco bindings, his
russia leather, his rare editions, his illuminated missals, his
black letters, his manuscripts, his breviaries and psalters. He
declares that he sells everything, and never refuses an order.
Each of these rooms contains priceless treasures, the value of
which is known only to the great man himself, for he marks the
price of each book. It is impossible to deceive Mr. Quaritch by
any flimsy pretence to book-learning. ' If I hear any one talking about Elzevirs and Aldines, *I know he is an ignorant ass.*'
Mr. Quaritch speaks plainly, and this outburst was, I must confess, *apropos* of an unfortunate remark of my own concerning
Elzevirs.   ' Elzevirs and Aldines, indeed ! a pack of ignora-
muses !' ' I suppose you like the excitement of a great sale ? '
' No, sir ; there is nothing I abominate so heartily as the dreary
hours I have to sit in those dreary auction-rooms.   Once or
twice one gets excited, and one's blood is up like the blood of a
gambler ; but how often ? No. I am happiest here.'"
The little intolerance as to the man who talks about Elzevirs
and Aldines " being an ignorant ass " is characteristic enough.
Many of this class are probably good customers. I fancy talking
about Elzevirs and Aldines betokens a taste for rare things, and
an amiable, well-meaning fancy to learn more. It was intended,
no doubt, in the sense of the rebuke to those who "talked of
Coreggios and stuff."

§ Of the Mazarin Bible.

HEN we think of our modern press, that of books there is now no end, being stacked away by the million in the libraries, it is surely with a feeling almost of awe and reverence that one calls up the earliest of the kind—the primeval Adam and Eve. But when we take in our hand the first of the "race" of books, and think of its age and its necessary vicissitudes, this leaves a strange mysterious feeling. On the eve of the famous Syston Park sale there were seen in the Sothebys' modest auction-room half-a-dozen volumes, laid out on the table under glass, on which one of the "old" booksellers made this speculation, not without point. "It would be a curious thing," he said, "to bring some of these country-folk who are up for the cattle-show, and show 'em these, and then put this question to 'em, 'What now would *you* fancy was the value of these half-dozen plain-looking volumes, and what are they likely to fetch?'" The rustics might think they were going ridiculously high if they named £5; but how dumfounded they would be if assured that £10,000 would probably be, and almost was, the figure realised!—the Mazarin Bible, its successor the "Codex," and some others fetching near that sum. It was a strange feeling to

c

take the volumes into your hands, turn over the
leaves, admire the long "black-letter," the mellow
satin-like paper, and then reflect—"And this is the
first, or first known of *all* the books ! And it has
survived all the storms and troubles, the kings and
princes, and armies and revolutions, and rough usage.
And further, this sheaf of leaves, in its modest, rather
common leather binding, will to a certainty survive
to the end of the world." A little volume might be
written on these now famous books, and it must be
confessed that there is a sort of flavour of romance
attached to them.

There is much disputing of a Dryasdust kind
over the origin of printing, the inventors and place
whence the first book was issued. As no dates
were attached to the first printed books, there must
be always something speculative in the discussions
as to priority of issue ; but it is marvellous what
comparative certainty has been reached owing to
the ingenious exercise of wits. The matter lies between two or three of those pristine efforts.

There are some three or four great and famous
books of the world, which are progenitors of the
millions that now, like the human population, swarm
over the earth. But it is a surprise to think that in
workmanship these fairly distance the most perfect
specimens of the modern press. The history of this
well-known Mazarin Bible, which attracted such attention of late, deserves to be told, like that of some
well-known historical personage. Other works issued
by the Mayence press about the same time—so far as
can be speculated—as the famous Bible, are not of
the same importance, such as the "Durandus," printed
about 1459, which exhibits the first specimen of the
smallest letter, and which a rapturous admirer de-

clares "strikes one as the most marvellous monument of early printing." This is indeed no exaggeration, and one does look with astonishment at the fancy and elegance displayed in the design and cutting of the type. Of the Mazarin Bible it is reckoned that there are in the world nineteen copies—*on paper*, mark; but on vellum, not more than five.

This grand book—the Mazarin Bible—was actually discovered, *dug up*, as it were, like a piece of antiquity, by an accomplished bibliographer, De Bure. In his own agreeable narrative he shows that this was almost an accident. " Mere chance," he tells us, " led me to the discovery of this precious edition, to which we have given the title of ' The Mazarin Bible,' and I do not hesitate an instant to give it the first place, not only above all Bibles, but above every known book! When making some explorations in the Mazarin Library, that is, of the College of the Four Nations, we were not a little surprised to find this first and most celebrated work of the press, which a simple impulse of curiosity caused us to open." It should be said, however, that the existence of such a book was long suspected, and there is an actual allusion to it in the Chronicle of Cologne, which speaks of the jubilee year 1450, when the first book, a Bible " of *the larger type*," *Scripturâ grandiosi*, was discovered.

It was at the Perkins sale, whose catalogue sells now for two guineas, held in the great library at Haworth Park in June 1873, that the *grand copy* made its appearance, and was thus gloriously described by the auctioneers, a prosaic firm of landagents (Messrs. Gadsden and Ellis). Kept as a *bonne-bouche* for the last lot of the last day, No. 864, no wonder it was regarded with veneration, for it was the first best-known regularly printed volume in the world.

It is a rather happy tribute to Christianity that this first printed book should have been the first issue of the Scriptures. But let us hear the auctioneer : " A most splendid and magnificent copy, printed upon vellum, with the capitals artistically illuminated in gold and colours, and in magnificent binding, with clasps and bosses." It was styled " Mazarin " from the first discovery of a copy in Cardinal Mazarin's library. It is printed in double columns, in large letters, much like those used in the Missals. " In contemplating this work," says our auctioneer, as though speaking of a statue or picture, "the mind is lost in astonishment that the inventor of printing should by a single effort have exhibited the perfection of this art." A very just remark, and what always strikes us when looking at any of these early works. Of the five copies known, all on vellum, " *not one is believed to be absolutely perfect.*" This Perkins one was considered "*the finest* of the few known copies, whether for amplitude of margin or purity of vellum, it being as clean as the day it issued from the press." It however was declared by Dr. Dibdin to want two leaves, which were " supplied in facsimile by Whitaker," one of those amazing persons who perform such feats, and so successfully that, as the auctioneer tells us, "a very careful examination has revealed one leaf which appears doubtful, but has quite failed to discover the second." * This copy came from the University

* There are in London now one or two persons who perform these feats. They seem amazing. I was shown lately by Mr. Toone of Leicester Square a little duodecimo of an old and rare Missal, but from which the title-page had been torn away. One of these artists supplied the loss, reproducing the red and

of Mentz, whence it was obtained by Messrs. Nicol.*
Three of the five vellum copies are in public libraries,
including one at Paris. A fourth belonged to Mr.
Grenville, who left it to the British Museum, and
the fifth came up for sale on this memorable day,
"unquestionably the most important and distinguished article in the whole annals of typography,
and a treasure which would exalt the humblest and
stamp with a due character of dignity the proudest
collections in the world." Allowing a little for "high
falutin" here, there is no doubt a modicum of truth
in all this, as there is no one but must look with
reverence on this true Adam of all the millions of
books that have followed. It was sold to Mr. Ellis,
in trust, for Lord Ashburnham, for the sum of
£3400 !

A copy on paper was next sold for £2690. It
was declared that "it is unquestionably the first
time, as it may with almost absolute certainty be the
last, that two copies of this work were sold in one
day." It was strange that a copy of so world-famed
a book was not secured for some foreign state. But
the price was prohibitive, particularly, as the auctioneers said, truly, it was virtually a unique, and no
other vellum copy is likely to come into the market,
as they are secured in public libraries.

black inks, the woodcut in the centre, the faded tones of the
ink, and nearly (but not so perfectly) matched the quality of the
old paper.
   * A Mazarin Bible was once sent over by Mr. Horne, and
consigned to Mr. Nicol. Dr. Dibdin describes the illumizations
as being "in a quiet and pleasing style. The volume is absolutely cased in mail by a binding of three hundred years'
standing, upon the exterior of which are knobs and projections
in brass, of a durability and bullet-defying power which may vie
with the coat of a rhinoceros." The style of the Doctor, it will
be seen, is vivacious and graphic.

In the same year Mr. Quaritch was offering his copy for 3000 guineas, describing it as "the original genuine issue of the book, printed on paper, as distinguished from the second issue made by Fust and Schöffer, to which all the copies on vellum belong, a perfect and extraordinarily fine copy, of the full size, most of the leaves being rough and uncut, so as even to show the ancient MS. signatures and chapter-numbers, as written down by Guttenberg himself for the guidance of the binder and the illuminator; in blue morocco extra, from the libraries of Sir Mark Sykes and Mr. Henry Perkins. Mentz, about 1455."

To appreciate this enormous price, we may trace the career of another copy, known as Count Maccarthy's, and which is now one of the glories of the British Museum. These volumes were originally in one M. Gaignat's library, and thence passed to Count Maccarthy, who secured it for a bagatelle or "song" of £85 ! At his sale, which was inevitable to take place (the only sure protection against the billows of prompt realisation being the safe harbour of refuge of a public library), it was purchased for that most elegant of collectors, Mr. Grenville, who paid for it just £250. He bequeathed his fine collection to the English public, who can every day walk through its spacious hall, lined with cases in which are enshrined these treasures, all handsomely clad. This monument passed with them, which had thus in about fifty years advanced to nearly twenty times its price.

On this romance of the Perkins auction, let us hear that congenial and competent judge and true bibliophile, my friend Mr. Sala :—

"With perhaps only one exception—and even this

is doubtful — of the magnificent collection by Mr. Thomas Grenville to the British Museum, the Perkins library has long been famous in Europe as the finest private collection that has ever been amassed by any English bibliophile; and when on Friday— the final and fourth day of the dispersion—the last lot was knocked down for £3400, a buzz ran round the room, which told that the entire proceeds of the four days' sale had been upwards of £26,000.

" It seems incredible—£3400 for a single book ! The money would buy a small estate; it would purchase a comfortable annuity; it would cover the expenses of a contested election. Yet the purchaser, Mr. Ellis, is a happy man, and one to be congratulated. Twenty years hence the precious volume will in all probability be worth twice or thrice the sum it fetched last week. The costly book was none other than a vellum copy of the famous Gutenberg and Fust Bible—' the most important and distinguished work in the whole annals of typography '—the first edition of the Holy Scriptures—the first book printed with movable metal types by the inventors of the art of printing. One such copy exists in the National Library of Paris, and but seven others are known in all, of which one, lamentably marred by the irretrievable loss of two pages, was sold in 1825 for no less than £504. Even paper copies of this wonderful and precious work fetch fabulous sums. Mr. Quaritch bought one on Friday for £2690. Nor was the price at all exorbitant. This very copy was purchased by the then Bishop of Cashel, and at his death in 1858 it was knocked down to Mr. Perkins for £596. It now fetches, in 1873, more than four times the price paid for it by Mr. Perkins in 1858, and fourteen times the price given by the Bishop of

Cashel in 1843. What, then, the vellum copy, for which Mr. Ellis has just paid £3400, will fetch in the year 1900 it is difficult to conjecture."

There had been, however, an earlier appearance of this wonderful volume in the year 1847, when it was thus introduced :—

" A remarkably fine copy of this splendid specimen of the typographic art. The margins of the first page are filled with rich illuminated borders, and the capitals throughout are finely rubricated, 2 vols., old blue morocco, gilt leaves, without name of printer, place, or date, but attributed to the press of Gutenberg at Mentz, between the years 1450–55.

" It is printed in double columns, in imitation of the large letters used by the Scribes in the Church Missals and Choir Books.

" On our first acquaintance with this extraordinary production [say the auctioneers] we were inclined to the opinion of Laire, that there existed *two perfectly distinct editions* of this Bible, printed with the same type ; but on a more minute examination and collation of the *two so-called* editions, we are perfectly convinced they are essentially the same. They are indeed the same book in different conditions of publication, occasioned by the cancelling and reprinting of certain sheets."

At Lord Gosford's sale, which took place a few years ago, there was but a tranquil interest excited by the appearance of what may be called an odd volume of the Mazarin Bible. It was only the first volume, and was arrayed in its old original monastic binding—" in an oak case, with twelve brass bosses." It brought a price that rather surprised the public, and was secured by Mr. Toovey of Piccadilly. This copy was sold for £500, so that we were then a long way from the days of huge prices. To illustrate further its rarity, it may be mentioned that the Duke of Sussex, who had an extraordinary craze for collecting Bibles in every known tongue and edition, had all his life been *striving* vainly to acquire one on vellum. Alas ! he died, unhappily, without attaining his desires, much as the late Earl of Derby failed to secure the " Blue Ribbon of the Turf." He had ruefully, we are told, to content himself with *a copy on paper*, for which he gave £100, and which at his sale in 1844 brought £190. In Mr. Pickering's shop hangs a single leaf of this curiosity framed and glazed, a great curiosity.

But it was now to figure in the most " sensational," as it is called, of modern book sales, and which rose to the dignity of a struggle, viz., that known as the Syston Park Library, which took place on December 12, 1884. Sir John Hayford Thorold had indulged his passion for books for nearly fifty years, from about the time of the French Revolution to the date of the Reform Bill. He had collected all the noblest "monuments " of printing, with such success, that it was said he possessed nearly all the "incunables," and certainly all the first editions of the Classics, with the exception of only two or three. The result was a grand and imposing collection, which, after his death, slumbered peacefully for nearly fifty years at his seat, near Grantham. These treasures—stately, impressive tomes—were magnificent in their calm dignity and rich but sober dress, and one could not but admire the taste which brought together such stately veterans of typography—notably that band of " Editiones Principes "—conceived and brought forth in days when the printer seemed to enter into com-

D

petition with the artist or painter, and to apply the
canons of art to his page.

For two days these veterans were gradually dispersed, some to meet again on a new friendly
shelf; but it was not until the fourteenth morn that
the "Mazarin Bible"—a work of which few had
even heard, but with which everybody became of a
sudden familiar—was to be contended for.   The
bibliophiles and critics grew excited as they dwelt
with pardonable exaggeration on its charms.   A
fevered excitement was in the air.   It was described as
"a superb work, the printing on paper as thick and
rich in tone as vellum, with glossy ink intensely
black, and very *uniform in the expression ;* in double
columns, the letters large, and similar to those written
by scribes of the Church missals and choral books."
"After a preliminary fever of excitement, as the
wonderful book was passed with great solemnity up
and down before the two rows of professional and
amateur bibliophiles seated in front of the rostrum,
the first bid of £500 was made, and immediately
met with one of £1000 from Mr. Quaritch, who had
to advance on the biddings on commissions made by
the auctioneer's clerk, Mr. Snowden ; and so the contest went on by bids of £50 ; the excitement rising
higher and higher, as £3000 was called for Mr.
Quaritch, followed by £3100 from his opponent, while
each seemed to get fresher with the fight up to the
fifty-seventh round, when at £3650 the commission
was exhausted, and at Mr. Quaritch's bid of £3700,
everybody expected the hammer to fall.   But here
Mr. Ellis, who had hitherto only watched the contest, joined issue with two or three splendid bids, and
a last one of £3850, leaving it to Mr. Quaritch to
possess this splendid Mazarin Bible at the enormous

price of £3900. There was a buzz of applause as the hammer fell, and there was some minutes before the excitement subsided."

Talking over his purchases, the enterprising Quaritch, then the hero of the hour, said :—"That of five copies of the Mazarin or Gutenberg Bible known, three had passed through his hands. The first he purchased when a young man in business, for what was then an enormous sum, £590. He had no commission for it, but offered it at the same price to the Earl of Crawford. The Earl (who had left a commission of £500 for the book) accepted his offer, and was always after a good patron of his. 'The present copy' (the Syston), Mr. Quaritch went on to say, 'I have also bought for my stock, and it is purely a speculation of my own. I do not expect to keep it long. A copy was sold to Mr. Huth for £3500, he himself securing the paper copy for £2690. This, from a bookseller's point of view, is worth more money than the vellum copy, from the fact that two of the five copies are on paper, the remainder being on vellum. The sum of £3900 is the largest ever paid for a book, the nearest approach being the £3500 above."

This extraordinary and extravagant price—which suggests the Dutch tulip mania—had scarcely ceased to be talked of, with much uplifting of hands and eyebrows, when the memorable day of December 19 came round, revealing a more startling sensation. For now the "Psalmorum Codex"—a portion only of the Scriptures, an older work, and fixed as belonging to the year 1459—was to be contended for.

Now, great as was the fuss and excitement produced by the appearance of the Mazarin Bible, this

was a yet rarer volume, and though only a Latin
Psalter or Codex, four years younger; there are supposed to be some five copies of the Bible for one of
this volume, but the latter is somehow not nearly so
"sensational" a volume, and, like many a modest
man of merit, had not been put forward.   Here is
its official description :—

"Psalmorum codex, Latine cum Hymnis, Oratione
Dominica, Symbolis et Notis musicis, folio, printed
on vellum, very fine copy, with painted woodcut-
capitals, in red morocco extra, borders of gold, gilt
edges, by Staggemeier, Moguntiæ, J. Fust et P.
Schoifher, 1459. This excessively rare edition is the
second book with a date, and contains the Athanasian
Creed, printed for the first time.   In rarity it equals
that printed in 1457, of which only eight copies are
known, and of this only seven, all printed on vellum.
The Schœffer Psalter [says Mr. Quaritch in his
Catalogue] (first produced in 1457, next in 1459) is
the first and almost the only early example of printing in colours, the large initials being impressed, each
in at least two colours, from wooden or metal blocks.
Of the seven surviving copies of the 1457 edition,
most are imperfect, and all but Lord Spencer's are
in public libraries.   Of the seven or eight (two or
three of the ten formerly known having now disappeared) extant copies of the 1459, all are in public
libraries except Lord Spencer's and the Thorold
copy.   Hence it was not surprising that the collectors engaged in keen competition to secure the only
copy of the book that is likely ever to come into the
market."

There has been much debate as to whether these
colours are hand-painted, but the best judges, with
the aid of magnifying glasses, &c., have decided that

at this early stage these wonderful printers were equal to this most difficult art of printing in various colours.*

The Codex was in vellum, and displayed five painted capitals with initial letters in red, and also musical notes. The second book in our wide world with a date, mark ! and, more interesting still, with the Athanasian Creed which thus made its first appearance in print. At the end was the usual printer's signature. There was no expectation of what was to come. Very many were present : there was no excitement. But there were bibliophiles there who knew what was involved.

There it lay—what perhaps is one of the earliest and oldest of printed books ! Four hundred and twenty-five years had elapsed since Guttenberg had looked on it. Its history was clear for nearly a hundred years. It had been in Count Macarthy's collection, where it had been been bought by Sir Mark for only £134, a great price : at the latter's sale it had fetched £2, 10s. more. Mr. Quaritch was heard to declare that " in his experience of forty years he had never handled a copy." The second book published with a date. It was indeed one of the "grand old men" of typography. Its grand splendid page was noted and admired—its vellum, its "painted capitals, its red letters, and musical notes." It was proclaimed as being " bound by Staggemeier, in red morocco, and is in an exceptionally fine state."

* Mr. Quaritch, the happy possessor of the latest sold copy now offers it—or did lately—among his numerous other costly treasures, for the sum of £4095 ! He thus seems to be paying about £150 a year—that is, loss of interest on the sum laid out —for the custody of the treasure ; just as the late Lord Dudley, who secured a famous pair of Sèvres jars for £10,000, was paying £500 a year for the pleasure of gazing on them.

Again the same graphic enthusiast describes the scene. " It was put up with a brief eulogy from the auctioneer, Mr. Hodge, at £500, and the biddings steadily advanced by fifties to over £2000, there being only three competitors in the field, Mr. Snowden (the clerk), Mr. Quaritch, and Mr. Ellis (the Bond Street bookseller), who, however, soon far distanced the commission, and brought the biddings to over £3000, while the audience looked on in dead silence, wondering if it could possibly beat the £3900 of the Mazarin Bible. To the astonishment of every one, this was soon not only reached, but surpassed by more than £1000, Mr. Ellis gallantly bidding £4900, Mr. Quaritch immediately topping it with £4950, at which, after calling this enormous price three times, Mr. Hodge raised his hammer for the last time, and sealed the purchase of the famous Codex to Mr. Quaritch amidst the loudest applause ever heard in the room."

There is yet another of this primeval company—known as the " CATHOLICON " of Johan Balbi de Janua—which is considered to be the fourth book printed with a date, two copies of which rarity have made their appearance recently. This distinguished work, " The *Catholicon*, was printed and completed in the gracious (*alma*) city of Mayence, of the glorious German nation, in the year of the incarnation of our Lord, 1460." This has been styled by an enthusiast, Lambinet, " souscription sublime."

" The date and place," says an enthusiastic auctioneer, Evans of Pall Mall, " are sufficient to excite the curiosity of the collectors of rare and ancient productions of the press." It is allowed by the most eminent bibliographers that this is one of the very few works printed by Gutenberg. It is interesting, too, as one of the works of his new press, after Fust had seized on his presses and established, as Mr. Quaritch says, "the second printing-office of the world."

Up to the year 1813 not three copies had been seen in England for fifty years. The paper is of surprising strength and beauty, making us acknowledge how little has been gained, or rather how much has been lost, in modern manufacture of this article, by having recourse to what is called chemical improvements. Mr. Stanley Alchorne, of the Mint, possessed a copy—sold in 1813 for £58. Mr. Quaritch, some seventy years later, was offering "a superb copy in old calf gilt, with the Royal Arms of Bavaria stamped in gold on the side," for £250; while at Sir Mark Sykes's sale, about fifty years ago, it brought but £50. Strange to say, within the last four years no less than two copies of this rare book have appeared. This, of the Syston Park sale, brought £400; the second, at the Woodhull sale—though boasting "painted capitals and bound by Roger Payne"—fetched but £310. There is a curious caprice in these prices.

§ Concerning the Incunables or Cradle Books.

ANY a "gentle" or unkindly reader, while feeling due respect for these antique books, has associated them with something musty and dusty, something more curious than beautiful—*magis admirandum quam imitandum.* A genuine old ecclesiastical library, where all the old calf volumes are grown rusted and mouldy, with its rows of vellum-bound things, mainly theological, their names and titles written in large characters on their backs, offers but a cheerless spectacle at best. But there are few who have seen and handled the splendid productions of the first presses. To the general they are *caviare.* Fewer will have seen them when enshrined in some great library, like that of Althorp, richly bound, waited on by guardians and menials, and sumptuously treated. But even under less favourable conditions, it is astonishing what splendid things these works are — perfect works of art, triumphs of unassisted genius, at a time when everything had to be devised. We look at them with wonder and admiration, as we would at some graceful and elegant memorial in some old

Italian city. And here is the further surprise.
While the first printed book of importance takes
rank also for design, execution, excellence of material, and price as one of the great books of the
world, viz., the Mazarin Bible, all those that followed it within so short a space as twenty years,
are about the noblest, grandest works that ever were
issued from the press. Vellum used for paper, with
magnificent effect, or paper almost like vellum in its
size and strength ; large and brilliant type, capitals
rubricated, and wrought by hand with a florid
variety ; other capitals " illuminated " in colours, and
golden miniatures with bindings to match—such were
the glories of the first printed books. Their size
was often two feet high, and as to their number, here is
one significant fact. In the Royal Library at the
Hague there is a collection bequeathed by a Flemish
nobleman, one Baron de Westreenen, and which
contains no less than twelve hundred of the rarest
editions, all printed before the close of the fifteenth
century—that is, during the forty years from 1460
to 1500. The works of Virgil in the noblest folio
shape, printed in large type, expands over a vast
surface, and makes a huge volume, printed with
labour and expense : yet a single library—that of
Althorpe—possesses no less than *fifteen* of these
great Virgils, all printed before the year 1476.
Fifteen great editions of a classic in eight or ten
years ! Again, among the delusions of centuries
one is that we owe the publication of the Bible to
the Reformation. But it is a fact that fifty years
before the Reformation there had been issued a
dozen editions in Germany, while over the world it
was a favourite " venture " with publishers. Koburger issued editions as early as 1476 and 1478.

It was natural, after so constant a use of vellum for MSS., that the same material should be adopted for printing. Yet almost at once we find that, in printing the first books, only a portion of the impression was taken off on vellum, and another on paper. To the close of the century this practice was adopted, and hence we find all the collectors of grand editions disdaining any save those printed in this splendid and costly form. In Lord Spencer's superb library there are nearly one hundred of these vellum impressions, worth on an average from two to three hundred pounds apiece. The National Library at Paris is said to possess more than any other. The expense of securing suitable parchment is an element in the value, together with the difficulty of working, drying, &c. In modern times we have occasionally a few copies of small works taken off on vellum, but this is merely a fantasy, and somehow, from the lean, attenuated character of modern type, the effect does not correspond to the trouble. The enthusiast, Dibdin, when publishing the magnificent *Typographical Antiquities*, on which no money was spared, determined to have a copy taken off on vellum for his patron's library, but after printing only twenty-four pages, was compelled to give up the task. "I attempted it," he says, "with every possible attention to printing and to the material, but I failed at every point. And *this single wretched*-looking book," adds the disgusted bibliophilist, "had I persevered, would have cost me about seventy-five guineas." The most important and ambitious attempt in this direction was made under the direction of an amateur whom no one would ever have expected to see figuring in such a capacity—no other, indeed, than Marshal Junot, Duke d'Abrantes. For this eminent soldier, Didot, the great publisher, took off a whole series of French dramatists on this costly material, over thirty in number. Many have, of course, had in their hands some small vellum MS., say a "Book of Hours," which, from its small size and liability to lie open and be crushed, will show much soiling and hard usage. But it is otherwise with a grand vellum tome that has calmly reposed for centuries in the libraries, and has been treated daintily, and petted, as it were. The spreading leaves have acquired a tone like ivory, and, indeed, seem of the texture of some precious metal, so stout and enduring do they appear. They are like veneer of ivory, and there is a golden mellow shaded tone over all. Then the ink seems blacker, and glistens like polished ebony. The gold and colours of the illuminated capitals and borders secure more effect on this ground. There is, too, the idea of costliness, of endurance, of skill and care in the working, for the printing requires infinite art and trouble.

What strikes us in these early works is their magnificent size and grand amplitude. They are indeed vast tomes, and it is curious that the first editions, or *Editiones Principes*, should be the finest of any. The publishers, in thus printing but one to three hundred copies, looked on each *volume* as a publication—it was a monument for the public library, or for the wealthy amateur. The miniaturist, now out of work, was called in to fill up the spaces left vacant for the initial letters ; while the scrivener, with extraordinary diligence, "rubricated" each page with a series of small "caps" done in a flowing, dashing style, which gave quite a free artistic air to the whole page. This decoration, while it added seriously to the expense, imparted a separate indi-

viduality to each copy. The front page was always
specially glorified with a fine border and arabesque
initial, and often had the escutcheon and devices of
the owner set out at the foot in gold and colours.
The sort of link between the fast decaying miniatur-
ists' art and the new-born typographer is curious and
interesting.

In England, Caxton and his successors had not
the same tastes. Their books seemed conceived in
a timorous spirit ; they were small, thin, and comparatively inexpensive ventures, as though they feared
to run risk. Perhaps the truth was that those
splendid foreign publishers, Fust, Gutenberg, Jenson,
Vindelin de Spira, Aldus, Pannartz, with others—
and what a melodious roll in their names !—could
justly count the whole Continent as their customers ;
whereas Caxton, with his English and French works,
could rarely reach beyond the shores of his own
country. Even now abroad Caxton's are regarded
with but a languid interest, and do not excite the
enthusiasm that the work of other printers do. The
same reasoning applies at the present time. English
works are printed for the English or Americans,
whereas costly books published at Paris or Berlin
have the world for a market.

It is wonderful to think that every incident connected with the making of a book was to be found
within ten years from the introduction of printing
almost exactly the same as it is now—the watermark, the system of noting and registering the sheets,
binding, &c. This grandeur of treatment, which
made a book a sort of monument, left its impression
on the men who conceived and carried out the enterprise. Many a noble tome is associated with a story
of energy, perseverance, or romance connected either

with the author or the publisher. In the days of Gutenberg, or Vindelin de Spira, curious tales have come down to us of struggles to raise money to complete some huge tome, as though one were striving to complete a house. As is well known, the founders of printing had to suffer cruelly. The story of the publisher's life has often been told, always chequered with a dogged perseverance, a generous ardour, if not enthusiasm, a venturesomeness, combined with tact and instinct. All this seems to suggest the career of a successful merchant.

The supremacy of German energy and enterpris has never been so triumphantly shown as in this development of printing, and the obligations of the world to this great nation are extraordinary. The old controversy between Mentz and Haarlem for the honour of the discovery may be considered as settled in favour of the German ; but it is really the German character of the early printing that is the most irresistible of the arguments.* It is calculated that there

---

* It is not known generally what escapes from destruction some of the MSS. of the classics have had. In a dungeon at the monastery of St. Gall, a writer in *The Fireside* tells us Poggio found, corroded with damp and covered with filth, the great work of Quintilian. In Westphalia a monk stumbled accidentally on the only manuscript of Tacitus. The poems of Propertius were found under the casks in a wine-cellar. In a few months the manuscript would have crumbled to pieces and become completely illegible. Parts of Homer have come to light in the most extraordinary way. A considerable portion of the Iliad, for instance, was found in the hand of a mummy. The Ethiopics of Heliodorus was rescued by a common soldier, who found it in the streets of a town in Hungary. The Thurloe State Papers were brought to light by the tumbling in of the ceiling of some chambers in Lincoln's Inn. The letters of Lady Mary Montagu were found in the false bottom of an old trunk ; and in the secret drawer of a chest the curious manuscripts of Dr. Lee lurked unsuspected for years. One of the most singular discoveries of this kind was the recovery of Luther's " Table

were over one hundred German printers established in the great cities of Europe within forty years of the discovery of printing. In Venice and in Rome we find the names of some twenty great German printers. More interesting is it to see how native force is thus tempered by local association and Italian elegance. Thus as we look at one of those portly Bibles of Koburger, the Nuremberg printer, issued in 1478 and 1480, we are struck with their rude stalwart proportions, the rough stoutness of the paper, the vigorous "blackletter," and blackness of the ink. The leaves lie in close together, board-like and compact. There is a general air of "burliness," owing to a lack of proportion between the thickness and other dimensions. But when we come to the work of Pannartz at Rome, or Jenson at Venice, we find a greater delicacy. The paging is laid out with more beauty and elegance, and the size of the volume more handsomely proportioned.

We are so accustomed now to this "Roman type" —almost always in use in England, France, and Italy —that we are apt to forget that the Germans to this day have merely retained what was originally the universal form of type, viz., the smaller blackletter, or "German text," though it has lately become the

Talk." A gentleman in 1626 had occasion to build upon the old foundation of a house. When the workmen were engaged in digging, they found, "lying in a deep obscure hole, wrapped in strong linen cloth which was waxed all over with beeswax within and without," this work, which had lain concealed ever since its suppression by Pope Gregory XIII. We are told that one of the cantos of Dante's Paradiso, which had long been mislaid, was drawn from its lurking-place (it had slipped beneath a window-sill) in consequence of an intimation received in a dream. One of the most interesting of Milton's prose works—the essay on the Doctrines of Christianity—was unearthed from the midst of a bundle of despatches, by Mr. Lemon, deputy-keeper of the State Papers, in 1823.

fashion to issue scientific works in the Roman letter. The earliest printed works, such as the famous Bible, were in the elongated blackletter, which speedily took the shape of the small German text, as we have t to-day, and which in that country has scarcely changed in shape to this hour. It was so in Italy, Belgium, and England. In the latter country the old blackletter lingered on in Acts of Parliament till a recent period. The bright, stout blackletter of Caxton was almost the same as that used in Belgium, and was brought by him from that country, and became larger and longer in the hands of Wynkyn de Worde.

It will not, perhaps, occur to many that these early forms of type were merely copies or imitations of the existing handwriting, as found in the MSS. Italy was the first to adopt another form of letter, which it had ready to hand in the abundant Roman inscriptions, said to be first used by the "eminent firm" of Sweynheim, in 1467. It is wonderful to think that only two years' practice should have resulted in the magnificent works of the Brothers de Spira, which shows a perfect familiarity with the handling of this new-born type. More wonderful, indeed, is it to turn the pages of their great Pliny, and think that the style of type displayed was but two years old. The well-known Aldine type—the original "*Italic*"— was simply copied from the "running-hand" of the time ; and it is said that it was Petrarch's handwriting that formed the model. These elegant works deserve their reputation, and the little thin quartos, with the well-known anchor on the title, the pretty turns and flourishes of the italic letter, are ever pleasing to the eye. The greater massive folios of the same publisher—ponderous armfuls, each page "packed" with

matter, yet clear and uncrowded—impress one with
the sense of a magnificent power. We feel that one
of these grand volumes was a storehouse or magazine
of learning. It was to its surroundings what the
chained Bible was in the church—a tome to be read
from, for the benefit of all.

But would we dazzle the careless inquirer, and
show him one of the stateliest, most imposing efforts
of the early press men, we would exhibit two noble
tomes, grand folios, the work of Zainer, grown ripe
and mellow with age, though literally defying "the
ravages of time." It came from his press, in
1474, and is a "Pelagius de Planctu," "thick Royal
folio." Here is Mr. Ridler's enthusiastic description :
"As large as the Nuremberg Chronicle, blackletter,
with woodcut borders, and large capital letters, supposed to be the first of their kind ever engraved.
SPLENDID COPY, the capitals filled in with red ink by
the rubricator, with old blue morocco extra, full gilt
back by Derome. A more glorious production of
the fifteenth century, or a more beautiful specimen
of early typography it would be impossible to produce. It is in the finest state imaginable, the paper
is of the firmest texture, and as clean as on the day
that it was issued from the press: it is so large a copy
that it might almost be emphatically called UNCUT.
—Thorpe's long printed article is inserted on fly-
leaf, which copy was priced £31, 10s." As these
grand volumes are taken down and laid open re-
verently, we are struck by the beautiful proportions,
the noble margins of the natural size—not artificially
or studiously *made* large, the dazzling brilliancy of
the Gothic letters, the sobriety of the binding, and
the curious woodcuts flourishing around the capital
letters, delicately coloured by some artist.

It would not be fanciful to say that the possession of such a treasure would have an elevating and
refining influence, and one would be almost bound,
like the possessor of the old china teapot, "to try
and live up to it."

One of the rarest of the early Greek books is the
" Lascaris Grammatica Græca," *the first Greek book
printed,* the first edition, which is a small quarto,
printed at Milan 1476.   Only five or six copies are
known.   The one in the British Museum was picked
up by Mr. Pryse Lockhart Gordon in 1800 for his
friend Dr. Burney, and was after his death sold to
the British Museum for the extraordinary price of
£600.

As one dwells on these grand books and grand
printers, we seem to be dealing critically with pictures or other works of art.   But it should be remembered that almost every copy thus had an individuality of its own, and was distinguishable, having
been "worked on," decorated, and otherwise glorified
as a true work of art.   There are, however, some
half-dozen grandly conspicuous works of this era,
which it is impossible to gaze on without admiration.
Apart from their typographical merits, there is a strange
feeling in the thought that these noble tomes are the
very first editions of Homer, Virgil, Horace, Dante,
and among them is the book that is second only in
popularity to the Bible, "The Imitation of Christ."
It is extraordinary to think that these noble volumes
—the first appearance of their authors in print—
remain, strange to relate, the most dignified forms
in which they have ever appeared.   They are grand,
solid, substantial, well printed, and well edited (for
the time).   Hear Mr. Quaritch on one of these
primæval volumes for which he demands the sum of

F

one thousand pounds :—" Its first page," he said,
" is decorated with a magnificent border, on which
architectories and arabesque ornament are combined,
with exquisite figures of winged and wingless angels,
those in the bottom painted with camien blue, the
whole picture radiant with gold and lovely with har-
monising colours of floreate scroll-work and ornamental vases, with entwined handles in green on a
gold ground. The initial to the first book "—and
this gives a good idea of the magnificent style in
which the threshold to one of these stately tomes
was decorated—" was a full-length figure of a warrior,
in pale blue, in a floreate letter in crimson, on a
golden ground ; in the centre of the right-hand margin
was a highly-finished miniature of a doge ; in the
corner a coat of arms upheld by Cupids—while some
of the epitomes were written in blue and gold." There
is mány an opening page thus set forth in this combination of pictorial and typographical splendour.

A short time ago Mr. Quaritch was in possession
of more book rarities than ever were found in the
hands of one single owner before. He was fresh from
the spoil of the Sunderland, Syston Park, Beckford
and Hamilton sales. There were to be seen the
Mazarin Bible, Psalter, Codex (before described),
and, above all, the first of the classics that was put
in print, namely, the Cicero of 1465. It is extraordinary all that is conveyed in this simple phrase,
for it was not only the first printed Cicero, but the
first of the classics printed. Then we turn the
catalogue of the British Museum, under the heading
" Cicero," and find some thousand editions. What a
leap ! He had also the first editions of Livy, and of
Bibles the first Polyglot, the first Greek Bible, the
first English, Latin, German, Icelandic, Swedish,

Welsh, and American-Indian; nine Caxtons; the (*rarissimus*) Boke of St. Albans; the Shakespeare, folio, fifteen of the quartos; the first edition of Don Quixote; Blake's Works and other rarities, to say nothing of all the great binding masters, and a host of books that had belonged to kings and queens.

Of the finest and most "desirable" of these patriarchs, and rarest of rare Aldines, is the Virgil of 1501, an ordinary octavo of no striking merit. But mark! " It is," says Mr. Quaritch, offering a copy, "the first book printed in italic type by Aldus Romanus, slightly wormed, else good copy, in red Italian calf extra, borders of gold, gilt edges. To find the first Aldine Virgil in perfect condition is *almost hopeless.* Neither Mr. Beckford nor the Duke of Hamilton, who would have become purchasers at any price, could ever secure even tolerable copies, those occurring for sale being defective." A sad state of things, but warranting the seller in asking for his small octavo £112. But this should be further noted. Even in these pristine days the forger and imitator was at work, and so desired and "desirable" was the Aldine octavo that there was issued at Lyons, to meet the demand : " The Aldine Counterfeit, with facsimiles of the title and last leaf of the real Aldine Edition, probably to pass it off for the original, the book being perfect without that imprint, red morocco extra, gilt edges, with Aldine anchor in gold on sides, 1501, £15, 15s." This volume was the first issued by the Lyonese forgers in imitation of the Aldine type, and is perhaps quite as rare, if not even rarer, than the original. Bishop Butler's copy sold for £22.

The next desirable of these grand old monuments is the Livy of the De Spiras of Venice, issued in the year 1470 in two great folio volumes. Everything stately and beautiful seems to have been lavished on these noble tomes. Dibdin's tongue seems to "grow wanton" in their praise. "This great printer," he exclaims, "is praised, not because he produced many volumes, but because he gave the world what was the most beautiful and best." This was a work of supreme rarity; on vellum, probably not more than three copies are known. It was one of the most superb works offered at all the recent sales. It was arrayed in contemporary oaken binding, covered with stamped leather, the first page of each volume exquisitely illuminated in choicest Italian style, and each chapter heading illuminated in gold and colours. Well kept and taken care of through four long centuries, richly yet soberly dressed, these treasures repay the kindness with which they are treated, and might be well enshrined in cabinets.

The sense of possession adds hugely to the power of enjoyment of such treasures. Shown so rare a volume in another's library, there is not time leisurely to weigh and appreciate its merits. Somehow a book in a *public* library seems to be beyond sympathies. It is under government, under the care of officials— not to be handled tenderly by *one* kind and anxious master. When it is your own, however, you can cultivate its acquaintance day by day, and get to know it. But to these grand "Incunables" or Cradle-Books, with their miniatures and capitals glowing with gold and colours, the ordinary book forager hardly dare raise his eyes. He may handle at auction-rooms Jenson's Pliny—the "glory of his press;" but £35, the price at the Woodhull sale, is too vast. The companion Pliny of the Venetian De Spiras seems a nobler and rarer volume, worth pausing over a few

moments as it strikes the spectator with more astonishment and admiration than any other work of its
day. It would be difficult to give an idea of its sumptuous and noble aspect. It is one of the monumental
works, and might be laid apart by itself, on a great
reading-desk, as though it were a Bible or Missal.
There was a copy on vellum with " painted capitals "
in the Sunderland sale which fetched £82 ; but Jenson's Pliny at the same sale, in its blue morocco
jacket, brought no less than £220 !

One day exploring the shelves of a favourite old
book shop in Holywell Street, and groping in the dim
mysterious light within, I came upon a maimed imperfect copy of this De Spira Pliny. Leaves were
wanting at the end, it was grievously mauled and
soiled in places, and it was execrably clothed, by
some profane vandal of an owner, in the commonest
of modern jacket—oh ! vile profanity !—in "half
calf," with marble paper sides ! But there was still
left many a painted capital, richly dight, though many
a one had been cut out—beautifully designed things
—the larger letter in burnished gold, brighter even
than it was 420 years ago, and encircled with lacer-
tine devices of an Irish pattern. These, I was
assured, if " *cut out* " and sold separately for mount-
ing in books, would have brought money as little
works of art ! The glory of the whole, however, was
the front page—the threshold of the volume—encircled by a florid bordering with burnished gold and
flowers and arabesque. The date of this huge volume
was 1469, and it was to be noted that the leaves
were without numbers, but a scribe had placed a
number at the head of each page. More curious
still, as Greek characters had not then come into
use, and words in Roman letters were used cor-

responding to the sound; exactly as Jenkinson is described in the "Vicar of Wakefield," when quoting his cosmogony. Rudely handled as it had been, I was glad to carry the old tome home, to pour oil into and bind up his wounds. He became mine for something about three pounds, which it was well worth. It is pleasant and refreshing to take him out occasionally, and think of the eyes and hands of 420 years ago. Not less pleasant is it to show it to a visitor as an illustration of what could be done in those days. His surprise is great, for he expects some rude and clumsy effort. Such "a find" as this more than rewards the book fancier. But all the De Spira books—and they are very few—have this elegant and romantic air.

§ Of the Elzevirs, Plantins, and Old Printers.

CCASIONALLY in his wanderings the old-book collector turns up in the book boxes laid out at the stall-door a likely compact little volume, about the size of a small Prayer-book, but prettily printed in close but brilliant type. This is an *Elzevir*, a charming little pattern of book, full of artistic merit in its title-page, "colophon," and in its paper, print, and legibility everything that can be desired. This famous house was a family of printers for many generations, and flourishing for nearly a century and a half. It began with Louis Elzevir, who was followed by Bonaventure, Abraham, Isaac, and others. They were originally fixed at Leyden, and a great deal of their work was the routine University business, the printing of theses, examination papers, and books necessary for education. They afterwards moved to Amsterdam, whence the more familiar imprint, Daniel and Louis Elzevir, was issued. In time business gradually fell away, owing to the neglect of members of the firm, and it was noted that their works became as remarkable for misprints and general carelessness as they had before been for scrupulous accuracy.

Towards the close of the seventeenth century they ceased to work, or adopted the modern principle of getting other printers to do their books for them. What first brought them into notice was the simple innovation of issuing small and portable editions of the classics, instead of the vast and ponderous folios formerly thought *de rigueur.* They went to the opposite extreme, issuing little miniature volumes handy and elegant. They brought thought, money, and toil to the task, which was of enormous difficulty, for such compression, as we have seen, might necessitate small and illegible type ; but they contrived by the clearness and beauty of their letters, and by bringing the rules of art and proportion to bear, to furnish all that could be desired. They imported the finest French paper, and employed a skilful engraver, C. Van Dyck, to design their types ; and the beauty of their work, and its hearty appreciation, shows that their labour was not thrown away. The painter Meissonier has devoted himself to small cabinet pieces, worked with an almost photographic minuteness, yet it has been remarked that there is as much dignity and "largeness" in the effect as if it was on a great scale. There is much the same result in this kind of printing, which, without art and taste, becomes mean, petty, and unpleasant to look at. The secret seems to be in avoiding the excessive "spacing," or intervals between words and letters, which is supposed to give clearness. The letters are put closely together, and each word has a massive air. Again, each letter is well designed and has a characteristic of its own, and there is an avoidance of those unmeaning hair-strokes now fashionable. There were also a great number of shapes of letters and pretty forms which lent a variety. Above all, the paper was close and strong, ivory tinted, and velvety to the touch.

There are three little works, which are considered their *chefs d'œuvres*, namely, the *Pliny*, the *Terence*, and the *Virgil*. These bring great prices; but the eager connoisseur looks jealously at the *Terence* to see that it is the genuine first edition. For two followed which are held to be spurious; that is, they were issued *bonâ fide* by the firm and reprinted line for line, but the old engraved title was used again to save expense, and without alteration in the date. The paper, of Angoulême make, for the three little books was exquisite, and used in no others, which, cries an enthusiast, "turns what is simply silver into pure gold." * Some idea of the operations of this great firm may be conceived from the list of their works, which reach to some hundreds, including all the Latin, French, and Italian classics, besides a vast number of light and curious books of the *belles-lettres* class. Here we find Rabelais, plays of Molière and Corneille, the " Provincial Letters," books of controversy, and some not very proper books. A few are ridiculously *recherché*. At one time it was assumed that a reprint of a French cookery-book, the " *Pastissier Français*," was truly " precious " and one of the greatest rarities. It may be said, *en parenthèse*, that this sort of rarity is often the creation of some

* So with the Virgils, which a passage from Mr. Quaritch shows us how to distinguish. " VIRGILII OPERA, 12mo. The genuine edition, with the two passages in red and buffalo head on dedication, vita and page 1, fine copy, ruled, in red morocco, gilt edges, by Roger Payne. Lugd. Bat. Elzevir, 1636.—Also VIRGILII OPERA. The reprint with the two passages in black, buffalo head only on the dedication and the errata. fine copy, ruled, in red morocco, gilt edges by Roger Payne, Lugd. Bat. Elzevir, 1636." For the first twelve guineas were asked ; for the second, only four.

rich bibliomaniac, who officiously announces that the
case is so, or gives some large price, which leads
eventually into the domain of ridiculous and fantastic
cravings, when the poor sufferer is more fit for re-
straint than many a regular Bedlamite.

There has at times been a "rage" for Elzevirs
akin to the Dutch tulip mania, but extending
only to the choice and rare copies, whose margins
were nicely measured in millimetres ; such as the
Montaigne, in three volumes, "thick 12mo"—it
is recorded that Beckford's copy sold for £200, and
Benzon's for more. Wonderful to relate, a copy,
"a large tall one," and bound by Courteval, and
whose only blemish was being "slightly wormed,"
could lately have been had for three guineas. These
fluctuations are marvellous. The craze will come again,
nay, is likely to come speedily. There is a literature
on this subject, and the History of the Firm, with
grave learned disquisitions on the merits of their
books, lists of every work, duly catalogued, has been
written several times. The judicious collector can
even now secure, at very low prices, charming specimens of these famous printers.

The fashion in which one or two of these little
volumes have attained celebrity has been revealed
to us. Thus of the "*Pastissier François,*" one of
the oldest cookery-books, it is said that a bibliographer named Bérard was the first to give it a
reputation by declaring that he knew of only two
copies in the world ! Instantly the cry of *rarity* was
raised, with the result that in 1843 nearly ten copies
were discovered, while a later writer was enabled to
count up no less than thirty or forty ! Still this is
about the same proportion to existing demand as
the two copies were fifty or sixty years ago, and even

now the matter is brought to a fair test in a copy being offered at the choice and wonderful sale of the Syston Park Library, when two copies were sold at moderate prices.

The little Elzevir *Cicero* is also much sought. But have a care, stall-fancier! for some are printed on a fine paper, the others on an inferior paper. These little books are actually appraised by measurement, the finest copies, we are told, being from 132 138 millimetres high. Count D'Hoym, whose golden library-stamp on the side of a book adds an infinite value, was the blessed possessor of a copy bound by Padeloup, and which sold for £400! Charles Nodier tells us that the genuine Elzevir of the old catalogues is beyond all price when it is *large*. A hair's-breadth increases its value in the proportion of carats in the case of diamonds. "We have seen," he tells us, "a *Cicero*, bound by Derome, sell for 600 francs, while next it was another scarcely worth 60 francs. In this increase 300 francs was put on for three breadths of white paper, and 240 francs for the binding."

At this moment I have in my hand one of their typographical feats, a small edition of *Livy*, to be carried in the pocket. It is of 12mo size, and the modern printer would lift up his eyes in wonder at the problem successfully solved of compressing into so small a space, as to be read with ease, the contents of the vast closely printed folios which this voluminous author fills. There are nearly 800 pages, and each page contains 144 lines, or about 850 words. When it is considered that an octavo of our day, with a well-filled page, contains about 30 lines, or 300 words, it will be seen what a feat has been here accomplished. Yet the whole is brilliant, clear, and can be read with comfort by ordinary

eyes. The effect is very different from those painful
"diamond" editions which used to be issued by a
few of our publishers. The little thing which I possess is charming in every way, bound exquisitely in
solid Mazarin blue morocco.

There is one antique printing house still standing,
whose history and associations add to the romance
of books. In the old printing city of Antwerp, close
to one of the new Boulevards, is an old, iron-grey,
picturesque building, with a tranquil air of monastic retirement ; not, too, without architectural merit.
This, for the visitor of taste, is the "sight" in the old
town which leaves the most pleasing agreeable impressions. It is the Plantin Museum, the offices of a
great printing firm that flourished for a couple of
centuries. Their chief function was supplying the
ecclesiastical world with those fine quarto missals
and office-books, printed in cheerful red and black,
which are still often found in old chapels and monasteries. Gradually the business decayed, though
it was continued until a recent period. The old offices
were left deserted until some amateurs, true artists,
exerted themselves to have the place purchased for
the town and preserved.

The effect of the grave, solemn place is extraordinary.
There is a strange tranquillity, a church-like shade,
that we never can forget. Never was printing so
housed before. The charming, spacious courtyard ; its
mullioned windows, struggling with leaves and nearly
obscured ; the creepers, the old vines, the 'scutcheon
—all on the iron-grey background—leave a soft con-
templative impression. A Renaissance colonnade on
one side suggests some of the colleges at Cambridge.
"The aspect of this place," as has been truly said,
"imprints a lasting impression on the mind of the

thinker and artist." The noise of the world outside
cannot penetrate to this solitude; and yet it is not
the solitude of desolation, but an isolation which
invites meditation. Time has indeed left his mark,
but has altered nothing and destroyed nothing. This
is no exaggeration, and many a traveller wearied with
the official shows of the Flemish town has testified
to the extraordinary and ever-enticing charm of the
old printing-office. We enter to the same solemnity ;
the shade awaits us within, in the suitable halls rather
than rooms, through whose diamond-paned windows
the light comes shaded by the vines.

Here everything is preserved as if from yesterday
—the old " formes," the black oaken desks, the types
and woodblocks, as if the workmen had but just gone
away. In these halls the dim light comes through
the diapered frames, and the greenery of the court
flutters before the windows. It seems some old
monastic retreat. Our thoughts fly back to the
modern Babel of a printing-room, with the whirling
wheels, the noise of the machine, the white walls,
and the general manufacturing air. But here there
is the grey and revered tone of age ; and so completely in order is everything, that one almost expects
in a moment to hear the old bell ring out, the
tranquil dream to come to an end, and to find the
Plantin workmen busy once more at their cases and
" pulling proofs " at the old presses. The whole
is certainly unique.

The work-rooms have a charm and grace that
must have lent a dignity to the work, and are decorated with medallions, escutcheons, paintings, and
other ornaments of the most refined and pleasing
style. Plantin was the great Catholic printer, as
the Elzevirs were the great Protestant printers, and

the works of both reflected these influences. From the former presses issued all the grand missals and prayer-books and religious works, while invocations to the Blessed Virgin and pious inscriptions graced the rooms in which the work was carried on. The Elzevir presses groaned with fierce controversy and abundant attacks on the old faith. The productions of both were almost on a level for typographical merit; but the Elzevir press has obtained a far higher reputation among book amateurs. The old presses, standing idle, but in excellent order, are notable for a certain artistic elegance of design and construction, and one is amazed at their number : in one room there being more than twenty-two. In the correctors' room—a noble apartment, where once Moretus, Rapheling, and Lipsius, all scholars, sat and worked—the drawers are filled with corrected sheets and old authors' manuscript, the furniture and armoires are all of fine design and solid make, and it is to be noted that the correctors sat upon a high platform to pursue their labours. It is a chamber worthy of the dignity of the calling, and very different from the little "den" so often allotted to that functionary with us. Upstairs there is the foundry, with the furnaces, the stores of matrices and type, and vast masses of woodblocks : three thousand for a single book, *The History of Plants*, reaching to some fifteen thousand in all. The curious have noted among the type some few of silver, thus giving support to what has been often stated, that certain books, either Plantins or Elzevirs, have been printed with silver type. This might seem a rather convincing proof of the fact, for to have cast only a few letters of this precious material would be unmeaning. The probability is that on ceasing business the silver type must have been taken away and sold or melted down. Otherwise it would have been like leaving so much money among the types.

Though their list of works printed is not nearly so abundant as that of the Elzevirs, it must be remembered it was a far older firm, and began its labours about 1555. Its grandest achievement was the great Polyglot Bible, in seven large volumes, and in five languages, Greek, Latin, Hebrew, Chaldaic, and Syriac. This was attempted in 1573, under the direction and patronage of Philip II. of Spain, and at his cost. Such a work nowadays would tax the energies of our most important printers, and it may be imagined how difficult it was to secure competent workmen equal to the duty of setting up such " outlandish " dialects. And yet it was accomplished in splendid style, in the course of only four years, employing the labour of forty men. The cost too was comparatively small, 40,000 crowns, or £10,000, equivalent, we may suppose, to about £20,000 in our day.

Combined with the printing-office was the dwelling-house of the family, which is exactly as it was in their day, with its rich yet chaste furniture, fine pictures, manuscript, and other treasures. The old printer who produced such grand works was an interesting and even heroic person ; the bringing out of some of his great folios was an enterprise—like launching a ship. He laid all his energies to the work, was often in straits for means to complete it : had to encounter jealousies and hatred, desertion and rivalries. He seemed to be carried through, inspired by a genuine faith and enthusiasm, as though it were a solemn thing to introduce one of these great things into the world. There was infinite thought, labour, and cost in the planning of such books, with also much anxiety and distress.

Such was the old printer's life—something of an art : for the workman brought with his strong arms and delicate touch a certain individual feeling. Many a compositor, as in the case of Franklin, would " set " the type of a book entirely by himself or aided by a companion : the pressman as he " pulled " the sheets made the task an individual, or separate art, carefully scanning and correcting defects for the next effort. He therefore strictly " printed " the book. So the work went on tranquilly and leisurely in the sober and comparatively silent buildings ; the Leyden scholars, sitting upstairs each in their calm retirement, officiating as " correctors." Now for a curious contrast, when we change the scene after an interval of say two hundred years.

It is the afternoon of a busy London day, and we turn out of Fleet Street into Bouverie Street, lined with ranges of great factories, all blackened and grimed, the rows of windows incrusted with the dirt of years. Nothing here but gloom. The cross lanes that join this street to its parallel neighbours are also lined with the factory buildings, behind which peeps up a stunted chimney belching rolls of smoke. Strange Cimmerian regions these—men in dirty caps and blackened arms hurry to and fro, and stray about the doors. The ground *throbs*, and in the cellars the pulses of engines beat. The perpetual clank, clank, clatter of " the machine " strikes the ear from all sides. Flywheels whirl, the presses strike and crash, and it seems a matter of labour, and often pain, to get an impression or " proof." For this is modern Printing Land, where the newspapers with " largest circulation in the world," &c., are engendered, books struck off at white heat, great ink-rollers glisten with jet ink, cobra-like; drying, boilers, flywheels, engines so many horse-power, men and boys like imps; and the "fair, white," unsoiled paper—one of the most delicate things—is produced, odd indeed! by such agents. Within nought but bare white-washed walls; the composing-room a vast cheerless factory, where there seems a sense of huddle and little ease; foremen seeming to work under temporary conditions, in accommodation knocked up, as it were; corrector hard by, in a rudely got-up enclosure; a tortuous stair, like that of the gallery of a theatre, perpetually promenaded up and down by the blackened boys and men aforesaid; pots of beer going up; a man keeping the "times" of the men in a little sentry-box hutch! Here is a suggestion of the "behind the scenes" in some great theatre; the rudely whitened walls, the revolving wheels aloft—ropes, "belts," &c., helping the idea. Here, as by necessity, everything is wrought by "the machine;" the boy stands at its mouth to "feed" it, the great white sheet is swept in, tossed out in a half second at the other end printed; nay, the setting, though done by fingers, is under machine influence, for the "copy" is cut into short slips, and a column distributed among a score, regardless of sense or sentence. What a contrast this to the old printers and their *art!* Yet this change is unavoidable, "cannot be helped," under the conditions; being, moreover, a wonderful spectacle of energy, "saving of labour," and unrest.

How often the character of the old printer seemed to answer to his work! The more eminent have invariably been men of force of character, "adventurers," as it were, and of a life that interests all. This may

H

come of the speculative cast that attends this venture, the need for sagacity and for making a *coup*. Their lives have been not without romance—there is something in the tone of the " chapel "—the intercourse with their authors—the busy workmen—that tends to this. The story of the very first of them all, Gutenberg, is a sad one of struggle and fortitude. How interesting and even exciting is that of the Italian Aldine family, and that of the French Stephens, the Elzevirs, and Plantins ! In England, too, the story of Caxton is full of interest; while in modern times we have the spirited careers of the Tonsons, Dodsleys, Strahans, Baskervilles, Boydells ; while the history of the Ballantynes and Archibald Constable lends much that is dramatic to the life of Scott. In our day the story of the Chambers's (Robert and William), Black, and Macmillan have been all told at length. The printers associated with Boswell and Johnson acquire a charming and original interest. So with the Dillys, Charles and Edward, the hospitable entertainers of Wilkes, and Johnson, and Bowyer.*

There is always an interest in the hard-working, painstaking, never-flagging "reader," who sits up

---

* A good tradition is handed down of the amiable delusion under which amateur writers labour as to the cost, sale, &c., of their productions. A simple country clergyman had written a sermon, in which he had exceeding faith, and came up specially to London to arrange for its publication. He waited on the worthy Bowyer, who was of the old type of publisher. The vicar was poor, but full of enthusiasm. The publisher asked him how many copies he would have taken off. " Why, sir," replied the vicar, " I have calculated that there are in the kingdom so many thousand parishes, and that, at the lowest computation, each parish will take at least one copy, and others more, so that I think we may venture to print thirty-five thousand, or say thirty-six thousand copies." The printer listened gravely, the matter was arranged, and the vicar returned to his parish. After waiting impatiently two months for the piece to get into fair circulation, he wrote for the account of sales, adding, how-

aloft, anywhere or anyhow, and does his work. Of him it was written :—

> " His brain must be cool,
>   As an eagle his sight ;
> And chained to a stool
>   From morning till night,
> He must read and correct
>   Typographical matters,
> Taking care to detect
>   All the wrong fonts and batters.
>
> He who seeks for the place
> Must have ' worked at case,'
>   Must be also ' well up ' in typography ;
> Of each science and art
> Must at least know a part :
>   Must be thoroughly versed in geography.
> German—French—Latin—Greek
> He must read (if not speak),
>   Must of course be a thorough grammarian.

---

ever, that there was no hurry as to the cash settlement. He received in reply the following account :—

" The Rev. ——, *Cr.*

		£	s	d
By sale of 17 copies of Sermon	.	£1	5	6
By printing, paper, &c., 35,000 copies	.	785	5	6
Balance due to Printer .	.	£784	0	0 "

In a day or two followed another letter from the worthy publisher, who was a good-hearted man.

" DEAR SIR,—I beg pardon for innocently amusing myself at your expense ; but you need give yourself no uneasiness. I knew better than you could do the extent of the sale of single sermons, and accordingly printed but 50 copies, to the expense of which you are heartily welcome, in return for the liberty I have taken with you," &c.

Thus was the poor vicar relieved. Yet those who take a cynical view of human nature and of authors' vanity, might be inclined to add a sequel, viz., the second thoughts of the disappointed vicar, when wounded vanity might begin to take effect. If a larger number had been put into circulation, *as he had directed*, why, the sermon might have sold. The publisher might surely have pushed it, instead of taking on himself to extinguish the work so effectually.

> Quite *au fait* to the rules
> Of the various 'schools,'
>   Not merely an Abecedarian.
>
> Then he'll read—read—read,
>   Till his eyes grow weary and dim,
> And read—read—read,
>   Till exhausted in every limb,
> 'Midst the clamour of boys,
> Interruption and noise ;
> The uproarious revels
> Of young 'Printer's Devils.'
>   Pray, how should you like to be HIM ? "

How this useful being pursues his monotonous
functions is shown in a pleasant sketch by a once
popular writer :—

"While the 'reader,'" says Sir F. Head, "is seated
in his cell, there stands beside him a small intelligent
boy who is, in fact, the reader—that is to say, he reads
aloud from the manuscript while the man pores upon
and corrects the corresponding print. This child—
for such he is in comparison with the age of the master
he serves—cannot be expected to take any more interest in the heterogeneous mass of literature he emits
than the little marble cupids in Italy can be supposed
to relish the water which is made to everlastingly
stream from their mouths. In our cell we find the
boy reading aloud to his patron a work or paragraphs
in the French language, which he had never learned,
and which, therefore, he was thus most ludicrously
pronouncing, as if written in English : ' Less ducks
knee sonte pass,' &c. (*i.e.*, '*Les ducs ne sont pas*,' &c.)
To the 'reader's' literary ears this must have been
almost as painful as is to common nerves the cutting
of a saw ; yet he patiently listened, and laboriously
proceeded with his task."

When the "*proof*" is returned to the compositor,
he amends it, and from it is printed another impres-

sion, which is styled a "*clean proof,*" also "*author's proof,*" which is sent to the author, and if he on reading it has no occasion to make many alterations, he may not think it necessary to require another proof (or "*revise,*" as it is termed), in which case he writes the word "*Press*" upon it; and having been finally "read" in the office, it is then printed off. But when the author or editor makes on it any alterations or amendments, the compositor is paid for the time occupied in so rearranging the type. Stower adds that if errors be discovered when it is too late to have them corrected, then the word "*Press*" is to the "reader" as the signature of the death-warrant of his reputation. It is absolutely required, therefore, that a "reader" should be a man of one business— always on the alert—all eye—all attention. It was a saying of Godeau, a bishop of France (*ob.* 1671), that to compose was an author's *heaven,* to correct his proofs an author's *purgatory,* but to correct for press an author's *hell.*

The following account of the various types will be found useful. These are *double pica, paragon, great primer, English, pica, small pica, long primer, bourgeois, canon, brevier, minion, nonpareil, ruby, pearl, diamond,* and *brilliant. Pica,* from being used in the pica or liturgy of the Church, was called by the French and Germans *Cicero,* the epistles of that writer being first done in them. *Brevier* had its name from being used for the Roman breviary. The French call it *little text,* and the Germans *maiden letter. Canon* was first produced by the French for works relating to the canons of the Church, to which the German title *missal* alludes. It came into use about 1695. *Bourgeois* also came from France, where it is called *gaillarde,* and was dedicated to the master printers there. It first appeared about 1529. Office-books of prayer suggested *primer* (from *primarius*), sometimes called *Bible text*. *Great primer* is the largest type ever used for books. The French call it Great Roman. *English* (or Old English—so called from its having been used in early times for printing our books of laws, statutes, &c.—one of the founts known among printers as " blacks "), is called by the Germans *mittel* (by the French and Dutch St. Augustin, that saint's writings being first produced with it). *Small pica* is called *brevier* by the Germans, and *philosophie* by the French. *Long primer* is called Little Roman by the French, the Germans *Corpus*, it having been first used for printing the *Corpus Juris*. *Union-pearl* is a letter of fancy created somewhat past the middle of the eighteenth century. It is said to have received this name from the pearls which grow in couples, to which the nodules in the letters were conceived to bear some resemblance. *Paragon*, or " perfect pattern," which the word implies, happening to turn out a well-shaped letter and better than the last, was so named by the French. It is the only letter which has preserved its name among all nations. *Minion*, a size between brevier and nonpareil, is so called from the French *mignonne*, or favourite. The Germans call it *colonel*. *Emerald* is a small kind of minion. *Nonpareil* (from the French and German *nonparielle*) so called because at its introduction it was without a peer in comparative size to the larger type. *Ruby* is so named by Mr. Hansard, he " having felt it absolutely necessary to give some distinguishing appellation to its size."

Of printers' errors, &c., there are innumerable good stories, and every busy writer could relate some piquant instances. Many, however, have the air of being manufactured. These American instances, however, are very good. A country editor, dwelling on the death of a village maid, whose obituary he was writing, detailed her dying injunction that no monument should be placed above her grave, but a plain slab, with the simple inscription " Mary." On reading the proof of his article, however, he became doubtful of the correctness of her Christian name, and hurriedly ran his pencil through it as a preliminary to correction. One of the townsfolk dropping in at that moment assured him that the young girl's name was " Mary," and he accordingly dotted a line below the erased word, writing in the margin of the proof the usual direction " stet " (let it stand). He was somewhat astonished the next morning on learning from the paper that the dying girl had requested, as a last favour, that upon her tombstone should be placed " the simple inscription, ' Stet.' " It availed him nothing that he endeavoured to explain to the tearful but indignant parents that the mistake, after all, was not so very bad. Many of the people believed that he had actually attempted to improve the poor girl's dying injunction with his " college lingo."

A widower in the same place wished his elderly wife to be celebrated, and he himself was allowed to write the obituary. In the proof the editor noted that the lady was described as " being remarkable for her *chastity* " —instead of " charity "—an odd commendation.

There is a work greatly *recherché* from a singular oddity :—Dr. Bonnell Thornton was passing through the press a splendid folio work. In a certain page a *space* (as printers term it) *stood up* : the Doctor (and this shows the misfortune of not understanding " printers' marks "), instead of writing or making the sign for *dele* opposite the line with the objectionable little mark, wrote on a head-page " take out horizontal line at page so and so "—the compositor inserted these words as a *displayed line* in the head-page whereon they were written ; the "reader" passed it in the revise, and it was so worked off ! Being eventually detected, the leaf was of course cancelled. Any copy, therefore, with these wrongly inserted words, is consequently eagerly sought after. Such errors arise, of course, from indifferent and bad writing, some of which is absolutely distracting. But it is a fact that no matter how indifferent or difficult to read, the printers, if they have to deal with much of it, soon learn to read it. They more protest against the confusion of alterations and insertions, which are often impossible to follow. Burke's " Letter to a Noble Lord" was printed off and the proof sent to him, but was returned to the printing-office with so many alterations and passages interlined, that the compositors refused to correct it as it was, took the whole matter to pieces, and reset the copy ; and there is little doubt that to the illegible caligraphy of many writers with their sometimes innumerable alterations, additions, &c., is to be attributed much of the "Errata" to be found in most publications. Truly some "copy" looks as if a spider had been dipped in ink and permitted to perambulate the paper, and so cover it with undecipherable hieroglyphics ; this was the character in which the poetry of the Rev. W. Lisle Bowles was written. Of the writing of Dr. Rees, the well-known editor of " The Cyclopædia," it is said it seemed as if he had used a burnt stick, and that on one occasion the printers clubbed their money and presented him with a hundred good pens, begging him to use them for their sakes if not for his own. The " Georgian

Era " states that there is an instance on record of three volumes of corrections being written to one volume of proofs !

In the history of the "chapel" or printing-office there are many strange incidents. How curious, for instance, are those beings who at their desk have "composed" their types without "copy," being author and printer at the same moment. The intermediate writing was omitted. There are many books which have been made in this fashion.

Thus, there was a book published in 1844 called " Colloquies Desultory, but chiefly upon Poetry, &c." —a volume of 250 pages, but not a word of it was really ever *written*. The clever author, printer, and publisher, Mr. Lordan of Romsey, set up the types as fast as he mentally composed the book, and the latter, as a critic truly says, is highly creditable to the author, who, however, never *wrote* it. It has been affirmed that Dugald Graham, the Rhyming Chronicler of the Rebellion of 1745, used to compose and set up his works in type without committing them to writing. There was a French novelist who, being like our Richardson, a printer, composed a volume in type, and thus this book was likewise printed without having been written. William Cowdroy, editor, proprietor, and printer of the *Manchester Gazette* (1814), whilst employed at Chester as editor and compositor, displayed this faculty of composing his paragraphs without writing them. The practice was first adopted by Thomas Jonathan Wooler, the printer of the *Black Dwarf*. He was also its editor and article-producer,—"composed" his articles (in a double sense of the phrase) at case. E. W. Forster, of the *Hants Guardian*, used to relate :—" From my earliest connection with

I

a newspaper, now many years ago, it has been my practice to compose all leaders from case direct, without the help of any copy whatever. I have followed this plan in many other ways connected with newspaper work ; and what it is desirable to communicate to the public is the fact that the rate of ' composing' coincides admirably with the flow of thought ; that to furnish a good leader, or anything else, it is a great advantage to produce it from the head direct, ignoring the use of pen and paper."

§ Of Caxtons and of the English Printers.

HE subject of our English printer Caxton is really a fascinating one, and has furnished food for the artist, the poet, and the story-teller. The learned and laborious Blades has written a profound account of his life and works in one of the most interesting of such treatises—a dungeon of learning, though perhaps too technical for "the general." Indeed, it is surprising to see what the indefatigable labour of antiquaries and expenditure of money have done both for Caxton and Shakespeare. But by this tremendous and assiduous toil, and the premium offered in the shape of costly prices, an astonishing number of the printer's works have been recovered, and will be preserved securely for generations born hundreds of years hence —unless, indeed, convulsions arise, such as the descent of barbarian hordes, or a revolutionary rising, when these libraries may be sacked or burnt, as in the case of the revolutions of 1830 and 1870.

One of the Spencer family, in an interesting lecture on the Althorp Library, gives a summary of the Caxton treasures in that wonderful library. Mr.

Blades has also enumerated ninety-nine productions of his press as in existence. The British Museum possesses the largest number of copies ever brought together, between eighty and ninety—of which twenty-five are duplicates. The collection of Caxtons in the Spencer Library is more complete, numbering fifty-seven separate works, of which thirty-one are perfect and three unique, namely, "The Four Sons of Aymon," "The History of Blanchardin and Eglantine," and a folio broadside of "Death Bed Prayers," which is in perfect condition, and measures 11 by 3 inches. An important relic connected with the house inhabited by our first printer, and affording the earliest known instance of a broadside printed in England, is to be seen in the Althorpe collection in the shape of an advertisement, of which only one other copy, and that an imperfect one, existed. It consists of a single paragraph of seven lines, the longest measuring five inches, and which read as follows:—" If it plese ony man spirituel or temporel to bye ony pyes of two and thre comemoracios of Salisburi use enprynted after the forme of this present lettre which ben wel and truly correct, late hym come to Westmonester into the almonesrye at the reed pale, and he shal have them good chepe." *

* From Mr. G. Sanders's laborious MS. notes I take the following curious comparison of prices, and of the rise in prices paid for Caxtons :—
"The Recuyell des Histoires de Troyes," fol. 1472, was sold by Dr. Bernard in 1698 for 3s., whilst at the Roxburghe sale (1812) the Duke of Devonshire gave £1060 for a copy. "Chess Book," fol. 1475, R. Smith in 1682, 13s. 2d. ; Mainwaring in 1837, £101. "Le Recueil," fol. 1476, Eames in 1760, £2, 12s. ; E. Spencer in 1823, £205, 16s. ; M. Libri in 1844, £200. "Propositio Johannis Rupell," quarto, four printed leaves, John Brand in 1807, £2, 5s. ; Marquis Blandford in 1819, £126. "The Dictes and Sayings of the Philosophers," fol. 1477, Osborne in

Mr. Quaritch, the possessor of many treasures, can of course boast some rare and choice Caxtons. Let him introduce—" The first book printed in England. Westminster, William Caxton, 1474. Caxton's 'Game and Play of Chess, Moralised' (translated 1474), first edition, folio, 65 leaves (of the 72), bound in old russia gilt. An extremely large, though somewhat imperfect copy of the first book printed in England, from Caxton's press. Mr. Blades quotes 9 copies (4 perfect, 5 imperfect), *and the*

1751, £1, 11s. 6d. ; Earl Spencer, £263, 10s. ; "Chaucer's Canterbury Tales," Joseph Ames in 176-, £2 ; Mr. Huth, £200. "Boethius," fol. 1479, Osborne in 1751, £1, 1s. ; Gardner in 1854 (imperfect copy), £70. "Mirrour of the World," fol. 1481, R. Smith in 1682, 5s. ; Duke of Devonshire in 1812, £351, 15s. (it cost the Duke seven guineas). "Tully of Old Age," fol. 1481, 15s. 3d. ; Dr. Bernard in 1698, 4s. 2d. ; Duke of Roxburghe, £115 ; Willett in 1812, £210 ; Mr. Huth in 1857, £275. Second edition "Game of Chess," Dr. Bernard in 1698, 1s. 6d. (!) Duke of Devonshire, £173, 5s. "Godfrey of Boulogne," fol. 1481, R. Smith in 1682, 18s. 2d. ; Dr. Bernard in 1698, 4s. ; Marquis Blandford, £215, 15s. "Polychronicon," fol. 1482, Ames in 1760, 14s. ; Sykes, 1815, £150. "Confessio Amantis," fol. 1483, Osborne in 1745, 14s. ; Mead in 1755, 26s. ; Duke of Devonshire in 1812, £336 ; Willett, 1813, £315 ; at Sotheby's in 1872, £670. "Golden Legend," 1484, W. Fletewode in 1774, 7s. ; Duc de Aumale, £230. "Troylus and Creside," fol. 1484, J. West in 1773, £10, 10s. ; J. Towneley in 1814, £252, 2s. "King Arthur," fol. 1485, Osborne in 1748, £5 : Earl Spencer in 1816, £320. "Fayts of Arms, &c.," fol. 1489, Rawlinson in 1756, 11s. ; Duke of Devonshire in 1812, £336 ; M. Libri in 1862, £255. "Eneydos," fol. 1490, R. Smith in 1682, 3s. ; E. Jeans in 1859, £100 ; B. Quaritch in 1874, £191 (copy wanting two pages), "Chastising of God's Children," fol. 1491 (?), Smith, 5s. ; Earl Spencer, £140. "St. Catherine," fol., Osborne, £1, 1s. ; J. Townley in 1814, £231 (now in the Grenville or British Museum Library).

At the sale in 1773 of the curious library of James West, Esq., the following were disposed of :—" The Prouffytable Book for Man's Soul," £5 (at the Roxburghe sale sold for £140) ; "The Mirrour of the World," £2, 13s. (Roxburghe, £351, 15s.) ; "Golden Legend," £12, 16s. (Roxburghe, imperfect, £31) ; "Tulle of Old Age," £5, 10s. (Roxburghe, £115 ; Willetts, £210) ;

present is the tenth known copy, and is TALLER *than
even the Grenville—hitherto the tallest known copy ;*
my copy measures 11⅛ inches in height by 8 in
width, whilst the Grenville body (also imperfect) is
only 11 *inches high.* No copy of this edition has
been sold for years ; in 1813, Alchorne's copy, wanting first two leaves, the last two leaves, and two
leaves in the second chapter of the fourth tractate,
fetched at Evans's, £54, 12s. The value of this
class of book has much risen since then, and may

"The Boke of St. Albans," imperfect, £13 (Roxburghe, £137;
"Fayte of Arms," £10, 10s. (Roxburghe, £336) ; "Passe Tyme
of Pleasure," £3, 3s. (Roxburghe, £81) ; "Tragedy of Sir Rd.
Grinville," 5s. (or 12s. 6d.), Bindley, £40, 19s. Here a 4to
volume of theological tracts sold for £3, 3s., but in 1856 six of
the lot realised respectively thirty-five times the amount, £110, 5s.
Caxton's "Mirrour of the World," 1481, in good condition, and
for a copy of which at the Duke of Devonshire's sale in 1812
£351, 15s. was given, was purchased in 1828 of a poor illiterate
widow for 2s. !

Dr. Morell tells a story "that Dickey Dalton, his Majesty's
librarian, in garbling the library, *threw out* several Caxtons *as
things that might be got again every day.*" The most beautiful
production of this press is thought to be "King Arthur," fol.
1485. The British Museum has eighty-five examples of Caxton's press, which is the largest number ever brought together ;
owing, however, to duplicates, the real number of works is but
fifty-three. Earl Spencer's collection is therefore more complete,
as it contains no less than fifty-seven separate and independent
works. Cambridge has thirty-eight separate works, the Bodleian twenty-eight, and the Duke of Devonshire twenty-five.
Mr. Blades gives a list of 540 extant Caxtons more or less
complete, some being mere fragments. These comprise ninety-
four separate works and editions, but out of these ninety-four
works no less than thirty-three are known to us by single copies
or by fragments only. With respect to the *sizes of early printed
books,* they were generally either large or small folios, or at least
quartos. Caxton printed 67 folios, 23 quartos, 2 octavos, and
one 12mo ("The Horæ," a unique fragment of eight pages).
His own translations into English amounted to twenty-two, containing upwards of 4500 printed pages. The total produce of
his press, not reckoning the books printed at Bruges, reaches to
above 18,000 pages, nearly all folio size.—*From the Sanders MS.*

now be considered as ten times greater." For this treasure the sum of £400 was asked. The same bookseller also offers :—

" ' Tour - Landry.' On p. 9, leaf a i, ' Here begynneth the book which the knight of the foure made, and speketh of many fayre ensamples and thensygnementys and techyng of his doughters,' small folio, splendidly bound in dark green morocco, covered with blind tooling, joints, blue morocco linings covered with gold tooling, silk fly-leaves, gilt edges, by Lewis, from the library of the Rev. Thomas Corser."

Next followeth its history :—" Excessively rare ; only three other perfect copies are known, of which two are in the British Museum and one in the library of Earl Spencer. There is besides one imperfect one which is in the Bodleian. It is easy therefore to conceive that the present perfect copy may be considered unique as far as the collector is concerned : Lord Spencer's copy is never likely to come into the market (why not ? more likely than unlikely), the other two are, of course, inaccessible, and the one now described is probably the only copy that can be offered for sale within the next hundred years. Since the year 1698 only one other copy has been seen in the public auctions ; it was purchased by Earl Spencer at Brand's sale in 1807. The present one was bought at the Marquis of Blandford's sale in 1819, by G. W. Taylor ; from him it passed into the hands of Mr. Jolly, at the sale of whose books in 1843 it became the property of Rodd, the bookseller. Since that time it has been in the possession of the Rev. Mr. Corser." For this treasure £616 is asked.

Again, let us usher in " ' The Mirrour of the World. Now at this tyme rudely translated out of

Ffrensshe in to Englissh by me symple p. sone William Caxton,' sm. folio, numerous fine woodcuts, *editio princeps*, with engravings, two leaves, and the last page in facsimile, otherwise a fine copy in brown morocco extra, gilt edges, by Bedford. Excessively rare. Mr. Blades enumerates fifteen copies, six of which are imperfect, while the other nine are *locked up* as follows:—in the British Museum (two), the Bodleian, and the libraries of the Duke of Devonshire, the Earl of Jersey, Earl Dysart, Earl of Macclesfield, Earl Fitzwilliam, and Earl Spencer. The Devonshire copy was acquired in 1812 at the price of £351, 15s.; and no copy of any kind has appeared in a public sale since an imperfect one was sold in 1835. Of the imperfect copies, three are safely laid away in the Cambridge, the Windsor, and the Ashburnham libraries; the other three are in private hands, and one of them is merely a fragment. The woodcuts are very remarkable as the first existing specimen of English engraving." For this £400 is asked.

He has also " ' Higden's Polychronicon.' A very fine and morocco copy in morocco extra, gilt edges, with joints, by Lewis, from the Dent and Perkins libraries. The last copy, even approximately perfect, which was sold, produced at Lord Charlemont's sale in 1865, the sum of £477, 15s., although it wanted two leaves. In fact, it would be difficult to name any perfect copies, except that in the Spencer library, and the fine one which is now under description." For this £500 is demanded.

When Lord Charlemont's library was offered, this " Polychronicon " was secured by Mr. Toovey, another spirited bookseller of Piccadilly. This "*wanting two leaves*" offers another marvel, as we may be amazed,

considering how these leaves are attached by the frail
" suture " of old thread, and how more frail still is
the paper, that they should have held together so
long, and that the whole had not gradually been
frayed away.

All these were thought great prices. But, as usual,
when we come to the year of grace and of sales,
1885, in the month of May, the great leap to vast
prices was taken. The rare Caxton, " Le Fevre
Recuyell of the Historyes of Troy," one of the
first books printed, was sold, and, as was to be
expected, the leviathan buyer was the hero of the
day. The book was put in at £200, and by bids
of £10 and £20, run up to the sum of £1820,
and fell to Mr. Quaritch for that sum ! Shortly
after, the auctioneer, Mr. Hodge, informed the buyer
that in 1756 the same copy was sold for £8, 8s.,
adding, " I wouldn't tell you before it was yours,
Mr. Quaritch, in case you would not bid." This
astonishing price was approached by that of Gower's
" Confessio Amantis, 1493," "a fine and perfect
copy, bought for £810 by Mr. Quaritch ; " while
" 'Vyrgle Boke of Eneydos,' reduced into Englysche
by me Wyllyam Caxton, black letter, perfect copy,
rare folio, W. Caxton, 1490," was sold for £235 to
the same buyer.

One of the most interesting features in the old
tomes of this era is the *variety* of type. Our modern
type is monotonous ; but these old printers seem to
have exerted their fancy, and yet, as we have seen,
printing had been but a few years discovered. One
of the most beautiful shapes is a sort of *small*
shortened text, only infinitely clearer, and which the
amateur will recognise in many of Caxton's books.
This was after a Flemish model, and Caxton adopted

K

it. It is curious, too, to find the same printer also adopting a very shabby form of type—a kind of elongated black-letter. He is often very careless about ink or paper. One of the most beautiful works of its size, modest pretensions and price, is a small quarto, Petrarch's "Rerum Memorandarum, &c.," printed in the year 1487, and now *penes me.* This is scarcely distinguishable from a Caxton, and is remarkable for its fine creamy vellum-toned paper and ebony letters of the small German text. The whole it set off with red and blue flourishes. It cost but £2, and is indeed a choice work. It was printed in Belgium, and shows clearly whence Caxton brought his types.

Caxton's books leave very much the same pleasing impression, and the unfamiliar reader who is shown one of his choicer volumes for the first time is astonished to see, instead of a rather rude, antique, and quaint-looking thing, showing age and decay, a fresh, clean, and brilliant work, wrought with elegance even, and lustrous with its cream-tinted paper and resplendent type.

Excellent, however, as are Caxton's best productions, it must be admitted that they cannot be put beside the triumphs of the foreign printers, neither in their sumptuously ambitious size nor in the style of workmanship. These seem to have become at once past masters in the art, and there is a perfect ease and variety in their mode of treatment. Caxton's are slight and unpretending efforts by comparison with their stately volumes, as though his establishment lacked resources, both of money and mechanism. The type and printing, too, will not bear minute criticism, which the foreigners seemed to invite or defy. This is clearly shown by the difficulties restored and reparators encountered—on which Dr.

Dibdin, an enthusiast in all that has typographical merit, declares "that some of Caxton's letters are *so riotous* and *unruly*, that the mere casting of a fount after his models would not ensure an accurate reproduction, while the 'setting' is decidedly bad and disorderly, the letters being set up irregularly and at unequal distances, leaning various ways, and altogether so rude and barbarous that *no printer could set up a line to correspond with the original.*"

About thirty years ago a beautiful and successful facsimile was issued of "The Game of Chess," with which enormous pains were taken, and much cost was incurred. It was not one of the common photographic facsimiles now in fashion, but a reprint or reproduction, letters being specially cast for the purpose. The paper and water-marks were made specially to approach the original as nearly as possible : the result is very satisfactory, and is really about equal to the prototype. In a hundred years or so, when it has duly mellowed, it will cause some confusion, but all imitations are readily distinguishable.*

The sad necessity of many a fine old volume wanting a leaf or title, or, it may be, a corner of a page torn away, has engendered an art of reparation and a race of doctors skilful in healing and restoring. It is a marvel what an infinite cleverness is here displayed —pages of print imitated, the tone of the paper copied, or a new corner joined to the frayed portion so as almost to escape detection. In the British

* A very curious instance is the case of the beautiful and celebrated "Giuntà" edition of the "Decameron," 1527, which so far back as 1727 Consul Smith at Venice had reprinted line for line and with the same title, tint of paper, &c., so that now, at an interval of 160 years, it is difficult to distinguish. But the skilled eye detects it.

Museum is often seen one of the reparators at his
work, for there he finds the original, which he can
copy. Some little old quarto play lacks the title-page
or a half-page torn across. A new title is traced, a
piece of old fly leaf is chosen, and with Indian ink
and a brush the whole is copied in a manner " to
defy detection." The joining of the leaves is contrived in a marvellous way, the edges being " pulped "
or softened, and then squeezed together in a press
with a little paste. The letterpress is then copied.
During the last century there was a person called
Whitaker, who worked for Lord Spencer and others,
and who performed prodigies in this way. His great
feat was the supplying of two leaves in facsimile
for a copy of the Mazarin Bible, and Mr. Nicol, its
owner, was often puzzled to point out which were the
two furnished. It is said that there is a lady who
now earns a livelihood by skilfully filling up *worm
holes* in old books, each leaf being separately and
patiently dealt with, the material being chewed or
" pulped," and pressed into the hole. The charge is
said to be sixpence a hole.

Whitaker's Caxton restorations were really works
of extraordinary labour and art. The inferiority of
a facsimile or photograph is evident ; for print is
an *impression* that is forced into the paper, whereas
the imitation is merely the *appearance* of being impressed. Hence it is readily distinguishable, and has
a disagreeable *sham* look. But this conscientious
person set to work in the spirit that became the
situation, so precious a book as a Caxton requiring the most exceptional treatment. His mode was
this. He had the missing passage traced from
a perfect copy, some founts of Caxton letters cast,
and each fixed in a sort of binder's tool. But then

came the difficulty—Caxton had no uniformity, and had sometimes twenty variations of the same letter. The restorer had then with his binding tools to stamp off every letter, guided by the tracing, and thus produced, at a great cost, certainly, what seemed all but identical with the copy.

From Caxton's day to our own, English printing has not been conspicuous, though, taken *en bloc,* there have been some admirable printers, whose work is of high merit. It may be said, indeed, that there is only one that has received the stamp of a foreign reputation or approbation, viz., Baskerville.* Baskerville was an artistic printer ; for to secure *beauty* in typography, art must be applied to the paper and tone of the paper, margin, ink, spacing, size of type, &c. The secret is the finding out an elegant *proportion* in all, *i.e.*, in a small book the type should not be thick or too black, nay even in the shape, cutting of a letter, quality and fitness is evoked ; it should harmonise with the mass of letters, and yet be distinct. Here was the beauty of the Elzevir type, each letter having a firmness and character of its own, and yet not offering harshness of detail. Uniformity having taken the lead in the commercial side of printing and "machining" with a vastness and rapidity that has no rival, the nation has sacrificed the other graces.

Baskerville, Foulis of Glasgow, Tonson, and Bulmer are perhaps the finest of the older generations of printers. Baskerville's types were purchased by a French company, and will be recognised by the

* The exhaustive monograph on this great printer, recently furnished to the National Biography by Mr. Tedder, the librarian of the Athenæum Club, should be consulted by all book-lovers.

critical in the grand seventy-volume edition of Voltaire's works, issued under the direction of Beaumarchais at the close of last century, where it has an odd masquerading effect. The bold, honest, English type is in protest, as it were, against the French *minauderies* and refinements it is compelled to express. So looks a Frenchman in English clothes. The force of expression goes deeper than might be supposed. There is something singularly odd in an English work printed in French type, and *vice versa.* Baskerville, it is said, produced his chief effects by rapidly drying his printed sheets in ovens before the ink had time to sink into the paper.*

Some of Tonson's folios have a noble air, the paper is so stout and thick, the type so large, black, and handsome. There is a Lucretius of his, which is sometimes met with arrayed in old crimson morocco *à la Derome,* which has an air of what the French call *distinction.* Bulmer's great quartos—the celebrated Boydell Shakespeare, Milton, &c., are fine ambitious works, but the type seems to lack force and dignity in the large expanse. It must be confessed that some of the Foulis folios have a greater dignity and are more impressive with less pretension. They are more after the stately sober pattern of the older progenitors—the pristine " Fifteeners."

English works, whether illustrated or otherwise, are little sought abroad, as any one who consults foreign catalogues may discover. One conspicuous work, however, always brings an enormous price, provided it be the right edition. This is Pine's Horace, a

---

* Baskerville lost heavily in his enterprise, and received but £3700 from the French for his splendid fount. These types finally descended to the base use of figuring as ordinary newspaper " print," and were employed for the daily *Moniteur.*

rather fantastic and stiff-looking book, which is illustrated on every page, and which is literally not printed with type. It is engraved on copper-plates, words and all, from beginning to end.

One of the grandest sets of books ever published was the Delphin Classics, a series of all the Latin and Greek writers, specially prepared, "for the use of the Dauphin." They run to many volumes, and bring a great price. An enterprising English printer, Valpy, reissued them about the year 1820, with *variorum* notes, in 152 volumes. A splendid copy was on sale not long since — a magnificent set of books from Colonel George Meek's fine library. The volumes bound in morocco and calf have his arms in gold on sides, the half-bound volumes have his book-plate. The work was published at over £400, and the owner must have paid Mackenzie nearly £200 for the binding. Yet Charles Lamb might have counted these books among the books which "no gentleman's library should be without." But this item shows what a terrible costly and serious thing a great library must be—from the vast amount required for such "long sets," their ponderous weight, and the cost of glass cases.

The Scotch, in truth, have always not only excelled in publishing enterprises, but have been conspicuous in bringing typography to its greatest perfection. Most of the great London publishing houses owe their prosperity to some sturdy plodding Scottish pioneer, and the names of Andrew Millar, Dodsley, Strahan, Foulis, Constable, Murray, Cadell, Macmillan, Black, Blackwood, and many more, show what success has attended these efforts. One Scotch firm belongs to the roll of the masters of the art, and the works of the Foulises of Glasgow bring fancy prices at the sales. Their fine folio Homer is " desired " by every collector, and their Virgil and other editions of the classics are as pleasing to look at as many of the older masterpieces of typography. There is a calm dignity, an unobtrusive harmony, in the large page and its proportions and tint, that at once excites admiration. These great printers took such a pride in the thoroughness of their work that, as the legend runs, they challenged all comers to discover a single error in their work.* This steady level of excellence has been maintained down to our time. The press of the Ballantynes, under the inspiration of Sir Walter Scott, issued marvels of brilliant and effective printing, which seem to ripen with age. A more beautiful, legible, and satisfactory edition could not be well imagined than that of the long set of the Waverley Novels, published about " sixty years since." The size, paper, illustrations, and extraordinary brilliance of the type, make it quite a favourite edition—indeed the famous tales seem to read differently in the " Abbotsford " and later editions of more show and pretence. This firm still pursues its labours, but has not equalled this feat.

Other later Scotch publishers have issued works that approach more nearly to the older excellence than anything that can be named of modern date ; and certain works issued by Messrs. Edmonston & Douglas are really astonishing for the nobility of the letters and the grand paper. It is uncertain, however, whether these will stand the test of time, or,

---

* So reasonably proud were the Scotch printers of one of their elaborate classics, the " Immaculate Horace," as it is called, that they set up on the gate of Glasgow College a notice offering a reward for the detection of any errata. Some, it is said, were discovered.

like the older monuments, improve and mellow with years. There is no guarantee for the excellence of modern materials, paper, ink, &c., and there is a hurry, roughness, and violence in the processes of machinery which are not found in the care and deliberation of the old hand-work. Each sheet was the distinct and separate result of the workman's labour. The making of a great book in the old early days was like making a monument, such as building a house; now it seems like a manufacture, and copies are turned out like so many " pieces " of cloth.

L

§ ⚙f tɦe Ꙇíbrarp.

EW things so effectually transport us
back to the older ages as the rare spec-
tacle of a library of *chained* books. In
the picturesque old Abbey of Wim-
bourne there is an antique chamber,
small, decayed, low-roofed, high up in the church.
Round it are arranged some rows of tall ancient tomes
in their mouldering calf and vellum, each secured
with its chain hanging down. The effect of all these
chains is graceful and bizarre, from the abundant fes-
toonings with which every tome is furnished. There
is also the accompanying shelf below; for the book
thus secured must be consulted in its own neighbour-
hood.* In one of the libraries at Cambridge, that of
Trinity Hall, the old-fashioned system of a seat that
drew out for the reader under the books, with a desk

---

* In the church of Grantham, Lincolnshire, was a library
remarkable for being one of the few remaining that had its
volumes chained to the shelves. The removal of Selden's books
(about 8000) from London to the Bodleian Library, Oxford, besides costing £34, the providing chains for them cost £25, 10s.
more. This charge occurs so late as 1751. In 1761 there was a
payment for unchaining 1448 books at a halfpenny each. The
Bodleian still preserves some of the loose chains as relics. Bodley
in one of his letters "advised the binding sundry authors together, that the multiplicity of chains might not take away the
sight and show of the books."

to place it on, is, or was, retained until lately. The system, too, of turning the books with the backs to the wall and their leaves to the front, on which was written the name of the work, is still to be seen in one or two old libraries. A bar with a ring and pad-lock ran in front, and gave protection to the long line of volumes.

There have existed, in our own day even, what seem to be appropriate tenants for these antique retreats. Such would exclaim, like Heinsius, " No sooner have I come into the library than I bolt the door to me, excluding Lust, Ambition, Avarice, and all such vices, whose nurse is Idleness, the mother of Ignorance and Melancholy. In the very lap of Eternity, amongst so many Divine souls, I take my seat with so lofty a spirit and sweet content that I pity all our great ones and rich men that know not this happiness." Such were these retiring men, whose studies have been as profound and interesting as those of the past. It has been the custom to point to old Burton as a miracle of quotation and display of omni-vorous research; but there died not long ago a student whose works offer far more astonishing exhibitions of reading and study. This was the late Kenelm Digby, whose " Mores Catholici" and succeeding works astound us, and almost take the breath away by their vast stores of wisdom and poetry, quoted from almost every known book. He appears to have read almost everything ; and the effect of the whole is not that of " scrappy " mosaic or patchwork. The body of the work is in itself a monument of good sense and thought, and the quotations are only used to illustrate the author's views, and seem to have been fur-nished from the memory, which must have been of prodigious power. The whole is conceived in a quaint antique strain. With these old scholars, limited and cramped in means, often dim-eyed, it is impossible not to have a deep sympathy. They seem to have grown into the very fashion of their idols, were mouldy, " fly-blown," wormed. One such is before me now—a worthy antiquary, and one that might have been treated by Dickens. There in his scant, curious library he sat, the dim, grimed panes of the old episcopal library, the atmosphere in which floated the dust of decayed leaves ; with gaunt shadows, the slumbering volumes, the long windows uncleaned for a decade of years, the complete stillness, and he, the old, absorbed librarian bent down to his folio ! Or I have met him on some country road, striding on to his duty—a strange Dominie Sampson figure—with invariably a tiny volume, an Elzevir it might be, held close to his dim bleared eyes.

Every important librarian of our day can tell his story of the pilferer, nearly always a person of respectable rank. Borrowing is often akin to robbery. The private individual who lends has almost invariably to bewail his good-nature. The borrowee himself knows not what has become of the volume. It is lost. There is a pleasant menace written for the benefit of such delinquents.

> " *Si quisquis furetur,*
>   This little *Libellum.*
> Per Phæbum, per Jovem,
>   I'll kill him—I'll fell him :
> In ventrem illius
>   I'll stick my scalpellum,
> And teach him to steal
>   My little *Libellum !*"

At the British Museum there often occurs an epidemic of unmeaning spoliations, a page or two, or a print, being found to have been torn out of valuable books ; and the reader will recall the time when one or two of these outraged volumes used to be set up on a stand as a warning and an exhibition. How often the librarian of some college at the Universities can tell his tale of volumes mysteriously abstracted in a steady course, and how at last suspicion rested on one much-respected scholar, perhaps an ecclesiastic, at whose rooms were found a whole shelf of purloined volumes. This distressing discovery is usually " hushed-up," as it is called—the offence being indulgently considered a sort of disease.

With the growth of modern libraries has arisen a sort of profession—a class of learned experts, well skilled in all the mysteries of books—an accomplished, and, it must be said, rare class of professors. The modern librarian is now recognised. There is a powerful guild of librarians, who hold their congresses and issue their Transactions. Reading these, one sees how truly *scientific* is the subject, and how necessary that the subject should be scientifically dealt with. In the enormous and overwhelming production of books, it needs a rare instinct and knowledge to know what books are to be selected as having a representative character ; and there are a thousand minor questions of arrangement, treatment, issue, checks, and the like.*

On the topic " Catalogue," what an elaborately scientific article might be written ; for the proper arrangement, disposition, &c., of a library have exercised the labour and speculations of some of the cleverest men. Some curious and unexpected reading on this interesting matter will be found in the

* Mr. Tedder, one of this body, has written an agreeable and scientific little tract, in whieh are set out the librarian's duties, with a view of all the various qualifications necessary.

Parliamentary Blue-book on our Museum. Classification is always perplexing, but the classification of books now reckoned by millions is the most perplexing of all. Would we enter " Coningsby," for instance, under Disraeli or Beaconsfield ? It might be said that the principle of modern cataloguing is to adhere strictly to an inflexible rule, even with the result of some inconveniences ; but to make up for this, out of pure good-nature they set up signposts to direct the searcher to the right road wherein he shall search. Thus, it being fixed that names, but not titles, should be used, we may conceive one searching for Lord Malmesbury's Diary. If he were ignorant of the family name, Harris, he could not find the volume ; but a sign-post, good-naturedly set up, points the right road " Malmesbury—*see* Harris."

The British Museum Catalogue is, like the Museum itself, one of the sights of London. It extends to nigh two hundred great folio volumes, ranged in convenient circular shelves, accessible to all. Considering that the books are pouring in at the rate of some thousands a day, and which have to be entered, one gazes with astonishment at the feat of a catalogue that remains the same in form, for daily use, and yet is daily expanding. This marvel of steady perseverance and ingenuity is thus contrived. The title of every work is written out in a sort of uniform " Museum hand," and by manifold ink some half-a-dozen copies are made. These slips are pasted into the folio volumes in their order. The folios are all bound with abundant "guards," so that when a leaf is filled with the slips, new leaves are attached to the adjoining guards. And here is shown the ingenuity. The slips are pasted in a peculiar fashion ; only at the ends, not at the top or bottom. A paper-knife will detach them in an instant; and such is the quality of the Museum paste and the handiness of the system, that the operation can be repeated again and again. When it is necessary for the purpose of rearrangement, as when a page is filled, that the new entry should have a place found for it among the others, in a few seconds the paper-knife has set free all the entries: the new leaves and the old ones are now all blank; the whole can be re-arranged, and spaces left here and there, &c. When all the guards have been filled, and the volume will absolutely hold no more, it is taken to the binder's, divided into two, each being filled up to the old measure with new blank pages and new guards. By a new system the printing of the entries has been adopted, thus making an enormous saving of space, a third or fourth of the old space now sufficing. This is making steady progress, many letters having been completed. The system is a costly one, but not so costly as might be supposed; and it is a further testimony to English spirit and energy that it should have been the first to carry out, on this great scale, a plan from which other nations have shrunk.

Of late years a fashion has obtained of giving exact reprints of first editions of such books as "The Complete Angler," Bunyan's "Pilgrim's Progress," Shakespeare, &c. One or two of Caxton's very earliest books have been thus reprinted. This opens a curious matter for discussion: the vulgar idea being that nothing can be more correct than thus to go back to the fountain-head, where you find the pure text. The truth is, these editions, with their simu-lated antique type, are no more than simple "curios." Little value is attached to the disorderly first folio

Shakespeare, with its antique spelling and mistakes, and queerly shaped letters. But even in the case of modern authors, the first - edition theory will not serve. The truth is, once the book is published, the text ceases to be controlled by the author, and he himself becomes one of the speculators and conjecturers as to his own text. This is one of the penalties of print. Even as to the meaning of a passage, it has been superficially thought that the author is the best judge of what was intended. But it is really what meaning the text will *bear*, not what he intended,—which, however, may be accepted out of compliment to him. " There are some books," says Mr. Palgrave in a pleasant essay, " of which we cannot tell whether the author sanctioned what was printed in his lifetime. There are many of which we cannot tell which edition represents his final intention. Simply to take the last published *coram vivo* would be a coarse and imperfect expedient; for by that time the copyright has often passed from his possession, or the works have been reprinted without his oversight, or he may add and alter many times." This has been done notably by Wordsworth, and in our own day by Tennyson, with bewildering effect, and many have not accepted the later shapings and changings.

We might fairly urge that his first imprint was final and complete—one might as well *alter* a face when born. The alteration of a verse is a new effort by the author, to be accepted *quantum valeat ;* " The Grand Old Gardener," for instance, has been reshaped—thought vulgar—but the author cannot unget his own. Then, again, it has been said by the same authority, that " it may be doubted if there are ten English poets of whose texts an editor could swear in court that they are demonstrably the exact mirror of the poet's intention." And many of Shelley's works were printed after his death.

"Elia" had an exquisite sense of the becoming *accidents*, as they may be called, of books ; and no one has expressed with greater delicacy the special charm of what seems indescribable and indeed impalpable. How common to hear some matter-of-fact reader, and an enthusiast too, say that all editions, pages, paper, print, are to him the same—matter, not manner, is for him. Yet it is a truth that certain authors "read better" in certain editions. So much in reading depends on "the humour" or *gusto* with which a book is taken up, that the costume and decoration of an author is not to be put aside lightly; as in real life we would have the friend whom we love costumed appropriately, and in a fashion that harmonises with his character. There are editions of Shakespeare, for instance—the stereotyped, double-columned, and in " one volume octavo, boards "—which no one that respects himself or his author could read with comfort or dignity—associated meanness and cheapness with cheeseparing, squeezing, huddling ; the contrast with the large ability of the author and the sumptuousness of his treasures, will intrude and disturb. On the other hand, the grand pompous edition equally distracts with its lavish amplitude of margin, vast " spacing," huge type, and large engravings. Here the splendid clothing diverts attention. But Lamb analysed these fancies with his charming touch. Thus he contrasts the older editions of "the Bard," with its ordinary unambitious "cuts," "which to him were more expressive, since they, without pretending to any supportable emulation with it, are so much better than

M

the Shakespeare Gallery *engravings,* which *did.* I have a community of feeling with my countrymen about his plays, and I like those editions of him best which have been oftenest tumbled about and handled. On the contrary, I cannot read Beaumont and Fletcher but in folio. *The octavo editions are painful to look at.* I have no sympathy with them. If they were as much read as the current editions of the other poet, I should prefer them in that shape to the older one."

In truth, an essay might be written by way of commentary on this pregnant passage. There is even a deeper significance in his praise of the older illustrations, which applies with even greater force to the illustrations of our own time. These older plates were all of the most general kind, of a rude imaginative treatment — warriors and tents, and flowing robes. They seem knights and heroes. Our modern illustrator makes all realistic, and copies from the men and women about him. This lends an *earthiness* and a prosiness inconsistent with the text. There is an air of old-fashion, too, about these older editions that is in keeping, and that being "oftenest tumbled about and handled," really means a human association, sympathy, or fellowship, which is always welcome. It must be said, too, that these old editions have merit, the paper and print being good. What Elia adds about not being "able to read Beaumont and Fletcher but in folio," is not purely fanciful. For these dramatic folios, the Ben Jonson, Beaumont and Fletcher, and Shakespeare, are exceptional volumes, convenient in size, and with an air of quaint antiquity that harmonises with the subject. There is a pleasant old fashion in the arrangement of the page, the double column, the

border, the catchword at foot, the old spelling and
lettering ; these being natural and belonging to the
age, not affectation, as the modern " old-faced " type
and imitation " old editions." The paper, too, is
grown tawny. They are really *interesting* volumes
these folios. There is a deeper philosophy, at which
we can only hint here, in the expansive page, into
which is gathered the substance of many pages.
There is *more* before the reader's mind ; his eye can
travel, and he can feel himself in company with
many more images and thoughts. He can have
anticipation and retrospect without trouble, and he
is not cribbed and cabined within the limit of a small
page holding a few lines. This sense of mental
space may seem a refinement, but it has its significance. The octavo editions, with which Elia had
" no sympathy "—he means doubtless those issued
by Gifford and Weber—being now nearly a century
old, would be more satisfactory in his eyes, as by
time and change of fashion they have an antique air
of their own.

Elia's other protest might well be taken to heart
by reckless publishers. " I do not know," he says,
" a more heartless sight than the reprint of the
' Anatomy of Melancholy.' What need was there of
unearthing the bones of that fantastic old great man,
to expose them in a winding-sheet of the newest
fashion to modern censure ? What hapless stationer
could dream of Burton ever becoming popular ? "
And a " heartless " sight it is, as any one who has
held the work in his hand will own. This grave
reverend " Don," now pedantic, now grimly humorous, now learned, the quintessence of the wisdom
of others as of his own, to be dressed up in " a
cheap edition," on mean paper, in a poor pimping

type ! The effect of the contrast between the antique diction and solemnity and the vulgar popular shape almost shocks. But who could express it so happily ? " Heartless " was the word exactly.

Few have an idea of the amount of industry and knowledge that has been brought to bear on the *science*, as it may be called, of books. Bibliography can boast its Owens and Buffons, who can classify and supply genus and species from a mere fragment. For centuries the fascinating study has engaged the attention of profound scholars, who have left behind them exhaustive works exhibiting vast research, and this too applied to everything that concerns the *accidents* of books. For these scholars do not regard the matter of which a book is the vehicle : just as I have known a first-rate philosopher and mathematician who mastered the whole science of music, and could compose you a fugue *secundum artem*, yet to whom musical sounds were unintelligible and odious. It was he who once declared that a fine melody " suggested to him the idea of chloride of lime ! "

It is pleasant to reflect that the first and earliest writer upon books and book-loving was an Englishman, the old Bishop Richard, of Bury, the popular author of the well-known " Philobiblion," issued in 1473. He was Bishop of Durham and Lord Chancellor, and wrote this ardent praise of a library : " In Paris he found delightful libraries in cells redolent of aromatics ; there flourishing greenhouses of all sorts of volumes ; there academic meads, trembling with the earthquake of Athenian Peripatetics pacing up and down ; there the promontories of Parnassus, and the porticoes of the Stoics. There, in very deed, with an open treasury and untied purse-strings, we scattered money with a light heart, and redeemed inestimable works from dirt and dust."

Him followed a long and respectable line of commentators and classifiers, whose works are quoted wherever the subject is dealt with, some writing in Latin, some in German, French, or English. Panzer is a dungeon of learning on " incunables " and early editions, followed by Hain. The French De Bure treats his subject in an agreeable popular style, but Brunet is the indispensable handbook and companion. For English books there are Watts and Lowndes, or Bohn's Lowndes, to which the present writer furnished some humble aid.

But apart from these solemn official treatises, there are some pleasantly garrulous little books, written with a light heart and out of pure love of the subject, and which offer very agreeable reading. Does not the following promise pleasantly as a " Book upon Books " ? " Book Rarities in the University of Cambridge, illustrated with anecdotes of bibliomaniacs, original letters, and notes, biographical, literary, and antiquarian. By the Rev. C. H. Hartshorne." More amusing is Davis's quaintly named " Two Journies Round the Library of a Bibliomaniac, with notes concerning rare, curious, and valuable old Books. Written in 1821." Dr. Dibdin's treatises are well known and unique from their exaggerated raptures ; his earlier works are little known, such as the " Literary Directory," or the " Bibliographical Miscellany : an Essay on Bibliography and the Love of Books," issued 1806. There is a little set of small octavos by Dr. Adam Clarke, which contain much curious information descriptive of old and rare volumes, and " Oldys' British Librarian," published in 1738. But this subject requires a treatise in itself ; and as, of course, there has been written a stout volume containing a list of all the works written on bibliography. It may be mentioned that not long since there was offered for sale for two guineas what appears to be the first attempt at classifying books in England, "A Catalogue of the most Vendible Books in England, orderly and alphabetically digested under the various heads, with the Supplement; by William London, 4to, calf, 1658, very scarce." It is added that this is "the first priced bookseller's catalogue ever compiled, and now of great rarity. The excellent ' Introduction to the Use of Books ' was generally considered to be by Bishop Juxon, but was really written by a Newcastle-upon-Tyne bookseller."

Bibliography being a matter on which large sums are invested and study and labour expended, has become almost scientific, with its systems and methods and tests. In the case of rare old volumes, whose lives are counted by centuries, troubled adventurous lives too, in which storms, buffetings, and ill-usage have been encountered, the purchaser may not venture to take their merits on trust. There are registered descriptions carefully and minutely made by which they must be tested. This is the "*colla-tion*," often a laborious process when it has not been already officially made. In the case of an old "incunable" or cradle-book belonging to the early printing days, there is often no paging, and the purchaser with his book, in good condition and old binding, cannot tell whether it has its proper number of leaves. The knowledge of the "Register" involves many intricacies, and it is often a complicated thing to investigate the state of a volume before it can be warranted sound and perfect. Bibliographers of the first rank do not disdain this labour, and their descriptions of rare volumes are founded on diligent and minute comparison with some rare and not commonly accessible copy. Here, for instance, is a good description of a very rare book :—" The Workes of | Geffray Chau | cer newly printed, with | dyuers workes whi | che were neuer in | print before : | . . . small folio, black letter, woodcuts, *editio princeps*, title inlaid, fine copy in old panelled calf. London, Thomas Godfray, M.D.xxxii (1532)."

COLLATION : Sig. A, 4 leaves, containing general title and preliminary matter ; B, 6 leaves, of which the first is the title to the Canterbury Tales ; C–T, V, X, Y, Z, in sixes ; AA, 6 leaves, of which the first is the title to the Romaunt of the Rose ; Bb–Pp, in sixes (of which Hh1 is the title to Troylus and Creseide) ; Qq, 9 leaves ; Rr–Tt, in sixes (Tt1, the title of Boetius de Consolatione) ; Vv, Xx, Yy, Zz, in sixes ; Aaa to Vvv in sixes (of which Ddd 3 is a title, " How pite is ded," and Lll1 the title of the Testament of Love). There are no blank leaves in the book, every folio bearing letterpress." With this before him, the purchaser of a copy of the Chaucer of 1532 would have no difficulty in testing the merit of his copy.

In the old Aldine folios, such as that of Georgius Valla (*penes me*), an italic " register" at the end gives the letter or signature, with the beginning word of every page, so that every page is, as it were, indexed. Often, however, the pages of "incunables" are found to be numbered in the handwriting of the illuminator. Many of the old MSS. are found to have signatures for the benefit of the binder.*

* The first printed signatures, according to Palmer, appeared in a *Terence*, 1470, and were introduced by Anthony Zarot, who started the first press in Milan. Others say they were invented by Koelhof at Cologne in 1472. They first appeared in Paris in 1476. Our Caxton first used them in 1480. (Sanders MS.)

The great "Nuremberg Chronicle" is numbered
in a stately fashion—ﬀolibm 3. or 133. being placed
on every page at the corner.*

It is remarkable that two of the most useful and
laborious encyclopædias of reference should have
come to us from America. The idea of these is
original, and entailed enormous drudgery. One is
"Alibone's Dictionary," in three portly volumes,
giving references and quotations dealing with every
celebrated person connected with letters. Thus in
the case of, say, Sheridan, all the more famous passages and criticisms of his speeches are given, with
references to nearly every book which gives information about his life. No one who has not yet seen
this work can conceive how Herculean was this task.
The merit of it is, that reference is made to many
recondite and little known quarters where information is to be found. The other work is "Poole's
Index to Periodical Literature." The author had
gone through all the long-protracted series of *Household Words, Macmillan's Magazine*, &c., and noted
everything under its proper head. This spirited
gentleman tells us that when he was a student at Yale
College, from pure love of work and humanity, he
prepared a MS. index to such periodicals as were in
the library, which was so much used, and became so

---

* Signatures are now put at the bottom of the right-hand
pages of sheets, and when the alphabet is finished a second
begins Aa (instead of a single A), and when that is terminated
Aaa are given for the third, and so on. In order to indicate
more correctly the order of each sheet, printers add to the initial
letters some figures on the third, fifth, and seventh pages. The
numbers of these figures which do not pass the middle of the
sheet point out the size of the edition—thus A2 on the third
page, A3 on the fifth, and A4 on the seventh page, shows the
work to be in octavo. In the duodecimo size A5 occurs on the
ninth page, and A6 on the eleventh page, &c.

popular as to be frayed into destruction. It was then printed, making a small volume; a larger edition was prepared, and finally, on the co-operative system, librarians agreeing to help him by indexing such periodicals as they had, it grew to its present size, nearly two thousand closely-printed pages.

Few who carelessly turn to the last pages of a thick volume " to consult the index" can imagine the art, not less than the labour, that is necessary to furnish a good index that shall be a guide to the contents of the volume. With some, it is enough to meet the name of a person to put it in the index. Thus : " Mr. Sheridan, after complimenting his friend Mr. Burke," would certainly be referred to as " Burke, p. 120." The difficulty of abstracting what is essential and of referring it to its proper head is enormous. The well-known story of " Best, Mr. Justice Best, his great mind," need only be alluded to. What can seem more drudging? And yet there is a certain meritorious charm in it. Thus poor Mr. Hodman labours on with a certain pride and purpose. There have been some prodigies of this sort of navvy-work in our day—

> " How index-learning turns no student pale,
> Yet holds the eel of science by the tail."

Fuller quaintly says, " Without an index a large author is but a labyrinth, without a clue to direct a reader therein. I confess there is a kind of learning which is only *indical*, when scholars (like adders, only bite the horse-heels), nibble but at the tables, neglecting the body of the book. But though the idle deserve no crutches, pity it is the weary should be denied the benefit thereof."

N

Alas! the drudges are not all so handsomely remunerated as were certain barristers who in 1778 were appointed to index the journals of the House of Commons, for which they received close on £14,000.

§ ᛗᚠ Binding and its Curiosities.

T is natural perhaps, when all that concerns "books" is so precious, *recherché*, and of exceeding interest, that the protecting *covering* (without which the leaves would all part company one by one) should become a subject of desire for the collector, ravening for what is collectable. Hence the rage for "BINDINGS," which has only comparatively recently attracted the gatherer of voracious appetite. In our own generation, opulent amateurs have entered this department, and "run up" prices to the most extravagant pitch. Few men, indeed, are above the influence of binding; for Roscoe, remarking on the taste for the decoration of books, says, "It is perhaps difficult to discern why a favourite book should not be as proper an object of elegant ornament as the head of a cane, the hilt of a sword, or the latchet of a shoe." Another says, "The binding is the robe of honour in which we invest a noble book, and upon the binding we impress its external insignia of rank and merit." Adam Smith, one of the least showy of men, confessed himself to be a beau in his books, and probably the majority of men of letters are so to some extent. Thomson, however, used to cut the leaves with the snuffers.

" Bindings " is one of the most fascinating and, alas! costliest of the many tastes or manias which pursue the bibliophilist. It may, indeed, ultimately become a *rabies*, when the unfortunate victim must buy regardless of cost, even unto beggary, until, by a fitting Nemesis, he is ruthlessly stripped of the treasures that beggared him. Old bindings of *the first class* are now ardently sought, and at huge prices, and the matter is complicated by an additional taste for gold scutcheons and devices on the outside, and for book-plates within ; nay, some of them, such as those with the De Croy arms and Grolier's, are secured at fancy and almost terrific amounts. We thus arrive at this odd inversion, that books are to be bought for the sake of the binding, not the binding for the sake of the books. There is indeed an air of romance about many of these old coverings, and we gaze with curiosity and reverence at the elegant and decorated volumes which have come from the libraries of those light and airy ladies, Margaret of Valois or Diana of Poitiers. Of late years a good many specimens belonging to these personages have come under the hammer, and these are distinguished by a charming elegance of treatment, set off with piquant devices. They are, besides, the handiwork of eminent masters. Clovis Eve was the artist who adorned the volumes of Margaret, and on his volumes, besides the fine workmanship, is to be noted her motto, *Expectata non eludet*, and that pretty device, the daisy. Many of them are classics and modern Latin works, giving us an idea of the owner's accomplishments. Thus even in the auction-room we can fortify or illustrate our history.

What associations come back on us as we take the dainty volume into our hands—say the " Cent

Nouvelles." There are visions of the League, Henry
the Fourth, all faded out, extinct, and dim ; and yet
the little tome was once in *her* hands ! Diana of Poitiers' piquant books are also coveted. Is there not
a melodious sound in the names of the old binders,
such as Clovis Eve ? At the sound the collector or the
dealer pricks up his ears, and his eyes kindle. It is
as though he were enjoying some full and juicy fruit ;
and "binding by Derome, *with his ticket*," to the
enragé collector has the melody of an organ chant.

This taste for beautiful bindings by *masters* of the
art has sprung up within the last few years, and
if not carried to extravagance, can hardly be pronounced an illegitimate one. For as binding is an
art, so there must be specimens some more beautiful,
and professors more skilful than others. At the
great sales of fifty years ago, it has been noted the
names of Pasdeloup, Derome, &c., were never quoted
as recommendations to a volume, though " English
binding " was a charm that might stimulate bidders.
About thirty years ago the eager pursuit of *bibliopegistic treasures*—is not this a truly absurd title ?
—began, set on foot, it is said, by a certain eminent
bibliophilist, Brunet. This connoisseur, the greatest
authority on all that is old and rare, was bitten in his
old age with this binding mania or phrenzy. His
new passion was said to have been really prompted
by a singular scene which took place at the Parison
sale in Paris, where a little obscure " Telemaque," of
the date of 1725, and which in ordinary course
might be worth a few francs at most, was put up for
competition. But one bibliophilist, or rather *biblio-
pegist*, had noticed that it bore on its cover a rich
device of the Golden Fleece, which had been selected
by a certain tolerably obscure dramatist. Brunet

saw a piquancy in this copy, and determined to secure it, but found that a wealthy financier coveted the book also. To the astonishment of the room, the two bid against each other furiously—*avec acharnement*, we are told. No one could understand it in those days of darkness. The bibliophilist finally carried off the "Golden Fleece" device (not the book) for the enormous sum of £68. "Madness!" "Folly!" "Ridiculous caprice!"—such were the criticisms, and the purchaser himself was much disturbed at his victory. But he was not far out after all. At *his* sale in 1868 it was sold for £88, and has since been on offer at £160. The same amateur was in possession of a La Fontaine, a "Farmers-General" copy, the rare edition of 1762, binding by Pasdeloup, described as "of a mosaic kind, laid out in compartments of red and green morocco, on a yellow ground of fruit and flowers." For this he had paid but £13, but the book was actually sold for £288, and finally passed to the cabinet of a rich amateur for £560!

Some of the finest existing examples are to be seen in the great libraries and treasuries of Europe, *e.g.*, the cloisonnée enamel cover of the Greek Gospels in the library of Siena; an ivory cover of Byzantine school at Würzburg, in Bavaria; the remarkable early pieces in carved ivory at Berlin; the Codex Wittikind; the very early cover in the Hildesheim Treasury, "open cut," studded with crystals, gems, and cameos; the most interesting ivory carved cover of the Psalter of Charles the Bald, preserved in the Imperial Library of Paris; the beautiful cover in copper-gilt and niello of the Sainte-Chapelle New Testament at Paris, besides several other remarkable examples in our own National Museum.

One of the most interesting and remarkable books in the world, both for its contents and its binding, belongs to the British nation, viz., the Bedford Missal, which has a regular pedigree, and whose history can be traced.   This work was a book of prayers, executed for John, Duke of Bedford, Regent of France, " containing fifty-nine miniature paintings, which nearly occupy the whole page, and above a thousand small miniatures, of about an inch and a half in diameter, displayed in brilliant borders of golden foliage, with variegated flowers, &c.   This rich book is 11 inches by 7½ wide and 2½ thick, bound in crimson velvet, with gold clasps, on which are engraved the arms of Harley, Cavendish, and Hollis, quarterly.

" It was in the year 1430 that Henry the Sixth is known to have gone on a visit to Rouen ; so it fell probably at the siege of Rouen into the hands of Charles the Sixth.   By Henry the Second of France it was subsequently decorated with the arms of Diana de Poictiers and Catherine de Medici.   From this period, and two hundred years later, it came into the hands of Sir Robert Worseley of Appuldurcombe, in the Isle of Wight, Bart., to whose lady it had descended from her mother, Lady Frances Finch, by whom it had been purchased in France for £100. Lady Worseley sold it to Edward Harley, second Earl of Oxford, who prefixed to it the arms of Harley and Hollis, and bequeathed it to his daughter, the Duchess of Portland.   At the Duchess's sale in 1786 it was purchased for two hundred and three guineas (George the Third having bid up to two hundred), by Mr. James Edwards, the bookseller, at the disposal of whose library in 1815 it was bought by the Marquis of Blandford, afterwards Duke of

Marlborough, for six hundred and fifty-five guineas (the contest for which is described in Dibdin's *Decameron*). The Duke afterwards parted with it, on consideration of a loan of three hundred guineas, to John Milner, Esq., who afterwards became the owner, it was rumoured, at £800. Mr. Milner disposed of it to John Broadley, Esq., F.S.A., and at the sale of that gentleman's library on June 19, 1833, it was purchased by Mr. Cochran, the bookseller, on commission for Sir John Tobin, Alderman of Liverpool, for the sum of one thousand guineas. In the year 1838 it became the property (by gift) of the Rev. John Tobin, M.A., Incumbent of Liskeard, near Liverpool, who sold it in January 1853, together with other splendid manuscripts, to Mr. W. Boone, bookseller, of Bond Street, who directly offered it to the Trustees for the sum of £3000." *

How say you, amiable and interested reader, is not this story of the vicissitudes of a book curious? And how strangely linked to the course of human life!

The common mode of binding in the sixteenth and seventeenth centuries was a simple parchment wrapper, with the edges folded down. Where oaken boards were used, "waste" leaves of other works were pasted in as a lining, while the boards were covered with sheepskin, marked with a pattern in circles, &c. Caxton is said to have adopted this mode, and Mr. Blades gives an interesting illustration of what may be gathered from so trivial a thing as the lining of a book-cover. For from a copy of Boece, and from some fifty-six half-sheets gathered from other volumes, it was found that these must have been fragments of three works of Caxton hitherto quite unknown.

Sanders MS., *penes me.*

As was to be expected, binding being a fine art, there are authorities and elaborate works on the subject —Dibdin, Peignot, and Paulin. There is also Jacob's " La reliure depuis l'antiquité jusqu'au dix septieme siècle," which is found in the author's " Le Moyen Age." Techener has an elaborate work, " Histoire de la Bibliophilie," with facsimile illustrations. Monographs on celebrated pieces of binding are to be found scattered about, notably in the " Bulletin de Bibliophile," and in catalogues such as that of the Libri Library. Finally comes the latest, the treatise of Mr. Zaehnsdorf, a pleasing work by a practical and tasteful workman.

The recent sales offered a goodly display of bindings. The Sunderland was notably rich in specimens —witness the noble folio " in Grolier style by Clovis Eve, distinguished as much by the exquisite style of the design as by the condition and extraordinary finish of the work, which is elaborately tooled and painted in compartments. It was bound, we are told, for a collector whose name it bears—R. D. Manaldi—but who is now unknown to fame, though his book has a pedigree from the library of Thuanus and the Marquis de Menars, who, however, was vain enough to stamp his arms in gaudy gold in the very centre of the beautiful design of Clovis Eve." The book itself, which measures 14 inches by 10 inches, is of no great merit. Another singularly interesting book is Grolier's own dedication copy of Rhodoginus, "Antiquæ Lectiones," with a beautifully painted large monogram of all the letters of his name in capitals interlaced, and on another page bearing the dedication and arms finely painted in gold and colours, with his mottoes. A more interesting and brilliant collection was now to come. The Duke of Hamilton had married the

o

daughter of the well-known Mr. Beckford, a virtuoso
of the old magnificent school, albeit eccentric. He
was a writer, too, of no mean capacity and much
picturesque power.   His son-in-law also had a taste
for rare and costly books, though in a different direction ; and the two splendid collections, after the
deaths of their owners, came under the same roof at
Hamilton Palace, though kept apart and distinct.*
The Beckford was noted for the superb collection of
bindings—beautiful bindings in themselves, but remarkable also as having come from the collections
of famous amateurs of binding.   Here were seen in
profusion works from the libraries " of Popes and
Cardinals, Kings and Queens of France, Grand Seig-
neurs of all kinds, whose books glittered in gold and
devices of their owners," folios from the Papal palace
and from cardinals' and bishops' libraries, usually
sumptuous-looking things, from their splendid golden
escutcheons, tiaras, and cross-keys, and the cardinal's
hat or mitre displayed on old crimson morocco.
Here, too, were seen the finest productions of the
finest binders — Le Gascon, Pasdeloup, Derome,
Thouvenin, Monnier, Desseuit, Nicholas and Clovis
Eve ; Roffet, Meux, Ruette, Boyer, Baumgarten, Kal-
teeber, Staggemeier, Walther, Roger Payne, Welkher,
Hering, Charles Lewis, and Bedford.   There were
many books from libraries of royal and other amateurs known to be luxurious in the matter of bindings
or sumptuous in their tastes.   Then there were books

---

* It may be mentioned, in connection with the subject of this
union of libraries, that the present Lord Malmesbury enjoys the
usufruct of no less than three libraries. His grandfather, the
well-known philosopher, had formed one in his own line ; his
successor, the diplomatist, made another abroad, chiefly of
foreign works and elegant literature ; while the present holder
of the title made another after his own taste.

that had belonged to Francis I., Henry III. and IV.,
Louis XIV., Marguerite de Valois, to famous Popes,
to Christina of Sweden, James I., Queen Anne, Queen
Mary II., and George IV. ; besides books from such
famous libraries as the Dukes of Grammont and
Montmorency, Villars, and Richelieu (what a ring in
these august names!), Prince de Soubise, Prince
Talleyrand, Duchess of Berry, the Italian families of
Cornaro and Contarini, " all arrayed in magnificent
coatings, displaying the exquisite bibliopegistic skill "
of every celebrated binder.

Here also were seen specimens of binding from
famous libraries, such as that of Maioli, which certainly brought absurd prices, solely for its devices
and bindings. Thus a " Boccaccio," in one volume,
with " Thomas Maioli et Amicor," and on the reverse his motto, *" Inimici mei mea mihi non me
mihi,"* very rare, brought £365. A " Book of
Hours," with " Grolier tooling," fetched £349. Of
all these choice works, those belonging to Grolier's
library seem to be most *recherché*, and fetch prices
that seem extravagant, if not ridiculous. The
" Toison d'Or," by the Prince Jasn, 1563, but having
the interlacing arms of the Duc de Guise painted on
the side, brought £405. A rare Scotch work, a poetical translation of the Psalms, a beautiful copy in
olive morocco, the sides and back covered with gold
tooling *in the Grolier style*, the first arms of Thuanus
forming the centre ornament, fetched £310. But
the following, for its associations and general
beautifyings, was one of the gems of the sale :—A
beautiful copy of the " Heptameron of Marguerite
de Valois," which belonged to Louis XIV., bound
in brown morocco extra, with elegant border, on
which are introduced the crown, fleur-de-lys, stag,

cock and star, having as a centre ornament the
arms of France, all worked in gold, lined with
vellum, covered with gold tooling, having "May,
1695," in the centre, gilt marbled edges by Ruette.
No wonder it brought £406.

At the Sunderland sale a specimen of Monnier's
binding brought £530.

Many years ago there was shown in the Stowe
Library a book of singular historical interest, and
which was also remarkable as a specimen of the old
fashion of binding. This was the "Book of Gospels," on which the early English kings down to the
time of Edward VI. took the coronation oath. It
was arrayed in ponderous oak boards an inch thick,
fastened by huge leathern thongs. The corners were
protected by huge bosses of brass, while on the
cover was a huge brazen crucifix which the monarchs
kissed. Brazen clasps mounted in leather secured
the volume. This interesting relic, after figuring in
the possession of a Norfolkshire gentleman, was
some years ago heard of as being the property of
"a lady in Belgravia."

The name of GROLIER ever kindles the eye of
the bibliophilist. The sight of one of this master's
books fills him with enthusiasm. Grolier really takes
rank with the painters, and excites a keen competition. He was one of the four treasurers of France
during the reign of Francis I., and the most celebrated of old book collectors. The binding he
adopted was remarkable for the fine character of its
interlaced ornament, which is said to have been
designed by himself in moments of leisure. We
find it recorded with astonishment, some twenty or
thirty years ago, that a bookseller gave £150 for
an Aldus, "rich and refulgent, yet quiet through

its Grolier tooling." Each volume of his library was adorned with the amiable inscription, "The property of John Grolier and his friends"—a curious contrast to that of another French collector, whose book-plate bears a text from the parable of the Ten Virgins : "Go to them that sell, and buy for yourselves."

The prices realised for specimens of the ancient bindings were perfectly marvellous at the sale of the choicest portion of the library of M. Libri, the most eminent of modern book-collectors, which took place in London in the beginning of 1860. "The collection exhibited specimens of the finest bibliopegistic skill from the fifteenth century to the present time, and embraced not only the magnificent samples of binding bestowed on the volumes by private amateurs like Grolier, Maioli, De Thou, Count d'Hoym, Longepierre, and others equally celebrated, but was particularly rich in books which formerly had been the private property of popes, emperors, kings, princes, cardinals, and reigning sovereigns of England, France, Italy, Germany, &c., all magnificently bound, and bearing either their arms or the devices known to have been adopted by them. These seem to have been collected with a view of tracing the history of ornamentation. They had availed themselves of the skill of the best artists to obtain designs or patterns, several of which are known to have been furnished by Giovanni da Verona, Andrea del Sarto, *le petit* Bernard, and even the great Raffaele himself."

The characteristics of the binding of this school were an elegance and delicacy of touch, the gilt lines flowing and interlacing with much freedom—a freedom that was secured by not sinking the golden lines so deeply as is done now; they were more on the surface. It may be conceived, too, that the leather

cannot be so indented or scored as to avoid break-
ing the surface; whereas by the lines being traced
lightly, the gold is shown to better effect. The work
of these old masters seems to have the freedom of
etching or engraving, so airy are the lines.

It would almost seem that the designs for binding
of Grolier, Maioli, and Clovis Eve, and kindred masters, were often suggested, if not copied from the
florid frameworks of the title-pages of the French
and Italian little quartos in the sixteenth century.
These seem again to be taken from the free-hand
carved frames and florid scroll-work of the day. The
idea seems to have been to decorate the sides as a
framing for the device. Grolier's library contained
about three thousand volumes, and it is declared that
each fetched about £120. Each side was decorated,
one with the device above quoted, the other with the
pious one—" Let my portion be in the land of the
living." The variety and ingenuity of his interlacing
of patterns of different shapes crossing and intersect-
ing each other is very pleasing. Bonaventure d'Ar-
gonne, an amateur of the day, thus described Grolier's
collection : " We might almost think that the Muses,
who had done so much for the inside of the books,
had striven to take their share in the outside, so much
art and *esprit* is seen in these decorations." They
are gilt with a delicacy unknown to later gilders.
The compartments are often painted in colours, are
admirably designed, and are all of different shapes.
Clovis Eve's style was more purely geometrical, while
Le Gascon is associated with the beautiful tracery
which covered the sides like a golden net, though the
effect was found at last a little monotonous. Often it
takes the shape of a golden spray. One work of his,
" La Guirlande de Julie," is considered a triumph, and

never to have been surpassed in the tone of the gilding, finesse, and workmanship.

The treatment of large quartos and folios by
binders of the present century has seemed always to
be directed by wrong principles. It is only when we
contrast it with the simple and perfectly effective and
legitimate system of the older masters that we see its
failings. English binders of this school were particularly favourable to a sort of buff-coloured calf, which
makes but an insipid contrast with the profuse gilding, scored at the edges with a rich flowery pattern,
so as to give the idea of a border. Most of the books
in the Syston Park Library were bound in a fashion
that has long since gone out, but which was in vogue
some fifty years ago, the principle of which seems to
have been an elaborate bordering, of a geometrical
kind, very broad bars, and rich gold. The effect was
unmeaning and heavy. It seemed to suggest an imitation of a raised or mechanical border. The fashion
of our day is to make the tone and workmanship of
the leather the main object. The light line of gilding
is adopted to set off the covering, as a light trimming
would a dress ; whereas the former system was the
reverse—to use the leather as a means of setting off
the gilding and decoration. The placing a golden
border on the edge of anything is as false a principle
as placing a rich lace border at the edge of a lady's
dress next to the ground, where rough usage and con-
tact with the ground would soon destroy it. The solid
lines of border should be traced at some distance from
the edge, and thus preservation as well as effect is
secured. Within, the linings were well tooled and
scored with parallel lines and flourishings at each
corner. These lines, much attenuated, lack force and
breadth, and the whole effect is poor. The leaves are

"shaved" smooth, and the gilding shows in one unbroken surface. Now, compare the olden style as displayed in some folio or spacious quarto handled by Derome or La Ruette. Here a well-grained fine skin is selected, of rich ripe plum colour, and the idea is to show that it is a leathern cover or jacketing for the volume. In the decoration the skin is treated *as* a skin. In the centre on this ground may be displayed the coat of arms, while the leather is allowed to be seen at the edges without gilding—a sign of practical purpose and use, besides being contrasted with the sinuous and irregular "old gold" leaves. But within a quarter of an inch of the edge are drawn three delicate gold lines running all round, which have a strange simplicity and elegance conjoined, and are infinitely more effective than the English bordering. The English boards of this period lie as square and stiffly as if made of timber : the foreign work has a flexibility, and offers curvings. Again, the ornaments used in modern binding are too meagre and stereotyped, and different from the bold, rich, and effective floweret, scroll, or fleur-de-lys. Leather is not suited to such fine lines or designs, save only when delicately touched and on the surface ; for even with Le Gascon's network the general effect is as of a mass of gold. The tendency of the binding of our time is in the direction of this olden simplicity ; large, expansive, and well-toned skins, treated with consummate workmanship, and with few or delicate "toolings" on the slightest and most modest scale.

The latter part of the eighteenth century saw English bookbinding carried to its highest pitch of celebrity by the remarkable skill of Roger Payne. He came to London about 1700, and soon acquired a reputation in his art which placed him above rivalry, notwithstanding his utter want of prudence and orderly habits. Towards the end of his life he worked for John Mackinlay, one of the most popular binders of the period in London, under whom many of the later English binders of chief note learnt their trade. David Walker was contemporary with Mackinlay, to whom Charles Lewis was apprenticed in 1800. To the skill and judgment of Roger Payne, Lewis added business qualities which won for him respect as well as admiration. Dibdin says of him, "The particular talent of Lewis consists in uniting the taste of Roger Payne with a freedom of 'forwarding' and squareness of finishing peculiarly his own. His books appear to move on silken hinges. His joints are beautifully squared, and wrought upon with studded gold, and in his inside decorations he stands without a compeer."

It is rather difficult to understand the admiration for the work of this most famous of English binders, Roger Payne. It has certainly the merits of a plain severity and simplicity, and of excellent workmanship; but there is a monotony in his favourite red and absence of tooling. There is also a lack of that elegance of touch and daintiness which distinguishes the old foreign binders. We note also the absence of that proportionate treatment which is the charm of artistic work. For we find that too often the little pocket Elzevir is treated on about the same scale as a large quarto, Roger using the same roughly grained red morocco and simple tooling as he did for some huge tome. Neither are the joints so free and like to a hinge, and there is a faint idea of clumsiness. His peculiar red tint is inharmonious compared with the rich mellow plum colour of

Derome, while his "tooling" is stiff, without that unobtrusive delicacy of the gold lines and borders of the French artist.

This binder, like so many other persons of talent and genius, was an eccentric enthusiast, never in possession of money, and fond of drink. His appearance was that of a quaint and attenuated old man ; but his work had an unmistakable *cachet* or "touch," and very little experience enables one to recognise a Roger Payne binding. There was a little roughness and clumsiness, as we have said, about the back, but there was a bold effective treatment about the rest of the volume, and he seemed to keep in view, what many binders forget, that the leather was the main element, not to be too much overlaid with gilding and decoration. It was a fortunate day for him when he secured the patronage of that munificent amateur, Lord Spencer, who trusted him with his finest and most precious volumes to dress. Some of his bills have been preserved, which are as quaint and eccentric as himself, and often embody a vindication of his charges. Thus, for binding an old edition of Petrarch :—

	£	s.	d.
The paper was very weak, especially at the back of the book. I was obliged to use new paper in ye washing, to keep the book from being torne or broken. To paper for washing	o	2	o
To washing. There was a great deal of writing ink and the bad stains. It required several washings to make the paper of the book quite safe. For tho' the book with one or two washings would look as well as at present, it will not stand the test of Time without repeated washings—carefully and quite honestly done	o	9	o
To siseing very carefully and strong	o	7	6

Æschylus. Finished in the most magnificent
manner, embordered with ermine, expressive
of the high rank of the noble patroness of the
designs, the other parts finished in the most
elegant taste, measured with the compasses.
It takes a great deal of time making out the
different measurements, &c. .   .   .   £12 12 0

Roger Payne ended a life of labour, poverty, and
intemperance in St. Martin's Lane, and was buried
at the expense of his friend, Mr. Payne the bookseller. This Æschylus is deemed his *chef d'œuvre*.
He was very singular in his conduct ; made all his
own tools, and never would work before any person,
but always in some secluded cellar, and only when
his necessities called upon him for exertion.

The late Mr. Bedford was perhaps the greatest
and most elegant of modern binders, combining the
characteristics of solid English workmanship with
the finish of the foreign school. Our present school
of binding is a good deal imitative, Zaehnsdorf and
others reproducing the Grolier and Derome workmanship with perfect success.

In binding, as in other departments of art, to produce success it is necessary to follow strictly the
aims and principles of propriety and good sense.
How often we see the whole *inside* of the cover lined
with morocco and "tooled," with the idea of adding
to the magnificence of the whole. Testing it artistically, we find that the first result is the enfeebling
of the general effect of the outside. The reflection
also occurs, if the leather is to protect and make
serviceable the outside, the same material must be
quite unsuited for what is within. It becomes so
much waste. Again, the inside splendour is *shut up*,
excluded from the air, and rubbed by the pressure of
the opposite pages, and this idea of friction or pres-

sure is at once hostile to the use of any precious or
decorated material. This suggests that one of the
most tasteful and beautiful effects produced by the
old masters of binding was the perfect *entente* between this lining and the outside decoration, both
being, as it were, harmonised when the volume was
opened. This lining in Derome's books was almost
invariably a richly mellowed and deep-toned marbled
paper, which suggested the idea of service as well as
of beauty. Many of his linings were exquisite in
their taste and rich harmony. The idea suggested
was that of something *subsidiary* to the purpose of
the outside. The common marbled papers of our
time are inferior and staring. Neither are the poorer
papers—speckled like plover's eggs—more effective.
The truth is, all should be designed together, lining
and outside. For large books a larger treatment
and larger pattern and bolder colours are requisite.

At the present moment the rage for collecting
bindings is at its height. There are amateurs, like
the Duke d'Aumale, who will give any price, not for
a fine piece of binding, but for pieces of a master's
work. One of the later binding fanciers was the late
Baron F. de Rothschild of Paris. This accomplished
man, who was remarkable as a financier, railway director, &c., and took a conspicuous share in the direction
of his great house, was cut off at the early age of thirty-
seven. His taste lay in the direction of early French
romances, poems, &c., of which he had collected a
vast number. His taste and knowledge was proved
by his extraordinary gift of endurance in that most
painful of all drudgeries, copying. With his own
hand he had copied an enormous mass of rare papers
and unique volumes. He was often seen at this
laborious task in our Museum, and he seems to have

taken pleasure in the monotonous duty. He was accustomed to say that this he found the best mode of reading and studying a writer, for he could remember the smallest detail of any manuscript or book he had copied, and this extended even to variations of the text, &c. When he had once undertaken to transcribe a work, he never omitted doing some of the copying every day. He had also a wonderful instinct for the true value of everything that was old and valuable ; he was not one of those magnificent purchasers who leave great orders at auctions, but always attended in person, and bid on rational principles ; not, as too many do, for the applause of "the gallery." There was a pleasant simplicity and honest enthusiasm in his " ways," for any day at a particular hour he was to be found at a bookseller's in the Passage des Panoramas, Morgand & Fatout's, surrounded by a number of amateurs, with whom he discoursed on this darling topic. At a later hour he appeared at Rouquette's in the Passage Choiseul, where we are told he met a class of fanatics devoted to the collection of illustrated romances published some sixty or seventy years ago, above all, with the original *paper* covers on. This foolish craze now obtains with us, and large sums are given for early " Pickwicks," &c., with their " green wrappers " on. These people he pleasantly satirised by purchasing a cheap copy of Hugo's poems in a villainous yellow paper cover, which he would not have bound or disturbed, but placed in a morocco case specially made for it. To some it seemed that this was genuine enthusiasm, but it was in truth a pleasant jest. He used also gravely to point out to them that they were neglecting a really important branch in not collecting the paper *backs* of these illustrated tomes, with their dates and inscriptions. His superb library, so rich in early French literature, was a monument of taste and erudition, of which a sumptuous *catalogue raisonné* had been prepared by his own laborious hand, with a title and proper description of each work. This sensible bibliophile, it is noted, never indulged in the usual exaggerated and unfounded encomiums of books, such as "very rare," "fine copy," "believed to be unique." He was a particular amateur of the old bindings, and here again he was nice and exigent, for he allotted no piece of work to Pasdeloup or Le Gascon on the testimony of their tooling, &c., but only on their official signatures. This fine catalogue, in thick and sumptuous royal octavo, is notable for some rather original illustrations of binding. Four or five exquisite specimens are shown, the covers, gold, &c., exactly reproduced, with even the raised embossing, the sunk "tooling," the actual texture of leather, &c., and the effect is really marvellous.

Jules Richard, a French amateur, tells us with much *gout :* "Like all great artists, great binders are intractable. We have not only to cover their productions with gold pieces, but must wait their convenience fifteen or eighteen months, even two years, be you king or prince, or even," he adds with sly sarcasm, "President of the Republic. You should always," our Frenchman goes on, "bind up with a book its printed cover, even though the cover be the same as the title. Every good bibliophilist will take care to add to his book everything that will enhance its price. You should have a copy taken on the finest paper, or, if this be impossible, one without blemishes. Then a portrait of the author should be got, his autograph, engravings made from

other editions, and in different states." Our bibliophilist then adds this emphatic declaration : " I
declare," he says, "that if a library were formed on
this plan, begun say in 1882, composed mainly of
first editions, and kept steadily up for twenty years
on this plan, at the rate merely of a hundred volumes
a year, it would be worth by that time fully £2000."

As a little indication of what collectors seek with
avidity, we come on the following :—" Thuanus, His
First Marriage.—Clamengiis (N. de) Opuscula Au-
reum, Paris, 1512–21, in 1 vol. sm. 4to, fine copy,
in old sage green morocco, with the large Arms of
J. A. Thuanus in gold on sides, and Monogram interlaced with that of Marie, his First Wife, in gold
on back ; " also, " Thuanus, His Second Marriage.
—Bossche, Historia Medica, fine copy, bright old gilt
calf, very neat, with the Arms of Thuanus and Gas-
parde de la Chastre, his Second Wife, in gold on
sides, and interlaced Monogram in gold on back, very
rare." This opens a subdivision ; for you may possess the De Thou monogram interlaced with that of
his first wife, but without the second you are utterly
incomplete ! To show how endless the business is, it
must be known that if you collect bindings, you must
display specimens of the grand libraries, such as that
of Colbert, Harlay, &c., and, above all, specimens of
that tasteful Marquise de Vielboisy, " Louise-Fran-
çoise d'Harlay de Celi," whose collection was noted
for being bound by the most celebrated bibliopegistic
artists of her time. Well might we covet her Delphin Livy, in six volumes quarto, dressed in fine old
morocco, extra gilt and marbled edges (pretty combination), and her arms and cipher stamped in gold
in four compartments.

A much-debated question arises as to the " plough-

ing " (as it is called) of the leaves, thus saving the
reader the trouble of using the paper-knife. This
seems a convenience ; but it is beyond question obtained at the sacrifice of artistic considerations and
injures the book.   Shaving or ploughing the edges
should properly not be done at all, that is, not with the
guillotine, which pares away wholesale with beautiful
accuracy.   Under the old system of a knife used
by the hand, it was possible to apply a certain delicacy, and do little more than trim the rough edges.
But when the book is *issued* with shaved edges, a portion of the margin is cut away; and when it is sent to
be bound formally, there is a second shaving, and it
becomes a maimed, cut-down, poor thing.   This smooth
edge, too, contrasts hideously with the cloth cover of
the unbound book ; it is like putting fine lace on a
frieze coat.   But, in truth, the making the gilt edges
as smooth as though they were *planed* is also a
falsely inartistic principle and a disguise ; for the
leaves are separate things and are details, and their
expression should be retained.   Nothing is more rich
than the effect produced by the old binders, such as
Derome, who allowed each leaf to express itself in
wavy lines with a dull " old gold " colour.

Intimately connected with this is the question of
margin.   It is foolishly imagined that a margin is a
thing of arbitrary caprice.   There is a law regulating
this, as everything else, based on proportion, and
arising really out of the mechanical arrangement of
the printer.   His " formes " are made to contain so
many pages, laid out according to the size of the
sheet ; the margin is the expression of the interval
between each page as they lie before him.   Margins
must, therefore, increase at the expense of the
page, till the absurdity is reached that a book's size

is regulated by the size of the paper space, not by that of the printed portion. Thus a duodecimo page might rank and fold as an octavo. But this is a technical view. " Large paper copies," as they are called, are a different thing from these exaggerated margins. These expensive luxuries are furnished by the printer, who, after the impression has been taken off, has to arrange his pages in larger formes, filling the additional space with wedges, an operation of expense. But it was worth the cost, and the effect was handsome ; a thicker or more solid paper was necessary, to be in harmony. Still the effect is often bizarre and odd, owing to the type, which seems out of proportion.

Vast margins are often ridiculous exaggerations— " rivulets of type running through a meadow of margin "—and present a greater superficial surface of blank paper than does the type itself, as though the fringe or border of the garment were broader than the garment.

Of course the extravagance in bindings has often furnished an opening for the display of fantastic tricks and fads, and the foolish have chosen to display their humour in this way, much as some vapid dame will dress up her honest dog and make him ridiculous. We have only to enter our libraries to find some of these exhibitions. A "Manual of Woodcarving" has been bound in wood by Bemrose & Sons. In a bookseller's catalogue we read of a Latin copy of Apuleius' " Golden Ass " (1501) bound in ass's-skin. The Duke of Roxburghe's library contained a collection of pamphlets (1724, &c.) respecting Mary Tofts (who pretended to be confined of rabbits), of Godalming, Surrey, bound in rabbit-skin. The Hon. George Napier had a work relating to the celebrated dwarf,

Q

Jeffrey Hudson, bound in a piece of Charles the First's silk waistcoat. At Perry's sale, a copy of the "New Year's Gift," also bound in a piece of the waistcoat of Charles the First, sold for £8, 8s. Mordaunt Cracherode, the father of the celebrated book-collector, wore one pair of buckskin breeches exclusively during a voyage round the world, and a volume in his son's collection (now in the British Museum) is bound in a part of these circumnavigating unmentionables. "Tuberville on Hunting" was bound by Whittaker in deerskin, on the cover of which was placed a silver stag. Fox's "Historical Works" were bound in fox-skin, and Bacon's works in hog-skin. It is said Dr. Askers had a work bound in *human skin*, for the payment of which his binder prosecuted him. One offspring of the horrors of the first French Revolution was this grim humour of binding books with the skin of human beings. A Russian poet is said lately to have offered to the lady of his affections a collection of his sonnets bound in leather—human leather—which the poet himself furnished ! On falling from his horse one day he broke his thigh, and being obliged to undergo amputation, he had the skin carefully tanned and reserved for some purpose of the kind. A public library in Bury St. Edmunds contains an octavo volume, consisting of a full report of the trial and execution of Corder, who murdered a young woman named Martin at a spot called the Red Barn in a neighbouring village about forty years ago, together with an account of his life and other cognate matter. This volume is bound in the murderer's skin, which was tanned for the purpose by a surgeon in the town. The human leather is darker and more mottled than vellum, of a rather coarse-textured surface, with holes in it like those in pigskin, but smaller and more sparse. A collector happened to be in a bookbinder's shop about twenty years ago, on St. Michael's Hill, Bristol, when he was shown several volumes which had been sent from the Bristol Law Library to repair. These were all bound in human skin, specially tanned for the purpose ; and some curious details were furnished of several local culprits executed in that city, who were flayed after execution to furnish forth the leather for binding together some contemporary legal lore. On May 15, 1874, was sold in Paris, by auction, the first part of the curious library of the late M. Lucien de Rosny, father of the eminent Japanese scholar. It was rich in fine and, above all, eccentric bindings, such as in skins of cat, garnet coloured and buff, crocodile, mole, seal, fur of the Canadian black wolf, royal tiger, otter, white bear, sole, and rattlesnake.

It has been often noticed that there is a physiognomy in books, which the very character of their contents enforces. Who does not recognise from its back or outside the " Poems by Tennyson," a small green dainty volume, or the Macaulay History ? Some books are intended for ornament. We know the gaudy volumes that repose at all the points of the compass on the drawing-room of the apartments to let, or those on the dentist's or doctor's table in the room where the patients bide their time sadly. Every judicious binder will have the decency to bind his volumes according to their degree and quality. He will not, for instance, dress the "Annual Register" or the "Year-Book of Facts" in morocco extra. These are surely Lamb's " things in books' clothing;" who justly complains of the disappointment, " To reach down a well-bound semblance of a volume, and hope it some kind-hearted playbook,

then, opening what 'seems its leaves,' to come bolt
upon a withering population essay." These indeed
are doleful and dispiriting experiences ; an idea most
eloquently expressed by Shakespeare, and linked by
his poetry to human sympathies—

> " O rare one !
> Be not, as is our fangled world, a garment
> Nobler than that it covers : let thy effects
> So follow, to be most unlike our courtiers,
> As good as promise."

So, too, Juliet, hearing that Romeo has slain Tybalt—

> " Was ever book containing such vile matter
> So fairly bound ? "

Each of the three daughters of Louis the Fifteenth
had her own library, the volumes of which are easily
recognised. Madame Adelaide had all her books
bound in *red morocco*, Madame Sophie's were in *citron
morocco*, while Madame Victoire selected *green morocco*. A somewhat similar practice is adopted at the
British Museum. There the great majority of the
books are bound in half morocco, with cloth to match
the leather. Historical works are in *red*, theological
in *blue*, poetical in *yellow*, natural history in *green*.
Besides this, each part or volume is stamped with a
mark by which it can be distinguished as their property, and of different colours : thus red indicates
that a book was purchased, blue that it came by
copyright, and yellow that it was presented. The
Bodleian use the following colours : arts and trade
maroon, theology *black*, medicine *light brown*, mathe-
matics and physics *light green*, history *dark red*,
poetry *dark green*, philology *light red*, classics *neutral
tint*, miscellaneous *dark blue*.

There is a device for giving effect to the leaves which
is scarcely worthy the dignity of the library. For this

purpose the edge of the book is well scraped and burnished; the leaves on the fore-edge are evenly bent in an oblique manner, and in this position, confined by boards tied tightly on each side, the fore-edge in this position receives a coat of colouring matter, generally red ; when this is dry, the boards are removed, the edges regain their ordinary position, and in this form are gilt (sometimes marbled), the gilding being afterwards duly burnished. When the book is closed, the gilt edge only is visible; when opened, the obliquity of the leaves shows the red or whatever other colour was adopted In like manner the same steps are taken when it is desired to paint a landscape on the edges instead of a whole colour. In the library of the British and Foreign Bible Society there is an old Swedish Bible that has a picture painted on the edges of the leaves, which is not to be seen when the book is closed, on account of the gold covering it ; but one cover being thrown back and the leaves slightly separated, the gilding disappears and you perceive an antique figure of Christian on his journey up the straight and narrow way to the Heavenly City, beside portraits, emblems, views, &c.

This brings us to one of those bits of facetiousness to which the scholar occasionally condescends, as if to lighten his graver pursuits. Most persons have seen in libraries those "dummy" things, after the pattern of backgammon boards, which, appearing to be ranged on shelves, simulate the titles of honest books, to hide a door. This system has exercised some of the best wits. Thus in Sir Thomas Acland's library we find "Friend's Right of Entrance," "Trap on Fictitious Entries," "Treatise on the Law of Partitions," "Noah's Log-Book," "Millington on Covered Ways," "Snug's the Word, by a Clerk of the Closet."

Near the hinges of the disguised door the titles run—
" Squeak on Opening," " Bang on Shutting," and
" Hinge's Orations."

In the Army and Navy Club library, Pall Mall,
are, or were to be found, quips in the same spirit.
" The Art of Turning, by Handle," " The Rape of the
Lock," " The Law of Substitutes," " Treatise sur les
Sorties Imprevues," " Essay on Woodbind," " Pasley
on Passages of Communication," " Viner on Stoppages
in Transitu," " Blacklane on Fictitious Entry," " Le
Livre Fermé," " The Blockade of the Sublime
Porte," and " Rien du Tout, in six volumes." These
are not over-sparkling. But of a very different kind
were the exercises of the ingenious Tom Hood.
He supplied to the Duke of Devonshire, for a door-
way out of the library at Chatsworth, some droll
titles :—" Percy Vere in forty volumes," " Dante's
Inferno, or Description of Van Demon's Land,"
" Lamb's Recollections of Suet," " Malthus's Attack
on Infantry," " Macadam's Views in Rhodes," " Bish's
Retreat of the Ten Thousand," " Pygmalion, by
Lord Bacon," " On Trial by Jury, with remarkable
Packing Cases," " Memoirs of Mrs. Mountain, by
Ben Lomond," " Boyle on Steam," " Rules for
Punctuation, by a Thorough-bred Pointer," " Book-
keeping by Single Entry," " John Knox on Death's
Door," " Designs for Friezes, by Captain Parry,"
" On the Site of Tully's Offices," " The Rape of the
Lock, with Bramah's Notes," " Haughty-cultural
Remarks on London Pride," " Lamb on the Death
of Wolfe," " Annual Parliaments, a Plea for Short
Commons," " On Sore Throat and the Migration of
the Swallow," " Debrett on Chain Piers," " Voltaire,
Volney, Volta (3 vols.)," " Peel on Bell's System,"
" Freeling on Enclosing Waste Lands," " Johnson's

Contradictionary," " Life of Jack Ketch, with cuts of his own execution," " Barrow on the Common Weal," " Cursory Remarks on Swearing," " Shelley's Conchologist," " The Hole Duty of Man, by J. P. Brunel," " The Scottish Boccaccio, by D. Cameron," " Cook's Specimens of the Sandwich Tongue," " Hoyle on the Game Laws," " In-i-go on Secret Entrances."

But at Gad's Hill, the late Mr. Charles Dickens, ever pleasant and mirthful, devised a series of sham titles for his shelves which are good of their kind, and to these his friend Mr. Forster added the following :—" Dr. Kitchener's Life of Captain Cook," " Adam's Antecedents, from the Family Papers," " The Poetry of Doctors' Commons (Proctor)," " Vestiges of the Unnatural History of Taxation," " Bishop Philpott's Wanderings in the Holy Land," " The Corn Question, by John Bunyan," " Retreat of the Ten Thousand, by the Earl of Cardigan," " Savage on Civilisation (2 vols.)," " An Impartial View of the Gorham and Denison Controversies, by Henry, Bishop of Exeter," " Mr. J. Horner on Poets' Corner." *

Librarians and others who give out large quantities of books for binding can record some amusing mistakes as to the " lettering " and titles placed or misplaced on the backs. Thus, such a publication as " Thomas Adam's Works on Private Religious

---

* A singular library exists at Warsenstein, near Cassel ; the books composing it, or rather the substitutes for them, being made of wood, and every one of them is a specimen of some different tree. The back is formed of its bark, and the sides are constructed of polished pieces of the same stock. When put together, the whole forms a box ; and inside of it are stored the fruit, seed, and leaves, together with the moss which grows on the trunk, and the insects which feed upon the tree ; every volume corresponds in size, and the collection altogether has a singular effect.

Thoughts," has been returned as "*Adam's Private
Thoughts*," and "Buffoon's Natural History" looks
like a practical joke. Recently Bishop King's disserta-
tion on the "Origin of Evil" was sent home from the
binders lettered "*King's Evil.*" Dr. Trusler's work
on "Synonyms, showing the distinctions between
words generally esteemed synonymous," was lettered
"*Trusler's Synonymous Distinctions.*" It has been
humorously remarked that the indorsements at the back
of books do not always intimate what is to follow, for
neither the "Novella of Leo," or the "Extravagantés,"
as edited by Godefroi, contain matter of a light, airy,
or amusing kind. "The Diversions of Purley" is
deemed the toughest book in existence. Edgeworth's
"Essay on Irish Bulls" was actually ordered by a
farming society. M'Ewan "On the Types," a book
treating of the types of Christianity in the old law,
has been deemed utterly useless by a compositor
or journeyman printer, who naturally expected to
find the book honestly descriptive of the tools of
his trade. There are an infinite number of pleasant
mistakes and misapprehensions connected with the
titles of books. The late Mr. Le Fanu, the novelist,
when a child, mystified the booksellers by ordering in
the name of his father, a clergyman, a work called
"Dodd's Holy Curate," and which could not be
found, though sought for "high and low."

Everything, indeed, connected with "Book" is
"collectable," or made a subject for the devotion of
the connoisseur. A pleasing custom that has long
been in vogue is that of the owner placing his book-
plate or registry in the beginning of his books.
They pass from owner to owner, from library to
library, and each new possessor adds his own plate,
which often gives a singular interest to a book thus

inherited.* Some of these decorations are exceedingly artistic and also characteristic; some of the older ones in a fine, bold, and flowing style. Others are in the nature of a "device" with a chosen motto, quaint and suggestive, some artist friend, such as Mr. Stacey Marks, having often designed them. Mr. F. Locker, in a note to his Catalogue, states that the late Sir W. Stirling-Maxwell designed nearly a hundred for his acquaintances and friends. It is pleasant to open some tome from an old library, and be greeted by a flamboyant coat of arms—it may be ducal—with supporters in all due state! It was natural that the eager, greedy eye of the collector should take note of these artistic adornments: why not collect, scour high and low, "lay down," neatly paste, classify into countries? Accordingly he has long been at work at his gruesome function, purchasing books—odd inversion—for the sake of their title escutcheons. The back in most cases is stripped off; but the more reverential have a deft mode of extracting the plate by means of a press and moisture.

It seems the most distinguished collector in the kingdom is the Rev. Thomas Carson of Dublin, who has gathered the most artistic specimens, and is deeply skilled in the lore and philosophy of such things. The specimens given by Mr. Warren show that there is a principle involved in such designs, and we are amazed at the boldness and beauty of some of the bookplates. There are innumerable forms — some

* The first who used armorial or other bookplates it would be difficult to ascertain ; they were certainly in general use on the Continent before the end of the sixteenth century. Mr. Hodgkin of West Derby has a 4to volume, printed at Strasburg about 1515, with a bookplate of H. Eck, of a date he thinks not later than 1530. However, in the December 1869 Catalogue of M. Bachelin-Deflorenne, bookseller, Garrick Street, Covent Garden, is a description of two bookplates dated respectively 1279 and 1314.

allegorical, some heraldic, and different styles, such
as the Jacobean, &c.   One very commonly met with
is what may be styled Chippendale, modelled on the
shape of the mirrors and other ornaments of that
designer.   Cardinals and bishops command a special
decorative advantage in the showy and effective hat
and tassels which serve as crest or canopy.   As a
matter of course, there is a system and handbook
for the subject, and the Hon. J. Leicester Warren has
issued a pretty little volume dealing with what may
be called the science of the " Ex Libris," for such is
the technical name.   Intimately connected with this
department is, of course, the subject of devices
stamped in gold on the sides of books, which
being more ambitious, are the desire of the opulent
collector.   There is something almost ludicrous in
the idea of having to secure some huge and heavy
folio on a dreary subject for the sake of the
escutcheon on the side ; but done it must be.   It
would not do to cut out the device, as it could not
subsist without the support of the book.   This, as
may be well imagined, opens up one of the most
costly of collecting departments ; for all the poten-
tates, kings, popes, princesses, have their arms
emblazoned with great state and splendour ; the
"masters," Clovis Eve, Le Gascon, and others,
" tooling " away exquisitely all round the emblazon-
ment, embroidering initials and monograms and
arabesques.

There is a Count D'Hoym whose device on a book
has been for some time the rage, and this a mystery,
for it is noted to be of an unostentatious character.

Yet another proof of the knowledge and skill expended on these trifles is that these arms and escutcheons, whether French, or German, or English, are

generally identified and their owners announced.
Connected with which a new craze has been recently
announced. Some one has discovered that the disused
well-worn engraved copper-plates have beauty from the
richness of detail. At least they can be collected,
framed, made into caskets, and the owner can point to
them as being the original of some famous engraving
on paper. But there is no end to these absurdities.

There have been a great many devices and sys-
tems introduced by the ingenuity of binders in
connection with the wholesale trade. It must be
remembered that binding also belongs to publishing, as distinguished from the other departments
affected by the amateur and collector, the latter
department only being artistic. In old libraries and
on the stalls we see almost every book of the last
century dressed in the invariable brown calf, the
livery of the publishers. All the books " which no
gentleman's library should be without " display this
dress. Who, for instance, has ever seen Goldsmith's
Histories or " Animated Nature," or Hume and
Smollett, or Robertson, or Fielding, or the pretty
little " Shandys," without these calf " jackets " ?
They seem to have been thus issued from the publisher's office, though copies could be had in boards.
Up to thirty years ago the circulating-library novel
was always in boards, covered with a sort of grey or
mud-coloured paper. It was only lately that a wonderful change was made, which really created a trade,
namely, the use of the now prevailing " *cloth covers*,"
the introduction of an enterprising and energetic
Scottish firm. This has developed in an almost
stupendous way, and has become universal in publishing. It has since become susceptible of decoration
and endurance, while the appliances of machinery have

been made so effective that "covers" can be turned
out as rapidly as the printed copies demand. In
1835 the late Mr. Archibald Leighton introduced the
use of *cloth* for covers, the first publisher to adopt
it being Mr. Pickering, and the first work so bound
being Lord Byron's complete works, with a little gilt
ornament. Most of our books at the present time
are cloth-bound, and many of them of a certain
elegance ; and amongst the names of the designers
are to be found some of the most noted decorative
artists of the day. In this we have created a style
the admiration and wonder of all foreigners—*toile
Anglaise* being known for its excellence of workmanship and taste over the whole world. In short, our
English cloth-binding is as superior to that of the
rest of the world as a Sheffield blade is to one of
Paris make. It would be an interesting speculation
to investigate why one nation, like France, invariably
prefers paper covers, and another the more perma-
nent cloth. The theory of the fashion after which
popular French works are sewn in paper covers seems
to be founded on portability (*pour la poche*), and a
saving in price ; with choice between preservation in
regular official binding, if the book be worth it, to
be thrown away if otherwise. The cost of binding
in thin staring paper boards of the railway novel would
be twopence or threepence, while the three volumes
of a novel can actually be done up "in cloth gilt" for
so low a figure as fourpence or fivepence a volume, on
a large number being taken. Much fault has been
found with the French system, the three - franc or
two franc yellow novel soon dismembering, the sheets
tumbling apart. But this seems exaggerated. The
book holds together long enough to be read by two
or three of the family, and even if the threads have

given way, it is still not inconvenient to read. But for decent binding the advantage is obvious. Our cheap "ploughed" railway novels cannot be bound without losing their already shorn margins. There is nothing meaner or more miserably starved in consequence than our two-shilling railway novel when bound, for it is then stripped of its gaudy picture cover, and, with its stunted margin, is positively degrading to read.

Some years ago it was calculated that the mere waste-paper shavings of the London bookbinders amounted annually to upwards of four hundred tons, while the consumption of leaf-gold amounted to little short of four million square inches *weekly*. Rags are used in removing the superfluous gold during the process of lettering, ornamenting, and edging. They are burnt, and the yield would astonish the majority of people. It is known in the trade as "skewings." There is a newly-introduced system of fastening the sheets together by *wire* stitching, which is being generally adopted, notably for such publications as Mr. Labouchere's *Truth*.

There were some examples of costly English bindings in the Exhibition of 1862. A book of Bedford's binding took some two months to finish, and cost forty guineas. Shaw's "Decorations" was lavishly enriched with tooling and jewels, said to be of the value of £100. Zaehnsdorf, of Brydges Street, exhibited Doré's Dante's Inferno in folio, the binding and decoration of which, after the Grolier and Maioli style, cost one hundred guineas. Messrs. Leighton, Son, & Hodge in later years introduced silver on the ornamentation of books, or rather, it should be said, aluminium, for silver too soon tarnishes to be useful. A unique specimen of binding was recently executed

by Messrs. Peacock.   It was a large quarto Altar
Service in crimson morocco, with massive side ornaments encrusted with precious stones.   A painting
on porcelain of our Saviour, framed in a band of
gilt metal studded with pearls, filled the centre.
This was surmounted by a cross, also set with pearls,
and with a large diamond in the middle.   Below was
the emblematic eagle of St. John, blazing with ame-
thysts, garnets, and diamonds, and a lily, emblem of
the Blessed Virgin Mary, set with black and white
pearls.   An elaborate border of gilt metal was thickly
studded with topaz, pearl, amethyst, malachite, and
turquoise, with beautifully carved cameos at intervals,
and large rock crystals mounted at the angles.   The
gems, several of which are of considerable size, were
alone said to be worth more than £200.

Turning to the comparative value of different materials for binding, Mr. J. Leighton (Luke Limner),
in a paper read by him before the Society of Arts in
February 1859, calls morocco "the prince of leathers."
Hogskin he considers "a nice and durable leather,"
though not much used, and it takes "blind-tooling"
admirably.   Russia leather, except extremely thick, is
apt to become rotten.   It is principally prized for its
odour and pleasant tone of colour.   It has been said,
indeed, by experienced binders, that the duration
of russia binding in the atmosphere of London is
but three years.   It is certain, indeed, that russia
backs always "go."   Vellum is extremely strong and
useful, but hard to work.   All the tree-marbles,
sponge-dabs, and other stained fancy patterns, he
also considers must in time injure the leather, on
account of the acids used in producing them.   Brown
and black are the only fast colours in cloth bindings.
Red, green, and blue are nearly so.   In calf-binding

yellow or tan is the only colour that will not fade.
It wears best. Blue calf fades and rubs white. The
quietest colours—neutral shades—will satisfy the eye
longest. What are called "purple" and "wine"
colours—solferino and magenta in binders' phrase—
have been known to fade out entirely in a month.
Wine — that is "claret" — is nearly a fast colour,
somewhat like green and red.

Paintings on the edges of books, or sometimes
with the edges of the leaves embossed, or the title of
the work written or impressed on them, have been
amongst the most interesting features of the ancient
ornamental art of bookbinding. At that time books
were generally kept flat on shelves or on appropriated
reading-desks, without any ornament or lettering on
the back. We frequently see such positions of old
books represented in the illuminations or woodcuts
of the period. In some places the practice of lettering books on the edges had not been discontinued
till comparatively recent times, for we find in a copy
of "Locke on the Epistles" a written memorandum,
made in 1711, stating that the "more convenient
manner of placing books in libraries is to turn their
backs outwards, with the titles and other decent
ornaments in gilt-work, which ought not to be hidden,
as in this library, by a contrary position, the beauty
of the fairest volume is;—therefore, to prevent this
for the future, and to remedy that which is past, if
it shall be thought worth the pains, the new method
of affixing the chains to the back of the books is
recommended, till one more suitable shall be contrived." What are known as "index edges," such
as we see in the huge Kelly's Post Office Directory,
are said to have been introduced by Messrs. Leighton.

§ Curiosities of Printing.

HE mere oddities and eccentricities con-
nected with books and printing are as
endless as the curiosities of literature
itself. There are books which exhibit
in their paper and print freaks and
"fads" of the strangest kind. One can hardly believe
the excessive length to which amiable fanatics have
indulged in their dealings with honest serviceable
type and paper. The most singular displays of oddity
have been in the choice and contrasts of paper and
print.

A French bibliophile, M. Peignet, has actually
published a work supplying a list of these fantastic
productions. Thus in the year 1822 we find the following : "Aristarchus, or the Principles of Composition," 1822, which was printed on about fifty different
coloured papers, and only twelve copies were struck
off. The most extraordinary of these caprices is an
"Elegy on the Death of Prince Henry," published in
1613, printed on black paper with white letters !
There have also been blue, yellow, and harlequin
papers. In the Bodleian Library is a copy of
"Textus Decretalium Bonifacii VIII." (1473), printed
on alternate sheets of vellum and paper. We also

find "A Sermon Preached before Charles the First," by the Rev. Joseph Howe, 1644, and thought to be the only known copy out of thirty printed, which is printed throughout in red ink. Other works, such as Chidley's "Complaints," 1652, Wilkes's "Essay on Woman," 1772, "Red Book," Dublin, 1790, are also printed in red ink. "Le Livre de Quatre Couleurs" (Paris, 1720) is printed in four different coloured inks. The "Book of Four Coulours," by one Caracicoli, printed in Paris in 1757, is printed in four different coloured inks, gamboge, ultramarine, sepia, and vermilion. Babbage's "Specimens of Logarithmic Tables" is printed with different-coloured inks on various coloured papers (to ascertain by experiment the tints of the paper and colours of the inks least fatiguing to the eye), in twenty-one volumes, 8vo, London, 1831. Of this work ONE SINGLE COPY ONLY WAS PRINTED. There were one hundred and fifty-one variously coloured papers chosen, and the following coloured inks were used : light blue, dark blue, light green, dark green, olive, yellow, light red, dark red, purple, and black. Vol. xxi. contains metallic printing in gold, silver, and copper bronzes, upon vellum and on various coloured papers.

"Le Livre de Demain" was printed on various kinds of paper with different coloured inks. The contents consist of selections in prose and verse, as well as an account of inks, paper, and the art of typography. The peculiarity of the book is the endeavour to suit the paper, ink, and type even, to the subject of the selection. The author, M. de Rochas, contends that a love-poem printed with light ink on rose-coloured paper will make a far deeper impression than if printed in black ink on white paper. There was a book published in 1832

S

entitled "Typographical Curiosities," printed on paper manufactured from white lead, and weighing two pounds. A curiosity, too, must be a book that appeared in 1800, being an account of "all the substances that have been used to describe events and to convey ideas," by one Koops, and which itself claims to be the first book printed upon straw paper.

Our great humourist, Sterne, in his first work, "Tristram Shandy," condescended to some fantastic tricks. Thus in Vol. i., at page 73, after the death of Yorick, we come on an entirely black page, in sign of mourning; at pages 169, 170, we find two pieces of marbled paper pasted on the regular page, "motley emblem of my work," he says; to say nothing of a chapter made to comprise two pages and left blank! At another passage, where Trim is described as making a flourish with his stick, a diagram of the flourish is represented on the paper. Stars are profusely used, sometimes for half a page, to convey the idea that something very emotional has been left out. It is remarkable, too, that in every copy of the two or three earlier volumes the eccentric author signed his name, which must have entailed much labour. Certain careful and fastidious writers have with their own hand corrected glaring misprints.

Indeed, there is no end to these curious tricks and devices, which are really unworthy of the great art. In the Exhibition of 1862 was shown a sort of typographical *tour de force* by one of M. Dupont's compositors—a statue of Gutenberg, a portrait of Beranger, and Cupid and Psyche (an odd company), all set up in "leads," and at a proper distance looking exactly like engravings. At the previous Exhibition of 1851, the printer of a Scotch newspaper, *The North British Advertiser*, displayed a view of the Free Church College, which was composed of twelve thousand five hundred pieces of type, and eighty feet of " brass rule," the whole at a distance being easily taken for an engraving.

Porro, born at Padua, 1520, is mentioned by Strutt as having engraved a print, " The Passion of Christ," in which the lines constituting the shading are found, when examined with a magnifying-glass, to be formed of small writing. In like manner, Strutt, in his " Common Prayer Book," 1717 (all engraved on 188 plates), prefixed an engraved bust of George I., the shading lines of which contain the Lord's Prayer, Creed, Commandments, Prayers for the Royal Family, and the Twenty-first Psalm.

In 1862 appeared Mr. Peter's machine for microscopic writing, whereby it is stated that the words " Matthew Marshall, Bank of England," can be written in the two and a half millionth of an inch in length, and it is actually said that calculations made on this *data* show that the whole Bible can be written *twenty-two times* in the space of a square inch ! The Lord's Prayer has actually been written this way in a space not exceeding the one-fifty-third of an inch square ; when examined with a high magnifying power each line of the letters was perfectly distinct.

The eccentric printer has always striven to distinguish himself by some vagary of this kind, and every age has boasted of its own special extravagance. Oddly enough, these feats, unremunerative to the projectors, have become profitable to those who come after. Thus, miniature volumes, printed in Liliputian type that can scarcely be read without glasses, seem to have had a fascination for certain printers, on account of their involving the solution of difficult problems. A large and respectable collection could be made of these tiny performances. The most tempting object of the printer has always been to produce little miniature volumes, which shall hold as much and be as legible as some of the huge and grosser tomes. The conditions attending on such a work are most difficult of attainment, legibility and thinness of paper being the chief. Minuteness of type is not, however, as might be supposed, incompatible with legibility, as the Elzevirs have shown in their dainty volumes. It requires extraordinary skill and thought to design letters which form words that shall be small and yet *clear*, and as the paper must be thin, to prevent the ink showing through on the other side. The problem has, nevertheless, always had a sort of attraction for printers, both in England and in other countries, and has been attempted frequently. One of the earliest attempts in this direction was the little Pindar issued in 1757 by the Foulis Press. Some fifty or sixty years ago, the printer Pickering issued a series of "Diamond Classics," marvels of minute typography, arrayed in silk binding, in which the whole of Virgil, Horace, &c, was compressed into a thin and tiny volume, very legible and "black in the type." These are now scarce and bring good prices. The Whittingham and Pickering "Shakespeares" are each in one substantial little volume, about half the size of the Globe "Shakespeare," but difficult to read, since the type, though brilliant, is crowded. There is another charming edition of the Pickering and Whittingham "Shakespeares," each in eight or ten volumes, legible and fairly readable, and illustrated with graceful and spirited cuts. The Pickering set is deservedly admired.

Didot, the famous Paris publisher, printed in 1828

a "Horace" in a remarkably small and exquisitely beautiful type called "*caractère microscopique.*" It is eclipsed, however, by another called *brilliant*, so named by its makers, Messrs. Miller & Richard, on account of its exquisite appearance when printed. Of this microscopic type, it takes 4000 i's to make a single pound, and about 6300 of the thinnest pieces for *spaces.* At the Exhibition of 1851, Gray's "Elegy," of thirty-two verses of four lines each, was printed in a space of four inches by three. Mr. Hotten issued a "Keepsake for Smokers" in this type, said to be "silver-faced," and the smallest type ever made. In 1884, Messrs. Field & Tuer published a tiny little book entitled "Quads," not more than an inch square, printed on "bank note-paper," and in what was pleasantly called "midget type." But all these *tours de force* were carried to extravagance towards the end of the last century, when some absurdly small books were issued in England and France. There is a little "Thumb Bible," as it was called, which contains some score of leaves, has copper-plate pictures, is bound *secundum artem*, and yet is no bigger than a postage stamp. I have also seen a French almanac of about the same size: in fact, there is no reason why a collector should not appear on the scene to devote his days and purse to gathering specimens of the Liliputian press.

The most thorough and rational feat in this direction was successfully carried out some years ago by Mr. Bellows, who planned a *waistcoat-pocket* English-French Dictionary, which was to be profound and scientific, and yet at the same time of the smallest dimensions for reference. The work is said to be admirably written, and a perfect success. The fact

of a dictionary comprising idioms, roots, &c., all on
the most elaborate scale, entailed the idea of vast
space. Johnson's vast and massive " huge armful "
and this tiny manual represent the two extremes.
The first point was to secure the very thinnest paper
consistent with stoutness, and by a consultation with
an eminent French firm of papermakers at Angoulême,
Messrs. Laroche, a very fine thin article was secured,
which was opaque, and firm enough to bear printing
on both sides. A special type was designed and
cast in Edinburgh of the sort known as " brilliant,"
only this was claimed to be the smallest ever cast,
even two sizes smaller than that of the smallest
Testament known. It was quite legible, and the
author considered that it would not try the eyes, as
dictionaries are not used for *reading* but for *consultation.* The paper was tinted buff, while a red line
ran round each page with pleasing effect. It is, in
short, a most singular little book, and the first edition
was disposed of in a very short time.

We may contrast with these tiny performances
some grotesquely Brobdignagian efforts, typographical
monsters made for the private reading of giants.
Some of the grand Aldines are enormous armfuls,
that require strong persons to handle, intended, as
we have said, to be read missal-like on a desk.
Perhaps the hugest work known is the vast Denon
collection of illustrations, which cannot be fitted
into any known library shelf, but require to repose
prone on their sides.*

* A pleasant traveller thus describes some gigantic volumes
at the Escurial, where it " seems there is an elephantine lectern,
weighing six tons, but moving very easily indeed on a pivot,
and on its ledges repose the books used by the choristers. The
volumes are about *six feet in height by four in breadth,* bound
in that famous yellow leather of Cordova, and heavily clasped

The most extraordinary feat in cheap printing in our time was the issuing of an edition of a substantial novel of Dickens's, filling three volumes octavo, in a pamphlet shape, for one penny. The paper was good and tough, and in amount was equal to three quires of cheap note-paper. In each page there were about fourteen hundred words. How it was done, or on what chance of profit or repayment it was based, it is difficult to say. For the very cheapest paper that could be brought into the market could hardly be supplied under the price of a penny a quire. Then there was the "setting," ink, working, stereotyping, &c. But there are wonderful and nice problems in these matters, and it was calculated that if the sale was only large enough the projectors would be repaid. The same difficulty occurs in the case of the *Times* newspaper, sold to dealers, I believe, at 2½d. a copy. Here the paper is fine, good, and stout, and the sheets that make up a copy, including supplement

and clamped with brass. The parchment pages, every one as big as the lease of the Castle of Otranto or Mrs. Shandy's marriage settlement, have the staves ruled blood-red, and on them rest, or rather ride, the notes. Such notes! such quadrangular blotches of glistening carbon! Every crotchet is as big as a blackthorn walking-stick with a knob at the end, fit to crack the head of Goliath. As for the words beneath the notes, so monstrous were those black-letter achievements, that, turning the crackling parchments over, it seemed that 'Non' took up one page, and 'nobis' two, and 'Domine' half-a-dozen. I never saw such books out of a pantomime." In the Royal Library at Stockholm there is shown a monster manuscript, the "Codex Giganteus," so called on account of its colossal size. It is two Swedish ells in height, and of proportionate breadth. This code is, in fact, a species of library in itself: it contains, besides a Vulgate, a collection of writings upon the Jewish Antiquities by Josephus, Isidorus, &c. Also the "Comes Pragensis Chronicon Bohemiæ." Many, struck with the enormous size of the volume, and with its singular illumination, have agreed in calling it "La Bible du Diable" or "Codex Diaboli."

and extra half-sheet, would be equivalent to some nine or ten sheets of good foolscap or "demi," which could not be bought under threepence the half-quire, thus leaving nothing for "setting" copy, money to editors, leader-writers, and reporters, or for working. Yet, as is known, there are vast profits. These arise, however, from the advertisements, which are thus all clear gain without deduction. In this connection it is evident that an excessive circulation beyond this proportion of profit must only increase the expense of production, while the advertisements remain a fixed quantity, and thus it would be conceivable that the expenses would exceed the advertising returns. And this accounts for what sometimes happens in the case of the Christmas numbers of the illustrated papers, where each copy costs a large sum to produce, leaving a slender margin of profit. Any fresh issue entails a capital expense, and the advertisements being already paid for and exhausted, additional copies become a matter of loss. Nor must we pass by, as a wonderful feat, Dick's humble edition of Shakespeare, sold at a shilling. The thought, organisation, and calculation necessary to produce this work successfully, required commercial talent of a high order. There is, or was, a bookseller's shop in Oxford Street, with which is associated a curious and perhaps unique incident in the trade. Mr. Horne, a poet of merit of the last generation, once published an epic called " Orion," and which, like many a good epic, was not as much appreciated by "the general" as it deserved to be, though by "the judicious" it was duly admired. One day he determined to prove that the cost, at least, of his work, should not stand in its way, and the front of the shop was covered with advertisements announcing

that the poem could be had within for *one farthing.*
I lately had this book in my hand—a rare one, and
"marked with three R's in the catalogues." It is
printed on the thinnest paper, is bound in cloth, and
filling more than one hundred pages. But on the
first day only three copies were sold, and by the end
of the week only a few more. The truth is, low price
will not tempt purchasers. A publisher once informed me that of a volume of poems he had literally
sold *two* copies, and these were purchased by a
friend of the author's. This, he said, was unique in
his experience.

Cheap literature, or books for the masses, has at
this moment been carried to the lowest point in the
great countries of France, England, and Germany.
France led the way with its "Bibliothèque Nationale,"
which was begun in 1863, and furnished for twopence-
halfpenny a series of little volumes containing the best
home and foreign literature. Since then some ten
millions of copies have been issued. Next followed
a Leipsic bookseller, Reclam (a good suggestive
name), who established the "Universal Library,"
at the same price, and has issued some eighteen
millions of copies. Finally, in 1885, came the
English attempt, started by the Cassells, who issued
little works at threepence a copy! Their series is
superior in paper and print to its foreign rivals, contains nearly 200 pages of print, and is issued every
week. It will be interesting to see the result of this
experiment.

The extraordinary results of machinery and divi-
sion of labour has of course been applied to printing,
and some wonderful *tours de force* have been accomplished in the way of rapid and cheap production.
There is nothing so wonderful in these feats after all,

T

as it only amounts to putting a sufficient number of workmen to the task. Thus, a three-volume novel may consist of some seventy or eighty sheets, and if a skilled workman could " set " a sheet in the day, the whole would be accomplished, on pressure, by seventy or eighty compositors in a single day. On the occasion of the Caxton celebration, a show feat of this kind was performed, which Mr. Gladstone, with a rather rhetorical flourish, described as " the climax and consummation of the art of printing." A hundred copies of the Bible were commenced at two o'clock on the morning of a commemoration meeting at South Kensington, and before two o'clock in the afternoon a copy was handed on to the platform perfectly finished. The book, with its 1052 pages, had been printed, dried, pressed, sent up to London, collated, sewn, rolled, bound in Turkey morocco, its edges gilt, the cover embossed with the University arms and an appropriate inscription, in less than twelve hours. Here, however, the " setting " had been done previously. Another fantastic performance was the issue of the Revised Version of the Bible, which was, in truth, an extraordinary commercial operation, admirably developed and worked. For one of the Testaments some 300 tons of paper were used, the presses were kept groaning night and day for months before issue, while a perfect dearth was caused in the leather market by the demand for skins for binding. Never was there such a foolish craze founded on pure curiosity, and it may be suspected, without breach of charity, from no burning ardour to be in possession of the purest and most genuine version of the sacred text. Nor must we pass that surprising feat of the Bible Society, the issue of the " Penny Testament," which, filling 240 pages, bound and sewn, and respectably printed on good paper, is issued for that sum.*

The mention of Bibles leads to that of certain extraordinary editions of the sacred text which have received names, or even nicknames, "in the trade," from some absurd mistake in the printing. These, of course, commend them to the notice of the ingenious collector. There is the well-known "Breeches Bible," which turns up frequently enough in an imperfect state. A Breeches Bible in fine condition is highly valuable. This sobriquet is owing to the quaint translation—"Adam and Eve made themselves breeches," &c. Nor must we omit the "Bugge Bible." There is also the "Vinegar Bible," the words "parable of the vinegar" being used instead of "*vineyard.*" A Belfast Bible, 1716, has "sin on more," instead of "no more." More curious is the "Leda Bible" of 1572, so called from the careless profanity of the publisher, who, wishing to adorn the work with illustrations, used an old block of "Leda and the Swan." Field's "Genuine Pearl Bible" of 1633, which has been described as "THE WICKED BIBLE," and is complacently recommended in the catalogues as "famous for its errors" (6000), deserves notoriety for its translation of a passage in the Corinthians—"Know ye not that the unrighteous shall inherit the kingdom of God ;" and also, "Ye cannot serve and mammon." These strange misprints were amended by cancelling some pages,

* "From the beginning of August 1884 to March 1, 1886," writes to me Mr. Brown, the secretary of the Society, " 1,310,000 copies of the Penny Testament were issued by this Society. The first million copies were sold *within ten months.* The cost of printing and binding the book is a small fraction under two-pence." The book was therefore produced at a loss of about three-farthings a copy.

which the collector rejects contemptuously, seeking copies "without the cancels." The well - known Catholic version, the "Douay Bible," issued in 1609–10, has been called the "Rosin Bible," owing to the translation of the passage in Jeremiah, "Is there no rosin in Gilead?" Even the folio authorised version (Barker's of 1611) has been termed the great "He" Bible—why I know not.

There have been, of course, collectors of Bibles—a really stupendous undertaking—of which the most serious and ambitious was the late Duke of Sussex, who sought them in every language, and amassed some two thousand. The catalogue of this wonderful collection no real Bible-collector "should be without." His Royal Highness was a fair Hebrew scholar, and his collection was rich in Hebrew Testaments.

It had long been established that the earliest printed Paris Bible was that dated 1570, and all accredited bibliographers and commentators, having settled this point, worked from it as a base. One day there was discovered in Archbishop Moore's well-known library a copy of a Bible with a date much earlier. The confusion and bewilderment among the cognoscenti was incredible. It was found impossible that such a thing could be; yet there it was, incontrovertible. An acute Mr. Johnson, however, scrutinising the date narrowly, "cried out that there had been an erasure, and that the new figures were written with printing-ink on the scratched part, otherwise no bad imitation, and upon the whole a very ingenious counterfeit." An ordinary piece of illumination had been drawn over the place for better disguise. There was also a rent, with a piece of thin paper pasted on the back, seemingly in a careless manner. "*Thus was exposed one of the greatest*

difficulties that have clogged the annals of the press."
It may be said that the wary eye of the modern old
bookseller would have detected the cheat at the first
glance.

As an illustration of the historical suggestiveness
of books, it may be mentioned that there was a copy
of Caxton's "Legende of Saintes, by me Wynkyn
de Worde," which had this inscription in the beginning : "I take this to be the edition of 1517. This
is one of the few copies which have escaped the execution of the remarkable inquisition of Henry VIII.
to expunge or deface the life of St. Thomas of
Canterbury, and the word Pope wherever it might
occur.—W. Herbert, 1827."

In the case of a work of Tyndale's, the "Penta-
teuch," it was directed by Parliament in 1540 that
all the marginal notes should be cut off, which was
actually done. The Grenville copy, however, escaped
the massacre or mutilation, and is therefore considered a choice rarity. Another book, "Fabyan's
Chronicle," was suppressed so successfully by Wolsey that only one copy survives.

There is a class of collectors who collect everything on a favourite and particular subject. These
elements fall under the denomination of "cuttings,"
and it is surprising how, with the diligent aid of a
pair of scissors, the mass soon begins to accumulate.
The accumulation is for the most part rubbish ; but,
to one writing on the subject, it often supplies valuable
indications of topics and matter worth investigation.
Some of these "dust-bins," which often contain a
stray silver spoon or fork, are of the oddest character,
as "A Collection of many Hundreds of Bills, chrono-
logically arranged, from 1741 to 1868, including
Astley's, Ducrow's, Coburg, Surrey, Tottenham Street,

Sadler's Wells, Drury Lane, Adelphi, Olympic, Covent Garden, Haymarket, Theatre in Guildhall (1758), New City, Garrick, Deptford, City Pantheon, King's, Soho, &c., Menageries, Exhibitions, &c., with a large collection, many thousands of cuttings from various sources, extending over a period of nearly 100 years, a number of orders and tickets of admission, with interesting autographs."

Another person with great industry brings together everything that can bear on " Waxwork Exhibitions, Panoramas, and other Shows of London, from early in the Eighteenth Century down to our times (a few country items included). It comprises a very large number of cuttings, bills, handbooks, catalogues, advertisements, admission orders, &c. &c., to Fantoccini, Shadows, Puppets, Marionettes, Automata, Tableaux Vivants, Penny Shows, &c., and represents the under-current of Metropolitan amusement with its frequent pandering to the morbid tastes of the last hundred and fifty years' populace. Of Waxworks it is believed that a larger collection does not exist in one body : in that branch are Anatomical Venuses, Chambers of Horrors, distinguished persons, scenes, &c., from 1729 downwards. Panoramas, dioramas, cosmoramas, sculpture, paintings, giants, dwarfs, monsters, entertainments, and very many items which, while legitimately belonging to the history of London life, and nearly allied to the lower stratum of the histrionic profession, are but poorly represented in even the richest collections relating either to our metropolis or to the drama."

Another curious collection is one on Dr. James Graham's exhibtions : " The Temple of Health and Hymen, the Celestial Bed, Exhibitions (Rare and Curious), &c., a curious collection of prints, views, songs, music, poems, manuscripts, matters, portraits, accounts of lectures and exhibitions, advertisements, &c. (including an account of Lady Hamilton), mounted and arranged in a 4to volume, new half-red morocco, cloth sides, gilt edges, curious and rare." And also the next on ballooning : "An Extraordinary Collection of 960 Engravings, Newspaper Cuttings, Autograph Letters, Documents, Advertisements, Broadsides, Handbills, Posters, Water-Colour Drawings, and other papers relating to Aeronautical History from 1724 to 1854. Arranged in chronological order, and very neatly mounted on 102 sheets of drawing-paper. The collection comprises 81 plain and 22 coloured plates, many of which are very scarce (and the large tinted engraving of Lunardi's balloon at the Pantheon especially so), 105 woodcuts, 8 caricatures, 23 portraits of aeronauts; 5 water-colour drawings, 20 large posters for walls, advertising fêtes at Ranelagh, Vauxhall, Cremorne, and other places of amusement ; 62 broadsides and songs, some with woodcut headings ; 45 autograph letters ; numerous admission tickets initialed by Green ; and 10 pieces of silk of various colours cut from balloons. The remainder are cuttings describing every event between the dates named, including the opening of London Bridge, the fête in St. James's Park, &c., &c. Having been formed by Mr. Green, the famous aeronaut, the collection is perhaps the most complete it would be possible to form. Several autograph letters of his are inserted, together with accounts of ascensions by him and Coxwell at Cremorne, Vauxhall, and elsewhere."

Among other strange and unexpected subjects, we have Willshere on " Playing-Cards " in the collection in the British Museum, which amounts to about forty packs of all nations. This is said to be " the most elaborate and authoritative of all recent works on playing-cards, containing a great many illustrations of all kinds. Also many interesting curiosities connected with playing-cards, including a facsimile advertisement of the patriotic American Decatur cards, of which the backs were adorned with a cut of Decatur's victory, various comic cartoons and caricatures in imitation of playing-cards, a lot of the internal revenue stamps issued by playing-card manufacturers, and specimens of the 'marked back' playing-cards used by gamblers." But there is a literature on playing-cards. The really grand work on the subject is that of the Society of French Bibliophilists, a grand folio volume, containing 100 coloured plates, and going back to the fourteenth century.

There is a well-known dictionary called " Men of the Time," which appears at intervals. The impression of 1856 is greatly sought because of a bizarre account of Wilberforce, then Bishop of Oxford, who was described as " a sceptic as regards religious revelation ; he is nevertheless an out-and-out believer in spirit movements." The fact was, this sentence had slipped out of the preceding article on Robert Owen, and got mixed up with the account of the Bishop.

Prince Ferdinand of Portugal recently made a collection of all works that had been *suppressed by governments*, the total amounting to many thousands.

Among the innumerable odd subjects to which books have been devoted, there is the odd one of caligraphy, or "flourishing" penmanship, once a sort of art, held in favour when schoolmasters cultivated drawing, with bold sweeps of the pen, swans, and other devices. Some of them are wonderful productions indeed, and the art was in demand for the preparation of addresses, &c., often seen hung up in old mansions and places of business.

It might be a fair speculation why it has not occurred to some collector to form a gathering of books each of which had some odd adventure or association. For there are numbers of books the very titles of which suggest some strange history, or have been connected with some crisis. Here, for instance, opening a catalogue, the eye falls on Henry VIII.'s famous work, with its full style and title :—"Assertio Septem Sacramentorum adversus Martinum Lutherum ædita ab invictissimo Angliæ et Franciæ Rege, &c. Henrico ejus nominis octavo. *Romæ, opera Stephani, Guillereti,* 1521.—Literarum quibis invictissimus Princeps Henricus Octavus, Rex Angliæ, Fidei Defensor respondit ad quandam Epistolam Martini Lutheri ad se missam. *Romæ, apud F. Minitium Calvum,* 1527. In one vol. 4to, *fine tall and clean copy in the original limp vellum,* £7, 10s. This original Roman edition of Henry VIII.'s famous book against Luther is still more rare than that printed in England, and contains in addition Pope Leo's letter to Henry conferring upon him the title of Defender of the Faith, which was not reprinted in later editions. This appears to be one of the earliest copies issued, as it has not the supplementary sheet containing Dr. Clerk's Address to the Pope. Concerning the second piece in the volume, the Grenville Catalogue says, speaking of the London edition, ' This original edition of Henry VIII.'s answer to Luther's letter to him is of great rarity. Strype says he once saw it in the exquisite library of the Bishop of Ely.' The Roman edition is probably even more rare. This volume is from the ancient library of the Altieri family, and bears marks of having been in days of yore in the hands of the Roman Inquisitors, for the name of Henry VIII. and Martin Luther are struck through with a pen, or have paper pasted over them."

There are some curious incidents connected with the first edition of Milton's great poem, which in small folio is readily procurable. But the informed collector knows that the publisher issued it with a series of different title-pages—seven or eight, if not more. You must describe your copy carefully, as the " first edition with the seventh title-page," or one with the third or fourth. But one with the first title-page and the first edition is priced by Mr. Quaritch at £40.

How curious to come on the quarto pictures of Lady Hamilton in her "attitudes"—a tribute paid her by her foolish worshipping husband. We think of Nelson, of her strange adventurous life, and her dying in debt and destitution at Calais. So to come upon a book printed that is "set" by the venerated hands of Benjamin Franklin. Such is "Cicero Cato Major, with explanatory notes. Philadelphia, printed and sold by Benjamin Franklin, 1744." For this small quarto ten guineas was asked many years ago ; now, with the "fury" for things American, it would be offered at double the money. In Mr. William George's Bristol catalogue, quaintly entitled "Bibliotheca Antiqua et Curiosa ; a descriptive and priced list of some old and curious books, being the fifteenth collection under that title," we find Milton's "History of Britain, collected out of the antientest authors thereof. Portrait by Faithorne. First edition. Quarto, original calf, 1670." On which it is pointed out that "the beautiful portrait of John Milton in this work is one of the few English portraits cut on copper from the life. Each impression has the rank of an original portrait of Milton, and, as such, an impression hangs in the National Portrait Gallery." Or here is a specimen of the minute fashion in which the bibliographer marshals evidence :—" Charles the First.—Eikon Bazilike, the Portraicture of his Sacred Majestie [&c., with two mottoes and date]. Folding frontispiece by Marshall. Tall octavo, original calf, 21s. 1649. The largest edition of the 'Eikon,' with fine impression of the folding plate, having engraved verses. This copy, *being in its original binding*, it is interesting to note that the place of the plate is *facing* its 'Explanation,' and *not* facing the title-page, which is preceded by a leaf on which the royal arms are printed."

A very odd and handsome book, published in 1754, is "The Gentleman and Cabinet Maker's Director, being a large collection of most elegant and useful designs of Household Furniture in the Gothic, Chinese, and Modern Taste, with proper directions for executing the most difficult · pieces, the mouldings being exhibited at large, and the dimensions of each design specified, 157 copper plates, folio, calf, by Thos. Chippendale." Now every one knows the merits of the "Chippendale furniture," the curious designs and carvings, unmistakable in their character. It is one of the scarcest of volumes, as Mr. "Rainy Day" Smith, after duly praising it, prophesied it would be. It now brings from fifteen to twenty guineas !

First editions of even living authors seem to become rare within a very few years. One of the most precious of volumes is the "Poems by Two Brothers," issued in 1827, which was the first appearance of Alfred Tennyson, and for which ten guineas is an average price. A copy of the "Poems by Alfred

Tennyson, 1833," has cost £14. A whole set of the green-coated volumes, first editions, would be worth a large sum, and there would be found plenty of opulent collectors ready to give what is called " any money" for the set. They could then have them dressed up in " crushed levantine" morocco, to form " a superb monument of the bibliopegistic art."

These early Tennyson editions are sought for chiefly by students and admirers, on account of the rather capricious variations the author is fond of making in successive editions. " The Grand Old Gardener" has thus been reshaped and altered many times and a new phrase substituted. " Timbuctoo," his prize poem, has been sold for five guineas ; but the rarest of his books remains the " Poems by Two Brothers."

Shelley's works attract the attention of the curious, such as the early editions of " Queen Mab," " Adonais," printed on rude paper and with ruder type. To this category also belong the works of Lamb, Southey, Coleridge, and many more, and their works are now greatly sought. These are elegant little volumes, set off with " plates by Westall" or by Stothard. There is an impression of grace and refinement left as we look at these illustrations ; they are conceived in an abstract and poetical spirit ; the figures, limbs, and draperies are elegant, and seem the work of masters. It is when we contrast these with the modern illustrations to Longfellow, Tennyson, &c., that we are drawn down to earth, so coarse and purely unpoetical are these things. Lamb's works in their original edition have an exceptional flavour. The " Tales from Shakespeare" derive an additional value from the plates being by Blake. A copy of the " Album Verses" was offered lately, and was of great interest. " Three copies, each

of peculiar and exceptional interest to the collector, all in original boards, uncut, viz., the original proof copy, with corrections in the author's handwriting (one leaf of which is missing); the copy formerly belonging to J. G. Towers (the friend of Charles Lamb), and presented by her brother (page 12 is composed of verses from the album of Mrs. Jane Towers); and the copy purchased at Samuel T. Coleridge's sale, with the following note on cardboard affixed to the fly-leaf in Charles Lamb's autograph:—
'At No. 64 New Bond Street is to be seen a capital picture of Milton, the property of C. Lamb, which he thinks would gratify Mr. Coleridge to see when he is in town and can spare a minute.' It is interesting to remark that this particular portrait found its way into a London auction about two years ago, and the advertiser, after a spirited competition, let it fall at £355." Rarest of all is the "Devil's Walk," a poem of which but a single copy was known to be in existence—I think in the possession of Messrs. Moxon. But one little work, "The Poetry for Children," containing some verses by Lamb and his sister, had altogether disappeared. For years a copy was sought; high rewards were offered, but in vain. Strange to say, it at last turned up in one of the colonies, was sent to England and reprinted. It should be known that poems and essays by Lamb are scattered about in all directions in such little books as the "Pocket Magazine," Selections from "The Champion" newspaper, and in Cottle's "Anthology." Very rare is the Coleridge little volume published at Bristol, in which are some of his friend's sonnets. His works extend, as may be conceived, to a vast number of volumes, all uniform in size and style.

The late Lord Houghton, among other fancies, collected all the poets of this century, great and little, and which were printed in this uniform shape.

In a previous page was detailed the fashion in which certain works have been saved from destruction. Boswell's entertaining Letters to Temple were discovered in a shop in Boulogne, in use for wrapping-paper. More extraordinary still, Mr. Gibbs of Bath related to me how, searching in some old house, he found Sterne's Diary kept for Eliza in a *plate-warmer!*

It is much the fashion now to *simulate* the old editions, mimicking, as it were, the paper, type, and general air of a favourite work. Mr. Stock has given us some curiously exact facsimiles, such as those of " Walton's Angler," and, more singular still, a tiny volume reproducing the original black-letter writing of the immortal " Imitation of Christ." The two little inviting volumes, the original " Vicar of Wakefield," retiring, unobtrusive—like the Vicar himself— have recently been revived, an exact copy in its boards, paper, and print. So with the first Kilmarnock edition of " Burns's Poems " and Bunyan's " Pilgrim's Progress," and many more. It would be an interesting speculation to think how these copies will mystify generations two hundred years hence. But with such things Time is the great distinguisher. As in painted imitations of wood, every year shows more clearly that it is paint and not wood, so in these volumes the points where likeness was attempted will become more glaringly revealed. One of the latest and most far-fetched absurdities of publication is a posthumous work of a popular writer, announced as the " last work of the late Hugh Conway." This is an oblong volume with facsimiled handwriting of this rather over-praised author. It is given with all erasures, &c., and is not, like all MS., very easy reading.

The modern devices for setting off books are end-less in their variety. Photography in its numerous forms—*photogravure*, phototype, &c.—is made to bring colour and mechanism to our aid, and it must be said with singularly pleasing and apparently artis-tic effect. The latest French works " of luxury," display on the finest paper the most exquisite draw-ings, printed in a rich blue, brown, or green tint, figures, arabesques, landscapes " embordering " the page. These are not engraved, but are the original drawings or water-colours reproduced by the process. They are, however, delusive enough. In course of years they will fade or at least " grow flat," for by a curious law of retribution all mimicries and pretences in time must prove their inferiority, and the weak places are revealed. The older finely finished engrav-ings are " impressions," *i.e.*, a magnifying-glass would show that every line is raised on the paper, which gives a sort of relief and the brilliancy of relief. On the other hand, a literal photograph of an engraving, the tone of the ink copied and every line reproduced, lacks this relief, or rather simulates it.*

* Here is a description of one of these bizarre works, which first brought this style into fashion. " Uzanne (Octave).—L'Eventail—L'Ombrelle—Le Gant—Le Manchon. Profusely illustrated with charming engravings by Paul Avril, exquisitely printed in various delicate tints, and having inserted sets of proofs on Japanese paper, printed without the letterpress, 2 vols. imperial 8vo, superbly bound by Rivière, in blue and orange morocco extra, *the original silk covers used as linings*, £40. Two remarkable books, illustrated in a manner entirely novel, and probably destined to effect a revolution in the art of book-illustrating. M. Brunox writes of them, ' Rarement livre fut accuelli avec un succès plus vif, et, disons-le, plus mérité que *L'Eventail.* Son apparition fut, pour les bibliophiles, un éblouis-sément.' Both works rapidly became out of print, and the publisher guarantees not to reprint them. Of the sets of proofs only 100 were printed, and that to *L'Ombrelle* is a picked set, bearing the artist's autograph." Forty guineas was the price.

During the last ten years another mania has obtained in Paris for issuing exquisitely printed little books with red-letter titles, it may be, and tiny etchings, of Elzevir shape or series. The paper is a little rough, the print "old faced," the margins large. Several firms have distinguished themselves by issuing these dainty books, such as Lemerre, Glady, &c. One would think it was a simple matter to do this, so many copies at such a price. But the jaded stomach of the bibliomaniac must be tickled by congenial devices. So : (1.) every copy must be numbered ; (2.) there must be a limited number, say 300. The numbering gives an individuality to each copy of the 300. Say thirty are printed on " Turkey mill-paper;" then for coquettish amateurs we have the following :—

Printed on choice grape-paper	.	.	.	1 copy.
,, ,, choice parchment	.	.	.	2 copies.
,, ,, Japanese quarto	.	.	.	30 ,,
,, ,, Imperial Whatman paper	.	.	.	50 ,,
,, ,, Chinese do.	.	.	.	50 ,,
,, ,, Van Gelder's Dutch	.	.	.	200 ,,

On this scale was the choice " Manon Lescaut " brought out. The English Whatman hand-made paper is highly appreciated in France. Most of these little books are designed to furnish opportunities for the binding maniac, who finds thus a choice subject to exhibit some exquisite exercise of the bibliopegistic skill.

Returning to other " oddities," the old halfpenny ballads have always had an attraction for the collector, and Macaulay's taste in this direction is well known. Playbills also are sought ; and there is something attractive "in the casual sight of an old playbill," the memories attached, its own frail texture contrasting with the stouter and more enduring tenure of those whose doings it chronicled, and who are long

since moulded away. Yet this shred and patch en-
dures. Mr. Halliwell Philipps has a bill of Dryden's
arrangement of " Troilus and Cressida," in the time
of William III., than which there is none older existing. As, however, there are no actors' names, this is
hardly a bill proper. Perhaps the scarcest of bills is
that of Garrick's first appearance. I myself possess
" a poster " of Mrs. Siddons's last appearance. The
most famous collection of halfpenny ballads is that
known as the " Roxburghe," partly formed by the
Duke of that name, and sold at his sale in 1812 for
£482. They are now in the Museum, having been
secured for £535. But this was exceeded at the
Brindley sale, when eight volumes of halfpenny ballads were disposed of for £837!

Yet another amiable craze is that for " chap-books,"
diligently collected, small pamphlets, things sold by
hawkers for a halfpenny and a penny, from ten to
fifteen pages long—" Goody Two Shoes," " History
of England," &c. There are those who boast their
" finest collection of chap-books in England." There
is a legend, moreover, that some of these have " cuts
by Bewick," and that some, at least certain children's
books, were written by Goldsmith. They are poor,
starved things, uninviting, on rough, villainous paper—
" wrapping," apparently—and wholly undesirable.

An odd and interesting department of which a collection might be made are journals and magazines
published at schools and colleges, and to which men
afterwards celebrated contributed. Among these are
" The Microcosm," published at Eton, to which Can-
ning furnished some lively, precocious trifles. Also,
at the same place, " The Eton Miscellany," by Bar-
tholomew Bouverie, now of Eton College (Eton, 1827),
" containing thirty contributions by W. E. Gladstone,

X

five by Arthur Henry Hallam, and others by Colvile, Doyle, Gaskell, Hanmer, Jelf, Law, Pickering, Selwyn, Shadwell, Skirlow, Wilder, Frederic Rogers, G. A. Selwyn, and others anonymous."

The familiar "Arabian Nights," delight of our childhood, one might fancy, was accessible enough. However, Mr. John Payne, of the Villon Society, conceived the idea of translating these old tales on the principle of calling a spade a spade throughout, with this result, that every judicious bookseller secures a copy when he can, and invites the purchaser on these tempting grounds : "The Book of the Thousand Nights and One Night, now first completely done into English prose and verse, from the original Arabic, by John Payne, 9 vols., very scarce, 1882–84. Intending purchasers are strongly recommended to lose no time in securing this valuable work, as every month it greatly increases in price, and the limited number printed quite precludes the possibility of its value decreasing. Only 700 copies were issued, each numbered and signed by the printer. It consists of a perfectly free and literal translation from the original Arabic, and was printed for the Villon Society by private subscription, and for private circulation only." For these nine volumes, now grown scarce, twenty-two guineas are asked. No doubt the attraction is what the French call "scatological" or "Pantagruelic." Captain Burton has *renchéri* on the idea, and recently published a new translation, and being still more literal, or, as our neighbours would say, "*naturalistic*," the demand is far greater. The copies are rising in price.

A recommendation often found in a catalogue runs, "The edition nearly all destroyed in the Fire of London." It has indeed been said that in this calamity

£200,000 worth of booksellers' property was lost. Whole editions were burnt on their shelves. In Lincoln's Inn Library is one survivor curiously preserved, viz., "Prynne's Introduction, or An Exact History of the Popes." Every copy was supposed to have entirely perished, until one was found to be in the library of the Duke of Buckingham at Stowe. It was never completed, but ends abruptly at page 400 in the middle of a sentence. The Benchers of Lincoln's Inn possessing the volumes comprising the body of the work (and which are of extreme rarity in a complete shape, "a large portion of the impression having been burnt in the Great Fire"), on the occasion of the sale of the Stowe Library in 1849, determined at any cost to possess this Introduction of two hundred fragmentary leaves. They secured it at the price of £335 !

Who would not hugely covet works of which literally there is only a single copy known to be in existence? This is the case in the instance of one of the old English writers, Barnfield, of whose "Lady Pecunia" there has been but one copy found. Some old bookhunter in the last century, prowling about the Barbican, saw it on a dust-heap and rescued it. Of other books there have been only a few copies printed, which has of course engendered an insane longing to possess them. Thus Lord Peterborough issued a work called "Succinct Genealogies," of which there were only twenty-five copies printed, a single one of which has brought £74, £98, and even £100. More extraordinary still is the French work "Tableau des Mœurs du Temps," of which only a *single* copy was printed. In such cases the book cannot be considered as *printed;* it ranks with things in manuscript. Dr. Madden's "Memoirs of the 20th Century," the bibliophilist Davis tells us, " published in 1733, is considered one of the rarest in the English language : it was intended to have been comprised in six volumes, only one of which was ever printed. In order to expedite the printing and delivery, three printers, Bowyer, Woodfall, and Roberts, were employed, and one thousand impressions of the first volume struck off, *but suppressed on the day of publication.* Eight hundred and ninety copies were delivered to Dr. Madden, and all were supposed to have been destroyed by him." In this short epitome, what a picture of reckless waste, indecision, and folly !

The second edition of Woolaston's " Religion of Nature " has deservedly an interest, as Franklin had a share in printing it, or rather in setting the types. The " Epistolæ Obscurorum Virorum " is notable, because Erasmus, on the eve of a serious operation, was seized with such a violent fit of laughter when reading it, that the " imposthume " burst, and he was saved.

There are two homely English books which at a sale would bring good prices—Mrs. Glasse's famous Cookery-Book, of *"first catch your hare"* notoriety, and " Cocker's Arithmetic," of *" according to Cocker "* fame. A living London journalist found the first edition of the first, " The Art of Cookery," folio, in the New Kent Road, and secured it for sixpence ! He had it superbly bound, and now values it as a unique at £100. The first " Cocker " was published so long ago as the year 1677 or 1678, and of this excessively rare book not more than three or four copies have been heard of. The twentieth edition appeared in 1700, and the thirty-second not long after. The indefatigable Dr. Dibdin could never succeed in meeting a copy earlier than this. The late Professor

De Morgan was all his lifetime engaged in trying to get together a series of the earlier editions, but could not succeed. Poor Professor! dying in despair! Rarest of this class is the famous "Joe Miller's Jests, or the Wit's *Vade Mecum* . . . . most humbly inscribed to those choice spirits of the age, Captain Rodens, Mr. Alexander Pope, Mr. Professor Sacy, Mr. Orator Henley, and Job Baker, the kettle-drummer. Printed and sold by T. Read, in Dog-well Court, Whyte Friars, Fleet Street, 1739. Price one shilling."

Our old friends Sternhold and Hopkins are cele-brated not for what had been their praiseworthy ambition, viz., versifiers of the Psalms, but as fur-nishing the happiest specimen of bathos or doggerel known. They suggested a happy jest to Tom Hood, who described a game of leap-frog by their familiar names. A desirable copy of these worthies' work was offered some time ago: "Booke of Psalmes, collected into English meeter, by Thomas Sternhold, John Hopkins, and others, in 1624, 18mo, bound in contemporary maroon satin, entirely covered in rich embroidery of gold and silver threads and pearls, gilt edges, and accompanied by a beautifully worked silk bag, embroidered in colours with trees, flowers, animals, &c., and gold and silver thread, the whole displayed in a specially prepared morocco case, lined with maroon velvet, with glass lid and lock and key." Thirty guineas was asked, and it was claimed that this was "a highly interesting historical relic, the volume and bag having been found in the pocket of Charles I. after his execution. In the early part of the present century it was purchased by Mr. Pickering, who sold it to the late Mr. Bedford, the eminent bookbinder, and while in the possession of the latter it was exhibited at the Manchester Exhibition. The bag is believed to have been the work of Queen Henrietta-Maria."

Should you come upon an old folio Livy, with portrait of Livy, and device of cat and mouse on title, large copy, original vellum binding, 1520, think of what the late Bishop of Ely used to say, " Whenever you see a book with a *Cat and Mouse* in the frontispiece, seize upon it, for the chances are as three to four that it will be found both curious and valuable :—admonition from such a quarter is not to be slightly rejected."—*Dibdin's Bibliog. Decam.*, ii. 231. There is something quaint in this piece of advice.

" Robinson Crusoe " went through more editions in a short space of time than any other book—forty-one editions in forty years. It has been translated too into every modern language. I have a few numbers of a newspaper, "The Intelligencer," in which it appeared as a serial. A popular school-book, however, goes through innumerable editions with a steady, certain progress that the author of genius might sigh for. In 1829 a book appeared known as " Butler's Spelling-Book," and it has since reached to nearly its 350th edition ! while the better-known " Mavor's English Spelling-Book " is advancing " by leaps and bounds " to its 400th edition ! It has been said that Longfellow's " Miles Standish " ran through forty editions in a month.

John Kemble, when an obscure actor at York in 1780, published a little volume of " Fugitive Verses," of which, when he grew into celebrity, he became ashamed, and whenever a copy was announced to be sold by auction, he sent to purchase it at any price ; and once had to pay an enormous sum, owing to the competition of a rival purchaser, who was determined to secure it. Hence it was considered to be exceedingly scarce. Now it would not be difficult at any time to secure a copy.*

* The veteran bookseller, Mr. Stibbs, one of the good old type, can relate many a legend of this kind. Once the Duke of Wellington wished to secure an old pamphlet written by Lord Wellesley, and directed his bookseller to purchase it for him at an auction. His brother, however, wished to have it, and also sent a commission. The shilling pamphlet was actually bid up to close on a hundred pounds, to the amazement and anger of the Iron Duke. He was appeased, however, when reminded by his agents that they had only "obeyed orders." Mr. Stibbs makes book-buying journeys through Holland in quest of rare "incunables" and mouldy tomes reposing in old dimly-lighted shops at Amsterdam and the Hague. His experience is that there is no level of price for these treasures, which, on the whole, bring far higher prices in foreign countries. There is an intimate communication between our dealers and the foreigners, who give commissions at auctions at Rome and Berlin.

§ Of Grangerising and Dickensiana.

RANGERISING" is a term familiar enough to the initiated, but possibly a mystery to "the general." There is many a book which a nice instinct feels ought to be illustrated, such as histories, accounts of persons and places. Hence it is that certain ingenious persons, with plenty of money and more idle time on hand, have devoted their lives to the Grangerising some favourite work. To this pursuit they have devoted energy and purpose, hunting up and hunting down, tearing and cutting out, ransacking generally, until they have secured what they desired. It is in this way, as Mr. Blades shows, that fearful havoc has been wrought, and thousands of fine books mutilated and destroyed by the Grangerites. And why Granger-ites? It seems that a Rev. Mr. Granger came into the world specially for the benefit of these Attilas, having written a large "History of England," in which he made allusion to every celebrated person and place connected with the chronicles of England. It may be conceived what welcome volumes these were to the collecting "Grangerite," and from that

time to the present there have always been a number
of persons diligently engaged in the task. Some of
these collections have cost fortunes. The " Bindley
Granger " was celebrated. The late Mr. John Forster
had two Grangerised copies of " Granger," one in
fourteen folio volumes, the other in seventeen. Together they contain between five and six thousand
portraits, many of which are singularly rare and costly,
and might count as originals. The incidental expenses of Grangerising are serious, owing to the nice
"laying down " of the prints on extra fine paper, and
of the " inlaying to folio size " of small printed pages,
which is an expensive operation.

Dr. Dibdin, in his most sarcastic vein, gives a
happy instance of this mania. " Take this passage,"
he says, "from Speed : ' Henry Le Spencer, the
warlike Bishop of Norwich, being drawn on by Pope
Urban to preach a crusade, and to be general against
Clement.' To be properly illustrated, (1) Procure all
the portraits, at all periods of his life, of Henry Le
Spencer. (2) Obtain every view, ancient or modern,
like or unlike, of the city of Norwich, and, if fortune
favour you, of every bishop of the See. (3) Every
portrait of Pope Urban must be procured, and as
many prints and drawings as will give a notion of the
crusade. (4) You must search high and low, early
and late, for every print of Clement. (5) Procure,
or you will be wretched, as many fine prints of
cardinals and prelates, singly or in groups, as
will impress you with a proper idea of a conclave.
The result, gentle reader, will be that you will have
work enough cut out to occupy you for one whole
month at least." He then adds that " a late distinguished and highly respectable female collector, who

Y

had commenced an illustrated Bible, procured for the illustration of verses 20, 21, 22, 23, 24, and 25 of chapter i. of Genesis no less than 700 prints ! "

It will be a surprise to know that even in the present time there is sometimes a wealthy amateur who, with a love or passion for a particular subject, determines to adorn it in a special fashion, and gives an order for a superb memorial to be prepared, set off with exquisite writing, a series of drawings and watercolours, the whole being bound with all the luxury "the bibliopegistic art" can furnish. It is thus that we find many a superb volume prepared, to celebrate this generous ardour.

One of the most tastefully printed modern works is Doré's famous Bible published at Tours, the English edition having but small pretensions. It is adorned with a vast number of illustrations ; but an enterprising Grangerite has gathered every Scripture print procurable, including all the most famous line engravings, each of which is a thing of cost and rarity, and has thus enlarged the work from two to ten sumptuous volumes.

Men the most unlikely have engaged in this fascinating craze. In the last century there was a Mr. Storer, one of the wild set led by the Duke of Queensberry, who never flagged in collecting, and left the result of his labours to his University.

An extraordinary monument of pains, patience, and expense in this direction is "Clutterbuck's History of Hertfordshire," which an enthusiast adorned and expanded in this fashion, regardless of expense. Starting with some fifty plates of its own of antiquities, seats, castles, plans, &c., proof impressions, superb copy on large paper, it was enlarged

from three volumes to ten volumes, folio, and " illustrated by eleven hundred original landscapes, architectural views, and portraits, beautifully painted in
water-colours by Buckler, Harding, and other eminent
artists ; also fourteen hundred drawings of coats of
arms, beautifully emblazoned by Dowse, and nearly
six hundred additional engravings, comprising views,
old buildings, antiquities, portraits, &c., by Hou-
braken, &c., fine and large mezzotints and brilliant
India proofs in folio, russia extra, gilt edges, by Hol-
loway." This, we are told, was " a magnificent monument of industry and liberality, and the finest copy
which has ever been offered for sale. *The work of
many years, it was executed regardless of expense,
and cost thousands of pounds to produce.*" The name
of this Grangerite was John Morice, Esq., F.S.A.
Eight hundred guineas was asked for this treasure
by Messrs. Robson & Kerslake, the vendors.

Another of these costly and stupendous enterprises
was the copy of " Pennant's London," illustrated by
a Mr. Crowle, and bequeathed by that gentleman to
the British Museum, where it now reposes. Pennant
is a favourite subject, as the prints of London buildings and London streets are to be found in enormous
abundance. But what was this to the prodigious
" Clarendon and Burnet," a collection of illustrative
pictures formed by Mr. Sutherland of Gower Street,
continued by his widow, and by her presented to
the Bodleian Library ? It has been said that this
is the richest and most extensive pictorial history
in existence, or ever likely to be in existence ; and
this will be admitted when it is stated that there are
nearly 19,000 prints and drawings. The scale on
which it is carried out may be conceived when we

find it contains no less than 731 portraits of Charles
I., 518 of Charles II., 352 of Cromwell, 273 of
James II., and 420 of William III. If we only
think how few are the portraits of Charles I. that we
ourselves have seen, mostly copies after Vandyke,
we shall have an idea of the labour and exploration
necessary to gather up the 731. Think also of the
labour, pains, and cost in cleaning, "laying down,"
"insetting," and "inlaying" these portraits, the
binding, arranging, &c., and we shall not be surprised to learn that this folly occupied the eccentric
and fanatical Sutherland forty precious years of his
life ; that it fills *sixty-seven* huge volumes, and cost
twelve thousand pounds ! We may conceive all the
visitings of print-shops, the turning over boxes of
prints, the visiting of wynds and lanes, the correspondence, and the endless paying of money. To
give a finish to his labours, a catalogue was prepared
of all the engravings, and which fills two great
quartos.

Portraits *en masse* have little value, as they are
mostly copies one from another. "There is a
charm,' it has been said, "in collections of the
human face divine," though it must needs be powerful to call forth, as it does, twenty or thirty or fifty
guineas from a collector's pocket for a coarsely
executed cut of some Meg Merrilees, or a con-
demned criminal of which the only value is being
"*mentioned by Granger.*" The illustrator of Boswell's "Johnson" will find allusions to a malefactor
called Rann, otherwise "Sixteen-String Jack," and
to Johnson, a circus-rider, whom the great Doctor admired for riding several horses at a time. There
are actually in existence some cheap common sketches

of these worthies, the latter shown riding the horses. These are singularly scarce, as may be imagined, and your "Boswell" would be halting and incomplete without it; so any price must be given, on the ground that all that had been paid would be thrown away without them. It might be worth while almost to have the plate re-engraved, and printed off on old paper, say the fly-leaf of some contemporary volume, and the result will serve. Not unfrequently, by a happy chance, old copper-plates turn up, and new impressions can be taken. Some such discovery has been made in the case of Bartolozzi, the mania for whose red-tinted oval plates has been to dealers one of the wonders known in modern times.

Boswell's "Johnson" is certainly the most favourable object on which this taste may be exercised. What can be done with this book was once shown by a splendid memorial made by Mr. F. Harvey of St. James's Street, whose pleasant *magasin* is as entertaining to the passer-by outside as to those within, for he liberally takes pains to put his best and dearest proofs in the window, no niggard evidences of what is in store within. The pages of Boswell are so full of allusions to persons and localities, and these again are of such celebrity, and have been so handsomely glorified by art, that the task may be undertaken under the most favourable conditions. Mr. Harvey justly terms his work "the grandest literary monument erected in honour of Dr. Johnson."

The "Life of Boswell" selected, was Croker's edition in five volumes, which was enlarged and inlaid to *sixteen volumes folio*, by the addition of autographs, portraits, views in water-colours, mezzotints and line engravings. A general dealer in pictures, autographs, prints, has immense advantages in his system; for

out of the great masses of "papers" which he purchases, the great portion is certain to prove useful
for some one or other of these purposes.   The number of articles illustrating them, including twenty portraits of the writer, are nine hundred and eighty-two,
each one of which has been inlaid and enlarged,
cleaned, and laid down with the greatest neatness,
care, and cost.

The supplement, a single volume, was enlarged to
six folio volumes.   How rich and curious the contents
are will be seen from the fact that it contains many
original MSS. of the Doctor, including the famous
letter to Macpherson, and which was worth £50 ;
the draft of the plan for his Dictionary, and which was
sold at auction for £57.   There were water-colours
by Pyne and others.   For the whole set of twenty-
two volumes, handsomely bound in morocco extra,
with the title-pages, table of contents, and printed
specially, the large but not excessive sum of one
thousand and fifty pounds is asked.   The Grangerised Kemble is enlarged from two into nine volumes,
with all the *luxe* of special water-colours, bills, &c.,
proof prints, &c., and is valued at £300.   But in
these instances, it need not be said, the outlay has
been purposely kept within measurable bounds.   But
the wealthy reckless amateur need only to give his
commission and the book can be illustrated regardless
of cost.

The pitiless Grangerite slaughters a book for a
few pictures, just as an epicure has had a sheep
killed for the sweetbread.   At the Bernal sale there
was a collection of pictures to illustrate Shakespeare :
"An Extensive and Valuable Collection of Engravings made for various editions of the Plays of Shakespeare, formed with the intention of illustrating the

Works of this *celebrated writer* (!) by the aid of pictorial art, comprising the series published to several
editions, viz., Bell's first edition, with the Actors in
Costume, large paper, 170 plates; Inchbald's Theatre,
23 proofs on india before the writing; Singleton's
designs, 44 plates; Pickering's edition, 39 large
paper, india paper; Smirke's designs, by Taylor, in
ovals, nearly all paper; Woodcuts to Scholey's edition (23); Jennings and Chaplin's series of 40 proofs
before the letters; Smirke's Illustrations (40); Sar-
gent's Landscape and Architectural Illustrations, 9
parts, 45 plates, india proofs; How and Parsons,
1841; The Union Shakespeare, 6 parts, proofs before
the letters; Theobald's edition, 39 plates mounted;
Bell and Kearsley, 106, mostly mounted; Kearsley's
edition, 75 plates mounted; with others from Ballantyne, Thurston, and Whittingham's editions; in all,
above eight hundred engravings. A choice collection,
mostly proofs."

But what is all this to the following stupendous
monument :*—" Blomefield's Norfolk Illustrated.—
Blomefield's (Francis) Essay towards a Topographi-
cal History of the County of Norfolk, new edition,
with Continuation, 11 vols., large paper, richly illustrated by the insertion of additional manuscript and
printed matter, the arms coloured throughout, and
many hundred drawings of arms, seals, and other

* In a recent catalogue was offered a volume of miniatures
and illuminated capital letters cut from the old MS., and about
150 in number. Conceive of the sacrilegious Goth at his work,
slicing and snipping from the reverent tawny leaves of the thir-
teenth century, it may be, and flinging away the useless vellum !
There is an instance, too, of another devastator who wished to
illustrate the History of Printing in the most effective style, and
formed a collection of *title-pages* cut from books, with specimens of ordinary pages. These he accumulated in thousands,
each specimen entailing the sacrifice of a volume.

interesting objects upon the margin ; half russia.
Original Drawings to illustrate Blomefield's Norfolk ;
also a very extensive Collection of engraved Illustrations, together amounting to about seven thousand
subjects, 29 vols. half russia, and 12 vols. in cloth ;
also a few additional drawings, unbound.   Yarmouth
Town Rolls ; ancient manuscripts, neatly laid down
and bound in 1 vol. half russia.   Original Deeds and
Charters, two hundred and twenty-four in number, in
1 vol. half russia.   Miscellaneous Deeds, about two
hundred and thirty in number, arranged in 11 solander boxes, russia backs, uniform with the rest.   A
Collection of 224 Seals, embracing conventual, paro-
chial, corporate, and private seals, many of high
antiquity ; arranged in trays, enclosed in a case with
russia back.   List of Norfolk Portraits, Manuscript,
1 vol. half russia.   Index of Illustrations, arranged
according to Parishes (royal 8vo, privately printed,
inlaid to a size uniform with the rest), with copious
MS. additions, 1 vol. half russia.   *Together* 70 *vols.
and cases.*"

" To speak of this article summarily as presenting
the finest illustrated county history ever formed would
perhaps be its only fitting and sufficient description.
It may, however, be stated that of the total number
of seven thousand illustrations (without estimating at
all those to be found in the printed volumes), about
four thousand are beautiful original drawings."   One
feels a sort of pity for this poor demented collector,
with his " eleven solander boxes," and his "trays with
russia backs," and his bills to the artists and binders,
and the jackals employed to search the country for
prey.

These " County Histories " are a favourite and invariable subject.   Sometimes the wealthy amateur,

full of his pet subject, has given an order regardless of expense for the illustrators by pen and pencil, gold and colours. This seems turning the clock backwards, as these modern imitators, from want of practice, lack the certainty and freedom of the older masters of the craft. It was thus that some one interested in the meeting of the Field of the Cloth of Gold commissioned artists and scriveners to prepare him an illustrated chronicle of the ceremonies, with the result of a superb volume :—" Field of the Cloth of Gold.— Le Champ de Drap d'Or ; or, Account of the Interview between Henry VIII. and Francis I. on the Field of the Cloth of Gold, near Guisnes in Picardy, in the year MDXX, with a particular detail of all the magnificent ceremonies there observed, from the contemporary chroniclers. A beautifully - written Manuscript, within borders of gold, by Adams, the caligraphist, containing 80 original paintings by Stephanoff, Cooper, Willement, R. T. Bone, Harlowe, and Kenny Meadows, royal 4to, purple morocco super extra, joints double with vellum, completely covered with hand-worked gold tooling in a remarkably handsome pattern, vellum fly-leaves, gilt gaufré edges, by C. Lewis, and preserved in a green morocco case lined with velvet." The price for this gem was one hundred guineas. " A volume which is in every way a superb work of art ; and it has been justly said that nearly two centuries and a half have passed since any manuscript so richly decorated has been executed. It formerly belonged to Mr. Hanrott, the eminent bibliophile, and after his death was purchased for £173, 5s. by Sir John Tobin, whose arms were drawn and illuminated on the first leaf." It con-tained portrait of Henry VIII. in water-colours by Willement, after Holbein ; portrait of Francis I. in

z

water-colours, slightly touched with oil, by R. T. Bone, after Titian ; portrait of Francis I. in chalks on blue paper by Harlowe, from the original picture at Paris ; three water-colour drawings by Stephanoff ; two water-colour drawings by Cooper, R.A. ; thirteen historical oil paintings by R. T. Bone, and eight smaller ones ; one water-colour drawing by R. T. Bone ; three water-colour drawings by Kenny Meadows ; illuminated title by T. Willement, bearing portraits of Henry, Francis, their Queens, and Wolsey, coats of arms, &c. ; and forty-seven exquisite emblematic and heraldic head and tail pieces, initial letters, and vignettes, very beautifully illuminated in gold and colours, by Willement.

Nothing would have caused so much amusement and surprise to the late amiable and brilliant Charles Dickens had he been assured that one of the fashions in which his posthumous fame would have been celebrated was to be a mania for collecting " early clean or uncut " copies of his works, in various " states " and conditions. This sort of compliment would have brought a pleasant twinkle to his eye, anticipatory of some quip more pleasant. Still, though careful to preserve for himself the series of his works in due order as they were issued, he had little toleration for the fads of the bibliophilist, as little as he had for " fads " of any kind. Thackeray, it is known, like many other copious writers, used to complain rather piteously that he could never lay his hand on, or keep a copy of, his own books, which were usually begged or borrowed, stolen or given away. On the other hand, the less-appreciated author has generally a stock on hand, and is ever ready to bestow a copy on a favoured friend, en-

riched with a presentation formula in his own autograph.

It is only within the last few years this eager quest
for early copies and first editions of Dickens's works
has developed to an extraordinary degree. Everything written by this master when in its "first state"
fetches extravagant prices. All sorts of refinements
or variations are carefully noted to enhance the
price. Within the last two years a new "sense"
has been created by two or three enterprising London booksellers, who have contrived to stimulate an
eager demand for rare copies and editions. Pos-
sessors of early editions will be astonished to learn
what prices can be obtained for these rarities, or for
a "Pickwick" in "fine condition." A "Pickwick"
arrayed in its green covers, it may be said, should
be bound up with these adornments, including all the
advertisements, the British Museum having ruled the
precedent, and binding up its magazines in this
fashion. A nice point is thus raised, it being urged
that these are legitimate and component parts of the
work, as being issued with it; more especially as
among them will be found "the two scarce addresses" of the author to the reader. "Nickleby"
and its successors cost from three to four guineas,
according to condition, while "Oliver Twist," owing
to the masterly plates by Cruikshank, reaches to five
and upwards; for here the claims of collectors of
Cruikshankiana and Dickensiana come into conflict.
Next comes "Great Expectations," a first edition of
which is almost impossible to procure, buyers having
to be content with a first or second volume, making
up the rest from the second or third. The reason
given for this scarcity is a curious one. The work
was issued in the "Mudie" or three-volume form,

and was thus promptly thumbed, torn, marked, and
even dismembered, by the professional reader ;
whereas works issued in numbers were bought by private purchasers and preserved for binding. It is
indeed pathetically complained, " We have had to
use fourth editions for vols. ii. and iii. Vol. i. is a
first edition, and very clean. A complete copy of
the first is of extreme rarity, and even when offered
is generally very dirty in all volumes. When it is
remembered that the whole of the first issue was
sold out the day of publication, and the greatest
number of them went to the libraries, its scarcity
is understood." The little Christmas stories, truly
charming volumes, gems of art and typography,
fetch five or six guineas a set, according to condition. We remember not long since when they could
be procured for three or four shillings apiece. What
is really *introuvable* is " The Story of the Bible,"
" written for my children," and which, though printed,
was, we believe, never published. The truth is, the
early editions of Dickens's works have great typographical merit, and are really handsome volumes.
Nothing now produced can compare with " Master
Humphrey's Clock," its large noble page and type,
and its exquisite Cattermole etchings set in the type.*

* Mr. Jarvis, an enterprising bookseller in King William
Street, has recently issued a little " Dickens Catalogue," containing all the works, with additional " Dickensiana," reaching
to some four hundred items, all richly bound in " crushed
green levant morocco by Zaehnsdorf," and which includes ''an
almost unique collection of portraits, some seventeen in number." Here we find the rare playbills of the amateur performances, the various farces and plays he wrote, and which Mr.
R. Herne Shepherd ventured to reprint in two portly volumes,
thereby bringing down on his head a swift and effectual stroke
from Mr. Wilkie Collins, who suppressed the work by force of
law. They are divided under heads, '' The Green Leaf Series,"
the " Bound works," and " Dickensiana," all the books and

This fancy for Dickens is therefore not so unmeaning or exaggerated as might be supposed. It seems to be founded on a certain intrinsic excellence in the articles that are so *recherché;* later editions, being "cheap" and thrown off hastily, have really few attractions. As I have said, some of the prettiest volumes ever turned out were the little Christmas annuals, in their gold and crimson "jackets," effective and dainty titles, and exquisite engravings. The way these are combined with the type, the romance and sympathy in the touches, the beauty and dreamy character of the whole, make these most charming little works, and quite account for the general desire to possess them. A set in fine condition is a welcome treasure indeed.

pamphlets that have been written *on* our author or in imitation of him. Mr. R. H. Shepherd has written a very interesting volume called the "Bibliography of Charles Dickens," in which he has noted all his works, editions, letters, &c., with the dates of publication. Here are found all the theatrical adaptations, the imitations, "catchpenny" and otherwise, such as "Pickwick Abroad," "Pickwick in America," "The Penny Pickwick by Bos," "The Peregrinations of Pickwick," "Dombey and Daughter," by the notorious "Chief Baron Nicholson;" "Nickleby Married," &c. Even an attenuated little volume of poems by the "horse-riding" Ada Menken is much sought, owing to a letter of our author which is given in the preface. A most curious feature is that his wonderful descriptive faculty has been found of value in describing scenes or buildings that have now been swept away; hence we have volumes on his connection with Old London and its demolished streets and inns —"Charles Dickens in Kent," "Rochester and Charles Dickens," "Dickens and London," "Dickens in England"—while one person has used his scissors to make up a pleasing little book of sketches of old streets, inns, houses, &c., described by the great author. In short, the fashion in which this wonderful master has leavened social talk, allusions, jokes, characters, places, &c., is one of the most singular phenomena of the age, and as unique as it is extraordinary. No other writer, save perhaps Shakespeare, has been so reprinted or so illustrated, and it now looks as though this prestige is entering on a new lease.

The " Sunday Under Three Heads," like all pamphlets of small circulation, is singularly scarce.   I
recall the delighted chuckle of a well-known collector
who at a sale bid carelessly for a small volume of
tracts, secured for a shilling or two.   He was presently showing his friends, in unconstrained delight,
the·" Sunday Under Three Heads," bound up with
the rest.   " Worth a couple of guineas," he cried ;
" the rarest of Dickens's works."   The merits of the
" Sunday Under Three Heads " are set out thus offi-
cially :—" By Timothy Sparks (the only instance of
the use of this *nom de plume* by Dickens).   With all
the woodcuts (early specimens of the work of H. K.
Browne, otherwise ' Phiz '), and both the wrappers,
fine copy.   The first and probably the scarcest of all
Dickens's published works.   £11, 15s.   1836."   But
for another copy £10 is asked, and this has merits of
its own, being " an exceptionally large copy, with
the edges quite rough and uncut.   It has been generally found in stiff boards, with the edges cut ; the
present copy is the largest the writer has ever seen."

The ordinary mortal might esteem himself fairly
happy in the possession of a good legible copy of
" Pickwick " which he can read with comfort.   One
more ambitious will show with pride his copy of " the
original edition, sir, very rare, and picked up for a
trifle—old gold."   Alas ! he has but little idea of
the knowledge, the necessary perfections and beauties that go to make up that really perfect and entire
chrysolite, a first edition of " Pickwick " in a good
" state."   That it should be " clean," " uncut," *i.e.*,
the edges not pared by the binder's knife, are mere
elementary conditions, but there are far more important questions.   Are the numbers in the original green
wrappers with all the advertisements ?   Has it the

"suppressed plate" by Seymour, or can it show the "Buss" plates? and, above all, the recently discovered Buss plate of the Review? Has it Alfred Crowquill's set of forty extra illustrations, or the set of thirty-two illustrations by Onwhyn in the "green wrappers as originally issued," or the "twelve curious ones" by Strange, or the original cover containing fourteen portraits of characters, or Sir John Gilbert's thirty-two illustrations, or Leslie's frontispiece, or, finally, Mr. Pailthorpe's twenty-four etchings, done lately, which it must be said are admirable and full of a Cruikshank spirit. When all these additions have been secured, and the whole splendidly and suitably bound in "whole crushed green levant morocco by Zaehnsdorf in the best style," then indeed you may sit down contentedly in possession of a real first edition of "Pickwick," that is not only "worth looking at," but worth a great deal of money. Such has been priced at £28.

In this connection may be mentioned the extraordinary Cruikshank controversy, the delusion of an old man—the claim to the invention or suggestion of part of the story and characters of "Oliver Twist." The same claim was made to some of Ainsworth's stories, and finally some members of the Seymour family put forward a similar pretension. Mr. Seymour's widow seriously urged the claims of her husband in a tiny pamphlet of a few leaves, but so scarce and almost *introuvable* that a copy was lately offered at *ten guineas*. To this unhappy and clever artist we owe the original sporting complexion of "Pickwick," but he committed suicide during its progress, and threw the young author's venture into confusion. These claims seem ludicrous. One of the last plates, "Rose Maylie and Oliver," was so inferior that it had

to be cancelled. " With reference to the last one,"
wrote Mr. Dickens to the artist, Cruikshank, " without entering into the question of great haste or any
other cause which may have led to its being what it
is, I am quite sure there can be little difference of
opinion between us with respect to the result.   May
I ask whether you will object to designing this plate
afresh, and doing so at *once*, in order that as few
impressions as possible of the present one may go
forth ? "   This change was accordingly made ; but it
will be undisputed that " the few impressions " that
did go forth have since become exceedingly precious
and rare.   An " Oliver Twist " with this cancelled
plate is a thing to be the collector's glory and
pride.*

The " Memoirs of Grimaldi," which Dickens
revised rather than wrote, is also much *recherché*
on account of its spirited etchings by the admirable
George.   It has become, too, a favourite book for
" enlarging " and illustrating.   The quaint old theatre
of Sadlers Wells, where many of its scenes are laid,
the old style of entertainment, the pictures of Old
London life, all furnish, as it were, so many pegs on
which to hang the dresses and properties of decora-

* It is the same with " Nickleby " and " Humphrey's Clock,"
for which various artists have furnished extra illustrations, viz.,
Sibson, " Charley Chalk," Hablot Browne with his " eight
scarce plates," Peter Palette, Onwhyn, &c.   These extra illustrations have an artificial and arbitrary air, for the first regular
illustrations were done under the inspiration and promptings of
the writer.   Hablot Browne after " Copperfield," fell strangely
away, and his figures seem to have little significance.   Yet still,
when a change of artists was made, none of his successors seem
to have caught the spirit of the great novelist.   It may be repeated, however, that those of Mr. Pailthorpe are excellent,
and the one of the Pickwickians leading the horse and presenting themselves at the roadside inn is in the best vein of
comedy.

tion.* Even the little green pamphlets prepared for the "Readings," "Dombey and Son," "Christmas Carol," &c., and sold at the doors for a shilling, are now grown to be rarities, and fetch a pound or pounds. The great "edition de luxe," issued at vast trouble and expense, is described as "splendidly printed in large type, and illustrated with upwards of 700 engravings, including the whole of the original plates by George Cruikshank, Seymour, H. K. Browne, Maclise, &c., executed on china paper in 30 vols., imp. 8vo, cloth, uncut, published at £40, and offered for £24, and of which the edition was limited to 1000 copies."

There live and flourish in London *littérateurs* whose industry, at least, cannot be contested—painstaking, industrious men, who make themselves specially useful in compiling what are called "Bibliographies" of these works—picking up with a pointed stick every scrap or *chiffon* of composition, and tossing it into the basket on their shoulders. A

* We thus find copies of this character :—" Grimaldi (Joseph). —A number of unique portraits, views, scenes, and playbills, illustrating the Memoirs, by 'Boz,' of the greatest of English clowns, consisting of engraved and artistically painted portraits in water-colours by the artist, H. Browne, representing Grimaldi in private dress and in his favourite characters ; the *Times* report of his last appearance, together with his farewell speech ; interesting scenes of himself and son ; views of Sadlers Wells, coloured ; an etching of the exterior in 1760 ; fishing scene by Woodward, 1794 ; exterior, 1813, 2 views ; races in 1826 ; the Clown Tavern opposite. Also 12 playbills, T. R. Covent Garden, in which Grimaldi is cast for clown in pantomimes, Harlequin Mother Goose, Earth, Air, Fire, and Water, Asmodeus, Whittington, Dragon of Wantley, Gulliver, Cinderella, Mother Bunch, Vision of the Sun, Mother Shipton, &c. These have an extra interest, as they contain the casts of many of Shakespeare's plays, with such notables as Kemble, Young, Cosway, Miss O'Neill, and others, a most interesting collection."

2 A

little work on Dickens is, it must be said, a monument of careful and useful labour, for here we have
every book and pamphlet of the great novelist, with
date, place, and number of the edition, while almost
every letter that he wrote is duly noted. This has
been exceeded by the final tribute, " Dickensiana,"
for which every conceivable fact and criticism has
been gathered by Mr. Kitton.

It is not unnatural that there should be curiosity
and interest about some of our novelist's earliest and
scarcely acknowledged productions. Who, for instance, is acquainted with the " Library of Fiction,
or Family Story-Teller, Original Tales, Essays,
and Sketches of Character," 14 plates by Seymour
and H. K. Browne, &c., 2 vols. post 8vo, half calf,
very scarce, published in 1836–37, and containing
the " Tuggs at Ramsgate," and a little talk about
" Spring and Sweeps," by Boz, pieces by Mayhew,
Douglas Jerrold, Stirling Coyne, &c. Rarer still is
what is open before the writer at this moment, a
number of the " Monthly Magazine," containing
" Horatio Sparkins," the second number to which he
contributed. It is a curious and melancholy sensation to look at the characters of this juvenile attempt.
We stretch back over the long, long interval, to the
gay, spirited, handsome youth, now first trying his
powers—the brilliant career—fame, honour, profit
—a name to be known all over the world and in
every generation to come ; yet here he was, obscure,
unknown, unthought of—making this first jocose
effort—and the tale unpaid for ! Rare, also, the
strange story he contributed to the " Picnic Papers,"
a venture on behalf of a publisher who had shown
singular greed in his dealings with him, and whom
he repaid, as Mr. Pickwick did Job Trotter, with ;.

" Take that, sir ! "—not a blow, but the most un-
wearied exertions for him, and for his widow and
children.

The most wonderful and flattering monument,
however, to the memory of Dickens was the work
of Mr. Harvey of St. James Street. This is the
" Forster Life," comprised in thirteen large folios,
and illustrated by all that industry and money could
acquire. To begin with, each octavo was expanded
into a folio by the process known as " inlaying " or
" insetting," a costly thing in its way, and which
requires pressing and delicate pasting with a " feather
edge," and which has to be paid for at the rate
of fourpence a leaf. Every notable name has its
portrait, and every place visited by our author an
illustration. Every portrait had its autograph letter,
and the author himself was glorified by a series of
no less than sixteen. Here were all sorts of interesting curiosities, such as his " Manual of Shorthand,"
written out by himself and dealt with in a very
original way, and a review of a pamphlet done in
the vigorous Crokerish style fashionable fifty years
ago. There are bills of his early plays, pictures of
the actors who created their parts, scenes and bits
of Old London, with even a water-colour sketch of
the " Fox-under-the-Hill," an old public-house on
the banks of the Thames, where the child Dickens
occasionally forgot his early miseries over a glass of
ale. It would take long to describe this wonderful
collection, which, I believe, was sold to a wealthy
American, and for which the comparatively small
sum of £350 was asked.

It is evidence of the extraordinary interest in his
works that several of his little early books have been
reprinted in *facsimile*. The " Sunday Under Three

Heads," before alluded to, has been thus treated by two publishers; so have the plays, in a fashion which can scarcely be distinguished from the original. Perhaps the rarest of these little trifles is the " Dance Round a Christmas Tree," a little story of a few leaves, which was, I believe, written for a bazaar, and is eagerly sought, and at an extravagant price.*

One of the least known of our author's works is " The Loving Ballad of Lord Bateman," with the plates by George Cruikshank, in which Dickens treated the ballad with all the gravity of a classical commentator, furnishing notes and "various conjectural readings " in a most diverting fashion; but we must see and get the "scarce original issue," and, better still, have "the original " cloth covers preserved. For his friend Miss Pardoe he was induced to write something for one of the volumes, gorgeous in crimson watered silk, that she edited; and in " The Keepsake " of 1852 is to be found a story by him, entitled, " To be Read at Dusk." This, of course, is rare. Some industrious ones have traced his very earliest productions, carried by their ardour

---

* Among the "ana" is a curious little book on the "Origin of Sam Weller," published by Mr. Jarvis, and which certainly supports its title in showing how Sam was suggested, It seems that there was an actor of the name of Sam Vale playing at the Olympic some sixty years since. His chief and most popular part was that of " Sam Splatterdash " in the " Boarding-House," in which he introduced those odd similes which made Sam Weller so popular, such as " 'Come on!' as the man said to the tight boot;" " 'Why, here we are all mustered,' as the roast beef said to the Welsh rabbit;" " 'Where shall we fly?' as the bullet said to the trigger;" " 'I know the world,' as the monkey said when he cut off his tail;" " 'There she is, musical and melancholy,' as the cricket said to the tea-kettle." This subject has been recently dealt with by my friend Mr. Charles Kent in a curious little volume—" Wellerisms."

into very speculative regions, as when it has been assumed that he contributed to "'The Town,' a journal of original essays, characteristic of the manners, social, domestic, and superficial, of London and Londoners, containing an interesting condemnatory notice of the 'Penny Pickwick,' edited by Boz, and has probably unrecognised contributions by Dickens." Another journal, "Figaro in London," was also considered to have "probably unrecognised contributions," and accordingly is priced highly. It may be added that "Bentley's Magazine," which he edited, has been found to contain many addresses and ephemeral contributions which the diligent collector will take care not to overlook. In the *Daily News*, in an odd company, are to be found several of his poems and letters. Then there are prefaces, such as he prefixed to Overs, the "working man's" book, and to Miss Procter's poems.

A no less extraordinary testimony to the popularity of this great and charming writer are the number of imitations, sequels, &c., to his works, attempts made during his lifetime to secure one faint puff even from the full gale of his popularity. These also have been collected, and fall into the ranks of "Dickensiana." To this category belong the "Sketch-Book" by "Boz," containing a great number of highly interesting and original tales, sketches, &c. &c., curious rough woodcut illustrations (*circa* 1837), very scarce ; "Pickwick Abroad, or The Tour in France," by G. W. M. Reynolds, plates by Crowquill and Phillips, 8vo, 1839 ; "Pickwick in America ;" "The Penny Pickwick," edited by "Boz" (the first 54 numbers of this very remarkable plagiarism, many rough woodcuts, has the curious original wrapper to

Part 1, many advertisement leaves, and the title, very rarely to be met with, 8vo (one page slightly defective), 1842; " The Peregrinations of Pickwick." The unfinished fragment of " Edwin Drood " has produced quite a literature in itself, and the commonly found being, who rushes in where a more supernatural power might fear to tread, has exercised his art freely in speculative continuations and arrangements, dramatic and narrative. There are many of these continuations, such as " John Glasper's Secret." There is also "Christmas Eve with the Spirits, or The Canon's Wanderings through Ways Unknown, with some further tidings of the Lives of Scrooge and Tiny Tim, with illustrations ; " and " The Mystery of Edwin Drood," an adaptation by Orpheus C. Kerr, 12mo, half morocco uniform, original illustrated covers preserved.

A celebrated but not distinguished character of forty years ago was the so-called or self-styled " Chief Baron Nicholson," who presided at the " Judge and Jury " Club. This personage, turning author, wrote a continuation of Dombey, which he styled "Dombey and Daughter, by Renton Nicholson, Lord Chief Baron of the celebrated Judge and Jury Club, with numerous engravings, the rare original edition, very scarce." And later, some one, issuing a series of " Sketches of Celebrated Characters," was pleased to include our novelist, who was complimentarily marked " No. 1 " in the gallery of portraits," a mark of favour that must have been distasteful to its object. The number of persons who have described him, recorded their " recollections " of him, sketched the places he resorted to, is enormous. We have accordingly his " Youth and Middle Age," his " Childhood," " The Story of his Life," " A Day with Dickens,"

" Charles Dickens as a Reader," the " Philosophy of
Dickens," his " Humour and Pathos," "About England," with him " In Kent," Dickens as a " Journalist," " In Rochester," also among the " Worthies
of the World," a title that would have amused him.
Then the adaptations for the stage is in itself a long
catalogue ; and it is remarkable that every one of his
stories have been dramatised, some of them many
times over.

The portraits of the departed master form another
department for the collector. Some of the early ones
show how bright and interesting was the face when
he was a young man, and the eager, quick eyes, so
likely to rivet attention. Maclise had a happy faculty
for reproducing this grace. It seems there was to
have been a portrait prefixed to " Copperfield," but
which, being " suppressed " for some reason, has, of
course, become desirable. The Laurence portrait, a
brilliant head, we are told, was " much esteemed by
the family." Some of Cruikshank's careless sketches
have been reproduced. Some years ago a pencil
drawing by Cruikshank was discovered and reproduced in facsimile by Messrs. Robson & Kerslake.
This characteristic sketch has an interest of its own,
though, of course, it is stamped with that curious air
of aerial grotesqueness which was the author's characteristic. We are told that it is " one of the earliest, if not the first, and perhaps the most interesting,
of all the portraits of Dickens. It appears that in
1836 or 1837 both he and Cruikshank were members
of a club of literary men which had but a brief existence, under the title of the ' Hook-and-Eye Club.'
At a meeting one night Dickens was seated in an
arm-chair beside a table, book in hand, conversing,
when Cruikshank exclaimed, ' Sit still, Charley, while

I take your portrait.'"   Finally comes the French translations, such as "Les Aventures de Monsieur Pickwick," which read strangely.   How, for instance, can Count Smoltork's broken English be translated, " How you well, Peek Veeks ? "   There was a regular series of translations formerly arranged for with Hachette on one of Dickens's visits to Paris ; but Amadée Pichot, a diligent writer of all work on the French press, was the first, we believe, to introduce him to the French public.

§ Of Illustrated Books and "Luxurious Editions."

N further proof of the wonderful growth of the art of printing, which seemed to escape, equipped, as from the head of Minerva, it can be shown that the now popular form of illustration and engraving reached almost at once a surprising perfection. The combining of wood blocks in the same page with type has always been a matter of much nicety and difficulty, while copper engravings offer greater difficulties. This seemed child's-play to the early printer, who essayed works of magnitude which even the most speculative of modern publishers would hesitate before attempting; and as we open their broadly spreading pages, we are amazed at the abundance, the wealth of resource and general effect. Some of the most extraordinary productions of those early days of printing are what many called the great "picture books," folios filled with copious illustrations in the manner of Albert Dürer and his school. These are rude but spirited, with little shading; and it amazes us to see the freedom and boldness of these things, and with what ease the difficulties of "working" them were overcome.

2 B

One of the oldest illustrated books known is an edition of Æsop's Fables, published about 1471, with numerous initial letters and upwards of 160 very curious woodcuts in the text, bound in the original thick oak boards covered with stamped leather. The "Libro di Monte Sancto di Dio," Florence, 1477, with three engravings by Baccio Baldini after the designs of Botticelli, so rarely met with in the book, is considered to be one of the earliest samples of engraving on copper plates for book illustration. But the most celebrated of this class is of course "The Nuremberg Chronicle," a huge portly volume, thus lately described by Mr. Ridler: "The Nuremberg Chronicle, best Latin edition, thick royal folio, with large and spirited woodcuts, all brilliant impressions, and uncoloured (except two genealogies that are coloured), very large sound copy, in old black morocco, very neat, the sides richly blind tooled, printed by Koberger, 1493. So fine a copy has not occurred for sale for several years past. The book is genuine, and perfect throughout; *no wash'd leaves*, and all the large capitals filled in by the rubricator in different coloured inks; it has the blank leaves, and six additional leaves at end, which Brunet says are nearly always wanting." This astonishing volume contains between two and three thousand pictures or impressions of the most varied, grotesque, and entertaining kind. There are large plates nine and ten inches square, one a well-known composition, representing Almighty God seated on His throne, and which the wary collector turns to, as it is often missing, cut out by the "spoliator." This was a truly astounding feat for a publisher, considering that printing and woodcutting were then scarcely out of their cradles. When we think of the difficulties that always attended woodcutting, the warping of the wood, the tools, it is amazing to see with what ease these obstacles were surmounted. In each of these there is good drawing, and a strange lurid imagination in the display of human forms with animals' head, or of human heads united by the neck of a snake with the trunk of a man. In the old cuts of this era, in initial letters there will be found a suggestiveness and display of dramatic action, within a space of perhaps an inch square. These little sketches will bear study and also repay study. The earlier numbers of *Punch* exhibit this minute and artistic abundance to an extraordinary degree, and in the floriated borderings in a single page the astonished reader will trace hundred of little fairies, goblins, beautiful nymphs, pursuing strange games and gymnastics among the capital letters; all drawn with an amazing spirit and originality by Richard Doyle.

Here is the style and title of another copy, and it should be noted what a difference in price the element of " condition," *i.e.*, size of margin, brilliancy of impression, &c., causes—the former copy costing only six or seven pounds ; this one five-and-thirty :—
" Nuremberg Chronicle, by Schedel (Hartmann), first edition, royal folio, with fine original impressions of the 2250 large woodcuts of towns, historical events, portraits, &c., by Michael Wolgemuth (the master of Albert Dürer) and William Pleydenwurff; very tall copy, measuring 18½ inches by 12¼, beautifully bound in morocco super extra, dull gilt edges, by Rivière, £35."

" A volume," adds the vendor enthusiastically, " of which Dibdin says, ' If Koberger had printed only this Chronicle, he would have done enough to place his name among the most distinguished of his typographical brethren.' Many of the initials in this copy are coloured, and the original owner's coat of arms, finely illuminated in gold and colours, is added. Probably *no taller copy exists*, as the edges of some of the leaves are in their original state, rough and uncut. Mr. Bedford's copy, in no finer condition, sold for £49. It is only upon comparison with the edition with German text, published later in the same year (a book of much smaller value), that the full beauty of the original impressions is apparent." *

Open before me now—mine own too—is a goodly exemplar of this monumental old tome, arrayed in solid oak, covered with a brown calf hide scored and tooled, with an escutcheon of some German baron deeply sunk, and the date of binding, 1583, a very rare thing, displayed below. Nothing can be finer than the title-page, flourishing away with its great German ecclesiastical letters more than an inch

---

* These are, in truth, the ordinary copies that come into the market, but they would not satisfy the collector of taste and long purse. Any one that has placed a proof impression of a fine engraving beside a later worn one, has to own that the two are as different as though they were of different subjects ; and so with a tall clean copy of a famous work, unblemished and in sound "desirable" condition. Who would not covet such an exemplar of the "Chronicle" as this?—"A very large, complete, and fine copy, with capitals beautifully illuminated in colours, *and all the blank leaves*" (this is a characteristic touch), "in the original oak boards." "This," says the enthusiastic writer of the catalogue, "is probably the largest and finest copy in existence after Lord Spencer's." In 1873 a copy measuring 18 by 12½ inches was sold as the finest then known ; but the present one measures nearly 18½ inches by 12½ *on the paper only ;* while along the boards it is 19¼ inches by 13, and 3½ *thick.* This belonged to Mr. Dunn-Gardiner, one of the most accomplished of collectors, a book of whose is always honourably distinguished as "Dunn-Gardiner's copy." Dibdin says, "Let me entreat you always to pay marks of respect to the productions of the first printer of Nuremberg, Anthony Koberger. His *ample margins* betray a thoroughly well cultivated taste."

long, and laid out with good effect. A good and true copy boasts the wholly blank pages near the close, which are yet duly paged; but the author thoughtfully explains that they have been left blank purposely, so that, after he had brought all down " to date," the " courteous reader " might *write in* any particulars he listed. In short, a grandly " designed " book, if one may use the phrase; and the very " amplitude " of the title, with its bold stately proclamation of what is within—the inscription on the portal—impresses us with respect, if not with awe. A book of this kind is surely a monument, and excites wonder and astonishment.

Yet another of these wonderful picture-books came from France in 1491, and is thus described :—" Orose (Paul).—History of the World (in French), with the Book of the Four Vertues of Seneca, black - letter, 3 vols. in one, thick royal folio, with very beautiful ornamental borders, large map, and nearly 300 large and splendid woodcuts, all fine bright impressions, illustrating history from the Creation, large sound copy in old brown calf neat, from the Sunderland Collection at Paris. Anthoine Verard, 1491." " This most rare volume," says the book-dealer " (which is the size of the Nuremberg Chronicle), is one of the most magnificent and splendid productions of the early Paris press, was fully expected to have produced over one hundred guineas in the Sunderland Sale; *it has a slight defect, corner of two leaves being mended*, otherwise it is *in fine crackling state*. Brunet could never have seen a copy. He states it was printed near the end of the fifteenth century, whereas the date 1491 is given at the conclusion of the second volume. It must be an almost unique volume, since the celebrated bibliographer only refers to the sale of one copy sixty years ago." Twenty pounds is surely not too much. A companion chronicle is that of Cologne :—" Cologne Chronicle.—Chronica van der Hilliger Stat Coellen, Cœllen, J. Kœlhoff, 1499. Gothic letter, folio, with a large number of curious woodcuts of battles, historical events, portraits of popes, emperors, kings, and others, all coloured by a contemporary hand, olive morocco extra, gilt and marbled edges by Zaehnsdorf, rare, £12.". Of this interesting and important volume Dibdin says, " There are few ancient books so rarely seen. I think there are not three copies of it in this country, and the evidence of De Bure leads us to suspect that no copy of it was known at Paris." It contains an important passage relating to the invention of the art of printing with metal types, in which the author says, " The beginning and progress of the before-mentioned art was told me, by word of mouth, by the worthy man, Master Ulrich Zell, printer at Cologne," &c. It contains the suppressed account of Pope Joan, with her portrait, carrying a child.

Passing by the " Ortus Sanitas," 1497, the " Ship of Fools," 1488, crammed with strange illustrations, we come to what is really the most important of these old illustrated books, and with which is associated some rather ludicrous incidents. This unpretending series has been the occasion of a craze that has lasted nearly two hundred years, and at this moment diligently excites the longings of first-rate collectors. I refer to the well-known DE BRY volumes— a sound at which the *bibliognoste* pricks up his ears and feels his heart palpitate between hope and despair. For he may see a volume of the well-known Voyages in a catalogue, but this will give him no satisfaction, for the same editions differ, and only

grading slavery. This same Picart brought out another sumptuous work, " Le Temple des Muses," the rare original edition, with descriptions in French, English, Dutch, and German, royal folio, large paper, sixty large and very beautiful plates, brilliant proof impressions, each plate surrounded with broad and elegant bor- ders, fine copy, French calf gilt, full gilt back, gilt edges, £5, 5s. Amst., 1733. Descriptions in French, Dutch, &c. ! This shows the *clientèle* to which the artist appealed. The fine "style" of the work, its beautiful borderings, all commend it to the amateur of taste, though the treatment, however classical, goes beyond the limits of propriety.

Perhaps the more imposing and more pretentious work is the " Gallery of Versailles," from Le Brun's paintings, executed in the old, large, bold sweeping copperplate style, on board-like paper. One always admires even the frontispieces of these fine pictorial volumes, with their gods and nymphs disporting, combined with some architectural work, the title mixed up with abundant scrolls and flourishings, the inscription seeming as though it were carved on the walls of some old monument. This truly regal work is worthy of the Grand Monarque and the creator of Versailles. I take the description from the Perkins Collection, where a copy was sold for £130 :—"Cabinet du Roi. A magnificent collection of engravings exe- cuted at the expense of Louis XIV. for presentation to crowned heads and ambassadors resident at his court. Bound in twenty-three volumes." These enormous volumes are in the binding of the time, secured between planks of wood, the paper like a " board," and the engravings in the fine sweeping masculine style so effective in these great books. The printing was no less splendid—large, solid letters, proportioned

centre of an elaborately florid decoration. Who would think that to possess " a set " was the longing desire of the first-class bibliophilist ? But a reflection or two will show that it possessed the proper elements for stimulating this craze, *i.e.*, almost insuperable difficulties in the way of getting a complete set. At great cost, and as the work of a lifetime, you may have secured all the successive parts, but you were only beginning ; *had* you the *parts with the variations*, or had you these parts with the variations in the different languages ; or, had you these, did you know that you had *all*? The best collection is likely enough to be incomplete. No one can conceive the lore, the discussions, the elaborate distinctions, the exquisite instinct and knowledge necessary to a genuine part from one that was issued "made up" of other editions. Mr. Quaritch had copies of the *same* editions, which, as he shows, differed, the one having an "*i*" more than the other. So if you had the "*i*"-less one you were undone. Some, too, of the same edition had the vignettes altered. Under the dreadful fascination of tracing these things, collectors since the year 1740 have been writing volumes on the subject—Camus, Brunet, De Bure, &c. Brunet has over fifty closely printed columns, De Bure the same ; while, latest of all, comes the Earl of Crawfurd with a splendid quarto full of facsimile illustrations. For thirty years he tells us pathetically he has devoted his labours to the scientific study of the innumerable DE BRY'S and their variation of copies, and in this work printed in three columns side by side these trivial changes and alterations. But the truth is, this investigation seems endless, and there is the secret of its fascination.

Almost from these times down to our own times,

the line of costly illustrated works has been maintained almost unbroken. The feebly monotonous character of the "trade" illustrated books in our day is well known, and has happily tired out the public. Indeed, there is hardly a single ambitious work of the kind that can be pointed to with satisfaction. Whether it be Shakespeare, or Milton, or Tennyson, there is the regular procedure. It is too often put into the hands of stock artists and woodcutters, and usually with the same result. There is little time to prepare the greater engravings. Indeed, one of the single flowing-line engravings out of the old works would take one of our engravers half a year to prepare. A curious note, too, of those moderns' illustrations is that a single glance seems to reveal all that is in them, whereas the older ones are full of suggestion and thought, and bear study. The French have introduced a class of work of this kind, under the auspices of Lacroix (the bibliophile Jacob), Charles Yriate, and others, who have "done" the "arts of the middle and other ages," Florence, Rome, Venice, &c., setting off their work with innumerable illustrations, all of the same weary pattern. Doré is accountable for a great deal of this "job" work, and though all admire the inexhaustible variety of the artist, there grew up at last a sort of sameness in his work, no doubt the result of the publisher's ceaseless calls on his imagination. His Bible is considered one of his most successful achievements, and the execution of this work by printer and publisher is a true specimen of what is artistic in that direction. As a good illustration of how the machinery of trade may vulgarise what is good and noble, it may be related that when it was determined to adapt this work for the English market, *clichés*, as they are called, of the engravings were sent over, and a well-known firm proceeded to bring the work out. Large type was selected, good paper chosen, and the book duly "machined" through one of the great presses. But the result was anything but effective. There was no homogeneousness. This compatibility between the various portions of a book is too often forgotten. The whole should be designed together, like any other artistic work, so that the smallest duodecimo may show signs of elegance of design as well as the greater octavo. It must be admitted, however, that moderns labour under serious disadvantages compared with their predecessors, for the grand folio and quarto engravings, after reproduction of the works of great painters, offer space for breadth of effect and imposing design which is quite lost in small efforts.

In the old French work, so exquisitely carried out by Eisen and others, the appropriateness of their *culs-de-lampe*, vignettes, &c., to the position in the page, was one of the charms of the work. Type, spacing, headings, all calculated on principles of proportion, make up the indefinable attraction of fine typography. It is thus that the little Christmas volumes of Mr. Dickens are so deservedly admired for their elegance and the harmony and appropriateness of their illustrations. In the "Chimes," for instance, we are struck with the fashion in which the delicate fancies of Richard Doyle are blended with the text—the old church, the bells, fairies, &c.—the eye wandering from the suggestions of the writer to those of the artist. But in latter days an idea was conceived of issuing "editions of luxury" on a large scale —the works of Thackeray, Dickens, Shakespeare, and others—and all the illustrations, great and small, were collected, and dispersed through the work on a large page "with all the amplitude of margin." Artists of different styles and era were mixed in confusion, and a picture meant for a small page was set in the centre of a large one. It is obvious that this was a false and inartistic principle.

Of the falling off in English typography, looking at it as an art, there can be no doubt ; and the late American bibliophilist, Mr. Henry Stevens, of Vermont, who has judiciously investigated the matter, concurs in this view in a production entitled "Who Spoils Our New English Books?—Asked and Answered." " The sinners who combine together to spoil our new English books are no less than ten, viz. (1) the author, (2) the publisher, (3) the printer, (4) the reader, (5) the compositor, (6) the pressman or machinist, (7) the papermaker, (8) the inkmaker, (9) the bookbinder, and (10) the consumer. In what proportion each one of the above contributes towards the spoiling of the books which pass through his hands, it would be unfair to divulge, for it would simply be taking the spirit out of the little book. Let every representative of the combination buy a copy of it for himself, and if authors are thus taught to admit their 'ignorance,' publishers their 'fussiness' and their desire to cheapen and 'shoddy' literature ; printers their carelessness and want of taste ; binders their greed of 'shavings;' inkmakers their shoddy inks, which turn brown so soon, then we shall have read them a very valuable lesson."

This is not merely a speculative opinion, but a deliberate verdict founded on investigation. Our author founds his opinions partly upon long personal observation, and partly upon discussions, in many of which he participated ; upon reports issued by the juries of the several great Exhibitions since 1851 ; and, finally, upon the verdict of the last three, held at Vienna, Philadelphia, and Paris, at which the best and latest books of all nations were subjected to the closest inspection of experts. Each of his associates, he tells us, almost without exception, " felt and expressed his disappointment at the comparative quality of English exhibits in this class." Finally, he hopes " the art of bookmaking will drift back into the practice of those same laws of proportion, taste, and workmanship so well settled and displayed in old manuscript and old books, large and small, long before and long subsequent to the birth of typography." This is a serious and well-founded indictment.

It has often been urged in regard to original work, that the round of subjects—novels and fiction—must have been exhausted, and that there is now no striking out anything that is original ; whereas the truth is that the originality is inexhaustible because founded on the possibility of looking at the same subject from ever so many different points. This view is oddly fortified by the instances of Doré and Gavarni, two French artists who came specially to London to portray for their countrymen " The English at Home." The result was most extraordinary, for the subjects are little recognisable as English. The two artists unconsciously brought with them the atmospheric effects and associations of their beloved Paris, and one would think we were looking at Frenchmen and French scenes. A more curious effect could not be conceived. It may be said that the system which has grown up of illustrating ephemeral scenes for the weekly papers has had prejudicial effects on art. We have grown so familiar with this sort of hurriedly done picture that we accept it ; but there is no doubt they are as unfaithful as they are superficial. There is no roundness of drawing—all is coarse "scratching," and those who have witnessed the particular scene will scarcely recognise it. William Harvey was the last book illustrator who seemed to possess sentiment, as all who own the early edition of Knight's "Shakespeare" will admit. There is here a grace and sympathy, a harmony and fancy, that is inexpressibly pleasing, and contrasts favourably with the utter inexpressiveness of our modern illustrations. Another cause of this modern failure is the *realistic* spirit in which all modern art works—most figures and scenes being sketched from living models, without any attempt at abstract grace. The older illustrators all aimed at elevating the reader and putting themselves on a level with the poetry of the narrator.

It is only those who are familiar with the grand libraries that can form an idea of the splendid scale on which illustration was carried on a century ago. The "spaciousness," the grand ambition, and even splendour, of the older school may be illustrated by a few of their huger efforts. What will be thought of a comprehensive work such as the "Grand Theatre Historique," 5 vols. folio, map of the world, and many hundred fine plates of battles, sieges, executions, historical events, many English in the style of Callot, very fine copy, in rich old crimson morocco extra, full gilt back, gilt and marble edges. Leide, 1703? It may be added that nothing can be more spirited than the battle-pieces often supplied to historical works of this kind. The folio "Strada's Belgian War" is full of dashing etchings, highly imaginative, no doubt, but curious as showing the costumes, arms, &c. Picart was one of the great and most industrious of artists for this class of work, his labours showing an infinite boldness and variety. One of his monuments is "The Ceremonies and Religious Customs of all Nations," a most astounding work for its elaborateness and finish of execution, to say nothing of the encyclopædiac knowledge and accuracy necessary, for it embodied "all ancient and modern superstitions." There are eleven great folio volumes, overflowing with finely engraved copperplates, representing processions, sacrifices, costumes, and the most extraordinary rites and ceremonies. Every figure is well drawn, finished, and studied. One might spend days and weeks over it and find ceaseless entertainment. A copy "bound in rich old red mococco by Derome" was sold at the Perkins sale, and fetched £98 ; yet not long since we "picked up," as it is called, seven volumes of the work on a stall for twenty-five shillings ! But of this class of work there is no end. As another illustration I will describe one out of my own modest collection, and which is a pleasant recreation to look at for a few minutes, so grand and noble is it. This is an enormous Venetian book, the size of a large atlas—a huge armful indeed—a collection of engravings of the antique statues and busts in the Museum, engraved in a fine "large" style. But the charm is in the pages of description, each set in an exquisitely engraved and more exquisitely designed border. All is worked on one side of the page only on paper like cardboard. It is heralded by a grand title-page, a portrait of the King of Sweden, to whom it is dedicated, with the favourite apotheosis, always a welcome introduction. It is bound in a massive style, and came from the Townley Collection, finding its way to the outside shelf of a stall, marked twenty shillings. As an old writer remarks, it is a pleasant humane task to redeem such captives from their degrading slavery. This same Picart brought out another sumptuous work, "Le Temple des Muses," the rare original edition, with descriptions in French, English, Dutch, and German, royal folio, large paper, sixty large and very beautiful plates, brilliant proof impressions, each plate surrounded with broad and elegant borders, fine copy, French calf gilt, full gilt back, gilt edges, £5, 5s. Amst., 1733. Descriptions in French, Dutch, &c. ! This shows the *clientèle* to which the artist appealed. The fine "style" of the work, its beautiful borderings, all commend it to the amateur of taste, though the treatment, however classical, goes beyond the limits of propriety.

Perhaps the more imposing and more pretentious work is the " Gallery of Versailles," from Le Brun's paintings, executed in the old, large, bold sweeping copperplate style, on board-like paper. One always admires even the frontispieces of these fine pictorial volumes, with their gods and nymphs disporting, combined with some architectural work, the title mixed up with abundant scrolls and flourishings, the inscription seeming as though it were carved on the walls of some old monument. This truly regal work is worthy of the Grand Monarque and the creator of Versailles. I take the description from the Perkins Collection, where a copy was sold for £130 :—"Cabinet du Roi. A magnificent collection of engravings executed at the expense of Louis XIV. for presentation to crowned heads and ambassadors resident at his court. Bound in twenty-three volumes." These enormous volumes are in the binding of the time, secured between planks of wood, the paper like a " board," and the engravings in the fine sweeping masculine style so effective in these great books. The printing was no less splendid—large, solid letters, proportioned

to the space covered—a matter utterly neglected in
our time. The very title-page, with its fine characters
and the royal escutcheon, is ennobling to look at.
This work was issued at twenty-five francs, and only
1000 copies were taken off, about 150 remaining over;
these were sold as a bonus for the engravers. In
works like this we are attracted by the vignettes
and tailpieces, conceived in a singularly free and
flowing style, full of fancy in the disposition of shields
and cupids and scroll-work—often, indeed, rising to
the dignity of a regular picture. It is of what is called
" atlas folio " size, with the royal arms on the side.
It contained the King's own pictures, each a finely
engraved copperplate; the battles of Alexander,
after Le Brun; medals, French and Roman; plans
and pictures of the Louvre and Tuileries; of Versailles (in itself a monument); ancient and modern
statues; the royal tapestries, fêtes, and " carousals "
(always an entertaining form of illustration, from the
admirable spirit, and crowds, figures, costumes, &c.
&c.); all the palaces and celebrated buildings in
Paris; the battles, sieges, marches, processions, &c.
of the Grand Monarque, &c. &c. It may be said
truly that each copperplate in the collection, in size
about three feet by two, is in itself worthy of being
hung up and framed, the lines are shadows so rich
and bold, and the whole effect so masterly. An
objection is of course the unwieldy, unmanageable
size of these monsters, and the difficulty of storing
them. On the walls of the long galleries in noblemen's houses we often find large prints of this character, and fine portraits of cardinals and French
statesmen hanging, each in its old-fashioned ebony
frame; and as we pause and survey them to our great
interest and entertainment, we scarcely think that

they have formed but one in an immense company, and have been separated from their fellows.

Another department of these grand art works is the glorification of theatres. This in England is unknown; indeed, there are not more than two or three English works on the construction or theory of theatres, and those of an unpretending sort. Abroad, where a theatre is a public monument for the city, as much as the Exchange or the Town Hall, the highest talent of the country is evoked to produce what shall be an ornament to the city and to the stage. Hence we have everywhere splendid and interesting buildings, each with a significance of its own; and almost every theatre of importance has been celebrated by a magnificent work, setting forth all the plans to scale, with views of the interior and exterior, front, sides, sections, &c. In these works the amateur finds a certain charm, a savour of the entertainment of the stage itself; and the style of engraving, in some instances, is of the highest order. The writer possesses a collection of these great works, the pleasure of looking over which is almost akin to that of seeing a play. One of the best is that noble tribute to a noble theatre —of atlas folio size—the account of the great theatre at Bordeaux. The San Carlo, the Scala, the Russian theatres, the new Opera House at Paris, and our Drury Lane, have all been illustrated in this sumptuous fashion. Besides the architectural plans, done minutely to scale, there are given views of the exterior and interior wrought in artistic fashion; and in the case of the Bordeaux house we see the audience, composed of innumerable figures in bag wigs and sack backs, the king and his courtiers in the royal box, the wax lights blazing away, the whole conveying an idea of elegant festivity.

Another department of sumptuous volumes, issued not for profit, but to minister to the glory of some opulent patron, is found in what are styled "Galleries." These noble works, of grand dimensions, noble type, lavish, if not exquisite art, are a reproduction, with fine plates and minute description, of the pictures in some public gallery, issued at the expense of the State ; or in some private collection produced at the expense of the owner ; or of some artistic palace like that of the Farnese or Pamphili at Rome. These fine testimonials to art would fill a library in themselves ; and on them have been expended all the treasure of printing, paper, engraving, and binding. Most costly is the well-known " Musée " of the Louvre, issued by Napoleon at a time when he had ravished all the museums of Europe and gathered them in Paris. The work fills many atlas folio volumes, and is, indeed, a cynical monument of plunder. For the Musée Français the Napoleon publishers received £307 as the subscription price, and a copy sold by auction at Sotheby's in 1860 produced £102. At the same time, by a proper retribution, it became a mere temporary memorial, as almost before its completion the works had been restored to their lawful owners. The engravings in these huge volumes are in that rather pretty style which was fashionable, and reflected the finish of David's pictures, then much copied ; but the effect lacks boldness and breadth. No expense was spared, but, like other productions of the Imperial Press at this time—such as Denon's great work on " Egypt "—there is not the general solidity and boldness of the older works. Its merit is the vast number of subjects, and the vastness of the enterprise. Still, these five grand folios are a surprising achievement, having been produced with a com-

parative ease which is astonishing to us. Every sort
of engraving is here found, including "line," *eau
forte*, worked after the fashion of regular engraving,
but all showing honest and finished labour. These
volumes do not often come into the market.

The successor of Napoleon was stimulated by his
example to produce the "Gallerie Royale," a work of
the same pretension, full of highly finished engravings,
and finely printed. The "Florence Gallery" and
many others followed, but none rival the state and
splendour of the works of the last century. Two of
the most elegant and finished form the "Gallery of the
Palais Royal," describing the collection of the Duke
of Orleans, a series of beautiful engravings in the
Moreau style, each plate having an elegant border,
while the description is engraved below. The "Dres-
den Gallery" is in two splendid tomes, full of the
finest *lithographs*, the best and most effective sort—
to say nothing of the "Gallery of the Pitti Palace."
The library of the Athenæum Club is particularly
rich in works of this class, boasting a large number
of these costly and entertaining tomes. Many were
bequeathed by the Rev. Mr. Turner. But, as I say,
none are so sumptuous or impress one so much as
those of the last century. Not less remarkable is the
variety of forms in which this royal encouragement
of art would display itself. Such noble patronage
seemed to be ingeniously lavish in devising opportunities.

Yet another sumptuous work was brought out to
minister to the glories of the Grand Monarque. Conceive of a fine, crimson-coated folio, stout, but well-
proportioned, in old raspberry-tinted morocco, by
the court binder, Ruette. The leaves display the
rich "old gold." On the sides is the escutcheon

of Louis XV., the collar of the St. Esprit and Crown, the back exquisitely tooled, the monogram " L.L." and crown elaborately repeated. This noble " piece,' intended as a royal present, is devoted to a series of pictures of medals illustrating the achievements of the great king. Each page is devoted to a medal, and there are 318 medals, and consequently pages, but printed on only the one or the *recto* side. Each page is in an exquisitely designed border by Coypel and Le Clerc, exhibiting a great variety of treatment. The medal is shown at the top, in two views, the obverse and the reverse—the first by Edelinck, the latter by Picart. Then follow a handsome printed historical description, while at the bottom is a graceful vignette. The whole was produced at the Royal Press, with a splendid frontispiece by Coypel, and makes, from its glorification of the king in every page, a most flattering and sumptuous picture. It is certainly worth possessing such a memorial, which is as entertaining as it is beautiful. To this class of work, so artistic, one can come and come again. Our modern editions of luxury will not bear these recurring visits. A more wonderful, amusing, and costly collection could not be conceived.

The Popes, too, have contributed some noble works to this category, such as the " Musée Pie Clementino," ten enormous vellum-bound folios, full of pictures of statues and antiques, wrought in the native rough Italian manner.

It is seldom recollected that the infamous Regent of Orleans, whose name is odious, was one of the most brilliant and accomplished men of any age—a fine musical composer, well and deeply read, a skilled politician, and an exquisite artist, whose works are said to bear comparison with some of the masters of his day. A translation of Longus's "Amours de Daphne et Chloe" was illustrated by his pencil, and engraved by Audran. This exquisite work, in an artistic sense a companion to the "Temple de Guide," is sold at a great price.

One of the most extraordinary and brilliant books of illustration is the collection of Piranesi's views. These immense etchings are remarkable for their brilliant coal-black effect. The surprising dash, certainty, freedom, and *chiaro-oscuro* effects are truly astonishing—not less surprising are the number. In many a country house we may find in the library two of the huge folios and spend a morning looking through them. But there are some twenty-six volumes —and there may be more—containing nearly *twelve hundred* of these great plates, "comprising," says one bibliopole, "the grand series of splendid engravings of the buildings and antiquities of Rome, the prisons, picturesque architecture, classical ornaments, Herculaneum and Pompeii, statues, vases, candelabra, sarcophagi, &c. ; remarkable Rembrandt-like compositions." And this praise is not overcharged.

An extraordinary feature is the taste the Dutch have shown for the great works illustrated with copperplates. Most of the leading engravers were Dutch or Flemish ; and it is a fact that there is hardly a town in Holland that has not its folio volumes of description, set off with profuse plates of its buildings, &c., devoted to its glories. One of the most exquisitely done of these tributes is Radamaeker's small quartos—a series of miniature views, done with a Meissonnier-like grace and feeling. The connoisseur should secure a copy when he can of this work, as I have done.

Thus gradually making our way down the bibliographic stream, we shall find that each era has a special taste and treatment of its own, and an originality quite marked. The French have ever been unrivalled in this elegant taste, and above all in this tasteful art of combining illustration in its proper proportion with typography. About the middle of the last century in France, there was introduced a species of elegant illustrated quarto, rather thin in contrast to the solidly abdominal English quarto, and something smaller. And here again we find the homogeneousness of which we have spoken, and which contributes so much to the artistic merit of a book. It would seem that in "designing" a book—and the term is appropriate enough—the publisher took all the departments—binding, type, illustrations, paper—into consideration. For we find that the binding is uniform—a sort of mottled calf, laid out with a sort of mixture of fruit colour, bordered with three close lines of gold, the edges of the leaves wavy, and of an " old gold " tint, each leaf being distinct, with richest effect. Such was the binding of the little " Barbou " volumes. Not so long since I redeemed from the stalls, for three shillings, a couple of pretty quartos—the plays of Crébillon, printed at the Royal Press in *such* style, with an exquisite vignette on the title of Cupids, &c., " composed and designed by Boucher, painter to his Majesty," and " engraved by Le Bas, engraver of the King's cabinet." There is even a delicacy in the way this little inscription is set down. And how jet-like the ink, how beautifully composed the page, how charming the general effect ! This book, as the author tells us, was printed by order of his Majesty, and is worthy of such patronage. Such works recovered from the stall are among the pleasant incidents of the book-hunter's pilgrimage. In this shape appeared a number of the

French classics, such as Racine, Corneille, and others, and which are all of the same pattern. But they bring large prices now when in fine condition.

Of all books, the French seemed to have honoured the graceful and ever-popular " La Fontaine " most, and the elegance and grace of the various editions are truly remarkable. It was in 1762 that the opulent Farmers-General of France subscribed to issue an edition of the *Contes* which is a model of taste and beauty. It was printed by Barbou, prefaced by Diderot, illustrated with " eighty exquisite plates by Eisen," one of the " little masters," supplied with fifty-seven elegant " tailpieces " by Choffard—a combination of printers, illustrators, author and editor truly remarkable. By a common fiction it was, oddly enough, supposed to be issued at Amsterdam. As may be conceived, the ordinary price of this work is large, and the two small volumes, with the additional merit of Derome's binding, were lately offered for £520 ! Seventy-five years before an edition of the Fables was issued at Amsterdam, which has become celebrated for Romeyne de Hooghe's vigorous but rather coarse plates.

Three years after the Farmers-Generals' edition another beautiful edition made its appearance. This was in six volumes octavo, illustrated with hundreds of beautiful engravings, vignettes, *culs-de-lampe*, by Monnet, Huet, Loutherberg, the letterpress being also engraved, so that the whole was printed from copperplates. But the collector must be warned that these names only belong to the " first state," and if the name of Deslaurier is found at the corner of the plates he must reject them as inferior, and not of the *premier tirage*. But the really remarkable edition of " La Fontaine " is the one in four folios, of the date 1755-59, and finely printed, with humorous and bold illustrations, engraved in the most spirited style, after Oudry, the French painter. This book is occasionally found in old libraries. The engravings are the work of Cochin, Tardieu, and others, and there is, sometimes lacking, a fine elaborate portrait of Oudry. From £60 to £200 has been paid for fine copies of his edition. It indeed adds to the entertainment to read the pleasant fabulist in this shape.

In our own way, in this country, we can point to enterprising and costly efforts to do honour to the great classics, and our publishers have never spared money or enterprise in great speculative ventures of the kind.

It is when we compare the manner in which Shakespeare has been honoured in England with that in which the great classics of France have been celebrated by their country that we see the extraordinary interest excited by the English bard. In England itself no other writer has been so dealt with, or in such costly fashion. I do not refer to the ordinary editions, stereotyped and others, brought out to satisfy the current demands, but to those " labours of love," grand editions, on which scholars have expended a goodly share of their lifetime, or to those more sumptuous volumes, set off with all the magnificence that paper, print, and illustrations could furnish. But first of all let us see what our neighbours have done for their Molière, Racine, and others of their leading and most popular classics. Of the first, whom they usually couple with Shakespeare—a compliment to us—there are literally not more than half-a-dozen important editions, set out with fine margin and plates.

At first there were some poor little duodecimo sets of Molière's plays, such as are seen on the stalls ; and not until 1734 do we find a really handsome edition, in six quarto volumes, adorned with cuts. There was another quarto edition in 1773, furnished with the younger Moreau's plates. In 1792 Didot issued a fine quarto edition. In 1819 there came an octavo edition in nine volumes quarto, with plates ; while in 1824 there was the Variorum edition in eight volumes octavo, with notes and plates. There have been one or two more important editions since, such as Tony Johannot's, and lately they have been issuing something like our reprints of the original editions of the separate plays. This exertion, spread over 250 years, does not argue much generosity or enthusiasm.

Not till 1760 was Racine glorified with a fine quarto edition in three volumes. Till the end of the century there were only three other editions, one of which was adorned with Gravelot's plates. Then the first year of the century was celebrated by a really splendid effort in the shape of Didot's magnificent Folios, claimed to be "the finest edition of any author in any country," and set off with nearly sixty plates by the first artists. Up to 1844 there were about seven more of any pretence, one of these being a superb folio edition in three volumes, printed by the famous Bodoni, at Parma, under the patronage of Murat.

For all these varied efforts due credit may be given to our neighbours, but they cannot compare with what we have done in our own sturdy, positive way for Shakespeare. This shows a sterling appreciation, unrivalled by any nation or time.

Mention has been made of Bodoni of Parma, certainly one of the most magnificent and elegant of modern publishers. Under the encouragement of Murat he produced some magnificent editions of the French classics—Racine, La Fontaine, and others, some of which were taken off on vellum. No one,

Dibdin tells us, had such an eye for laying out or composing a page. These charming duodecimos, somewhat after the pattern of Barbou, often turn up on the stalls. I myself possess, with nearly every known edition, some forty illustrated editions of " the Bard," each extending from six to a dozen volumes.

We shall conclude this view with two specimens, and which perhaps for expense and luxury deserve to be placed at the head of the list, " Bastard (Comte Augustus de) Peintures et Ornemens des Manuscrits Français, depuis le Huitième Siècle jusqu'a la Fem du Seizième, twenty parts (all at present published), in five portfolios imp. fol. Par. 1835, &c." " This is," says a panegyrist with a reasonable pride, " without exception the most sumptuous, unique, and costly work that has ever been produced. Each part contains eight splendid plates, copied from the most beautiful examples known to exist, coloured and finished with gold and silver equal to the exquisite originals. The whole series extends to one hundred and sixty engravings. No perfect copy of this magnificent work has occurred for sale in this country prior to the present."

" This wonderful performance is remarkable for the price at which it was issued (and to subscribers only), as well as for the extravagant patronage it received from the government of the ' citizen king.' There were twenty parts published, but the work was to have gone on to a much greater extent. Each part cost £72, so that the subscriber had to pay nearly £1500 for his ' five portfolios ! ' This, as we have said, was but a tithe of what was intended, for there were to be two other sections devoted to France, which would have brought the sum up to £4500. If the succeeding portions dealing with other countries were carried out, the luckless or insane subscriber would have been bound for some £10,000. The French Government patriotically subscribed for sixty copies, representing a donation in money of £90,000. One copy, put up in an English auction saleroom, M. R. Cutler-Fergusson's, brought only £200." Yet another of these gorgeous works, coloured sumptuously in a style that puts our modern efforts to the blush, is Du Sommerard's " Les Arts du Moyen Age," in which all the most striking works in the Hotel Cluny and the Roman Palace at Paris, and in other collections, were reprinted. This was in five superb volumes, and contained over five hundred illustrations, all " so accurately coloured as to convey a lively description of the exact appearance of the originals." This, auctioneers boast, is more than warranted. These are all, as were the illustrations of the time, coloured *by hand* in the most masterly style, and here one is struck by the difference of the action of time on works of this kind and on the modern printed colours. The latter gradually fade and become hard and flat, and even disagreeable. " A magnificent copy of this most splendid work, admirably bound in smooth red morocco extra," was sold twenty-four years ago for £92.

All know the celebrated column of Antoninus at Rome, round which runs to the summit a spiral band containing hundreds of groups and figures all cast in bronze. To draw them correctly from top to bottom must have been a task of amazing difficulty and inconvenience, yet it was accomplished in a most minute and thorough fashion nearly two hundred years ago ; and we have a splendid folio, by one Peter Bartoli, containing "seventy-eight large plates of battles, processions, thousands of figures that adorn this column, brilliant impressions, and descriptions in Latin, quite complete." What astonishes us in this class of work, of which there is an abundance, is the laborious, conscientious thoroughness with which the task is carried out, contrasting strangely with the perfunctory, hurried style in which works of the same kind are attempted now. Such labour indeed could only be secured at an enormous cost nowadays.

There is a whole department of illustrated works devoted to "costume," to the dress of different nations. There are some sumptuous volumes on this subject, France being conspicuous—even the military dress of this nation being pictorially represented from the earliest times. The theatrical costumes are also separately dealt with from 1600 to 1820 in 104 coloured plates.

So with scenery. Forty or fifty years ago there was a fashion in England for issuing in quarto parts views of the different countries, under the name of "The Beauties," while there was a distinct class of writers engaged in "writing up" "to" the plates. These are generally insipid representations done on steel. Of course there were brilliant exceptions, such as Turner. Nothing, however, can be compared with the older works.

Any one who set himself to collect books with architectural illustrations of town churches, cathedrals, castles, &c., would require enormous and vast library space indeed. There are booksellers devoted to this one branch alone, notably Parsons in the Brompton Road, who within his shop has costly treasures galore, while outside there is a curious survival in the shape of a bookstall, with boxes (" all at threepence ") and loose prints of all kinds strung together, "from a penny each." This suggests the " Omnium Gatherum " on the Quai D'Orsay. Among these old strangers and pilgrims there is of course much that is artistically bad and mediocre, but the true connoisseur should never fail to secure the fine series of views abroad of old Flemish and French cities and churches, done on a grand scale by one Coney, now forgotten, but a man of singular taste and power. These are a series of large etchings, atlas folio, represented with a singular breadth, considering they are in outline, and not in the elegant blackness of the modern school. There is a poetry, a feeling, a tone of the place shown, and a dramatic animation ; to say nothing of their value as records of what has long since been altered or what have passed away. The courteous reader, securing his " Coney "—soon to become scarce—for thirty shillings, will be grateful for this piece of advice.

Such is a glimpse, and a little more, of this vast domain.

§ Of the Auction-Room.

 ITH what mixed feelings one regards the book auction-room! Many a biblio-philist might look on it as the scaffold whereon his darling "hobby" will one day be done to death. Like death itself, he may think the idea is remote and will not affect *him*. Yet each recurring sale seems to say "to-day for me, to-morrow for thee!" Consider-ing the costly nature of these operations, the vast sums involved, the "drawing and quartering" of whole libraries, it is astonishing how prosaic is the scene, how homely the properties, going little beyond a general tone of "green baize," and rude, raw-looking shelves. There must be a secret dramatic history connected with many a book or library that has found a few weeks lodgings in these rooms. One collection, and now another—comrades once, during a century's span—arrives; a glorious compact com-panionship, in all honour and distinction, in a few days to be disintegrated, sold into captivity, scattered or adopted into a new collection. With them the late owner's soul is associated. How has his long life been bent or coloured by their familiarity; how has he stinted or spent for them, to ruin almost; or it may be

some inheriting prodigal who is delighted to find an asset on which money can be obtained, and which he at once despatches to the auction. Then the smaller passions of greed, longing, envy, recklessness, all exhibited in the biddings ; the contrasts of character —the opulent collector with few real treasures to boast of ; the poor, rustily-clad one who can yet boast rare and splendid things at home. Then the " seamy side," the craft and scheming, the wrecking of a sale, and the robbery by " knock out." The dealer can tell you strange legends of the capricious fate of many a rare volume. One wonders as some mouldy fellow tells the craft of his journey three hundred miles, it may be, down to the country to attend some obscure sale of a " gentleman's effects," for here he draws in his lottery or lucky bag. Here he may win for "a song" or a shilling or two some rare volume worth many pounds.*

The rooms where these holocausts are offered up in London are the well-known Sotheby, Wilkinson & Hodge's in Wellington Street, Strand, and Puttick & Simpson's in Leicester Square. These are the historic marts where all the great sales have been held time out of mind. To the Sotheby's

---

* There are stories of a first Shakespeare folio " knocked out " for twelve or sixteen shillings and resold for £400. It is in country sales of Great Britain that this system of " knock out " is brought to bear with fruitful effort. The " knock out " is a nefarious proceeding, and is often carried on in country sales. The principles of the knock out are two—combination against the innocent buyer and combination against the seller or owner. In the first instance the book is bid up against the outsider, who is not allowed to buy save at some extortionate price, and if it be bought by one of the conspirators at an extravagant figure, he is indemnified by the rest or the book sold after the sale. In the second, where it is purchased for some ridiculously low figure—for "a song," in fact—it is allowed by sufferance, and a fresh sale takes place at some public-house among the dealers themselves, where it is bought at a dealer's price.

modest rooms you scale a steep ladder-like stair. The place is small and unpretending, the business is transacted in a quiet fashion ; but it is astonishing what sums have been here transferred in the course of a few days. More interesting are "the rooms" in Leicester Square, where the august genius, the shade of Sir Joshua, hovers over the scene. For this, as is well known, was his residence and studio, the latter a noble spacious apartment, serving now as the saleroom. Worn and somewhat roughly used as it has been owing to the traffic, the visitor will note the elegance of the town mansion of those days, the airy stone stair and rail, its graceful *pente*, the classical doorways, the fine proportions (it is probably a work of Sir W. Chambers), and the genuine air of dignity. Here we see the collectors and the " dealers," and if a field day, some notable buyers from Paris and Berlin. The collectors now give their " commission," but formerly the noble gatherers attended themselves and did their own buying. As we survey this interesting scene, one of the most fantastic bibliographical tricks, one connected with the auction-room, played in the year 1840, recurs to us, when the sale of the Count J. N. A. de Fortsas' rare and valuable collection was announced all over Europe. " The sale," says a pleasant bibliograph essayist, writing in the daily paper, " was advertised to take place at the office of a notary residing at Binche, an insignificant town in Belgium. The catalogue covered only fourteen largely printed pages, and contained a list of the fifty-two books forming the Count's collection, each of which was unique. It was added that M. de Fortsas would keep no volume if he found it mentioned in any bibliography. The catalogues were sent to the great book-collectors of France, England, and the United

States, and each recipient supposed himself to be specially favoured, and kept the secret to himself. Two days before the sale, Brunet, Nodier, Techener, and Renouard met accidentally in the diligence which ran from Paris to Brussels, and each hoped that his neighbours had heard nothing of the wonderful auction which was about to take place at Binche. It was related that M. Castian, of Lisle, took great interest in a work said to have been published by Castman, of Tournay, on the subject of the Belgian Revolution of 1830, the entire edition of which had been suppressed, although M. de Fortsas had been so fortunate as to gain possession of a single copy. Being a little incredulous as to a library of which he had never heard, M. Castian stopped at Tournay and called on the publisher to inquire if such a work had ever been issued by his firm. M. Castman had himself forgotten all about the edition in question, but his foreman recollected it and its author, M. Lecocq, perfectly—a fact which at once silenced the inquirer's suspicions. The Baron de Reiffenber, director of the Royal Library at Brussels, asked for a special appropriation to buy some of the Count de Fortsas' treasures, which was immediately granted. One ardent bookseller made the journey from Amsterdam to Binche in order to see a single volume—the "Corpus Juris Civilis," printed by the Elzevirs on vellum. The Princesse de Ligne, anxious to preserve the reputation of her grandfather from obloquy, wrote to a commissioner to buy "No. 48" for her at any price. The Roxburghe Club was represented at the sale ; and, singularly enough, there were books in the catalogue which appealed to the taste of every distinguished collector. On the day before the sale the good people of Binche were astonished at the number of mysterious

2 F

strangers who had suddenly appeared in their midst
without any ostensible cause. At last the eventful
morning arrived, and in the newspapers circulated at
Binche there appeared a curt notice that the library
of the Count de Fortsas would not be sold, as the
Municipal Council had resolved to keep it in honour
of its collector, their distinguished fellow-townsman.
It now came out that the Count de Fortsas was a
myth ; his chateau and his library were both apocry-
phal."

As we walk through the auction-room ghostly figures
seem to rise before us, the old heroes of many an
exciting contest. It would almost seem that for them
the spirit of competition was the charm. The shades
of Lord Spencer, Heber, Bernal and others must
haunt these places. The glory of English collectors
was certainly the Lord of Althorp, who, from the
calm retirement of his library, regarded his son as he
fought political battles ; and waged many a contest in
the auction-room when his heir was " taking divisions "
in the House. Never was collecting pursued under
such magnificent conditions. A fortune splendid as
his taste ; a noble mansion to contain his treasures ; a
period when books were to be " picked up " cheaply ;
while he was guided by an adviser and agent of remarkable ability, taste, and knowledge—such were
the advantages that favoured the noble amateur. The
adviser and agent was the well-known Dr. Frognall
Dibdin, F.S.A., and never was such talent so encour-
aged and supported. The enthusiasm of this enthusiast
seemed to gather every hour. Appetite, "growing by
what it fed on," became at last voracious and incon-
trollable. No bibliophilist had so enjoyable a life.
He was sent on missions to France and Germany,
visiting all the libraries, and monasteries, and shops,

and bookstalls, tempting the monks and librarians to dispose of their treasures by a display of his noble patron's gold. He published accounts of his travels, produced in royal style, and sumptuously illustrated. These noble volumes, set forth in all the epicureanism of "large paper copies," are now precious things when found in a "fine state ;" and a set of Dibdin's works fetches a very startling sum indeed.

It is pleasant, as it is interesting, to read the amiable ravings of this honest collector, who by living in one long dream came at last to persuade himself that he was dealing with precious stones, and all that was rare and costly in the world ! His style, from this generous ardour, was passionately expressive—full of quaint and gorgeous turns, with a power of delineating character that wins his readers. His career and story is valuable as exhibiting the very highest and most expressive form of which bibliophilism is capable.

So sumptuous was the system on which his catering for the Earl's taste was carried out, that merely good copies of any work were almost considered little better than having no copies at all, or at best but a substitute, *en attendant* a *fine* one. Again, a fine one was unsatisfactory should a finer appear in the market. This fastidiousness required the deepest purse, but the result has been a collection that is unequalled. It was thus that the Earl purchased a superb Livy from the collection of another amateur, magnificent in ideas as himself. ("It was, I believe, this book," says his Doctor, "and the Psalter of 1457, that the Abbé Strathman, librarian to the Emperor, declared he would carry away with him, one under each arm, should the French come.") Notwithstanding this enthusiasm we hear that "*his Lordship threw it out*" of his collection ; the truth being that he had found another whose charms surpassed it—a noble copy truly, bound in blue morocco. This system of "throwing out" culminated in a formal sale by auction of a collection of "incunables"—in itself enough to form a distinguished one, but rejected by the Doctor and his patron as not up to the standard of their library. "Our failures," he might call them, like Brummel's valet.

The Doctor devoted some of his magnificent tomes to a detailed account of the Althorp Library and its contents. He described the rooms, and gave the history of each rare work, too often straying off into raptures—as when dealing with a certain " Pliny upon Paper." " How can I convey an idea," he exclaims, " of its condition and amplitude. Think, enthusiastic collector, *of the uncontaminated snow* upon the summit of the Apennine peaks, and you will have an idea of the size and colour of the Spencer copy. The press work of this surprising volume is quite perfect." *

By way of contrast it is pleasant to reflect how much can be done with small resources, but large indeed in their efficacy, without outlay of little beyond trouble, time, and patience. In a provincial town of some note I recall the figure of a retiring man of modest means, but sufficient—and with nothing to do—who spent his days during the past forty years in a sort of unexcited, though careful, sensible, and diligent attendance at auctions. For him the sale day was a regular gala. Forty years have been thus spent, and he still pursues his quiet labours. He had a calm, accurate judgment, and a quick eye. The city he lived in was but indifferently stored with " curios,"and our friend's purse,

* A collection of the Dibdin publications, all tall splendid volumes, is rare indeed. One such (large paper) was the glory of a great American collector's library.

as I said, was but indifferently lined—I doubt if he laid out twenty pounds in the year. But during these forty years he pursued his course unflinchingly, securing now the print, now the rare play, the old book, the unique pamphlet, the playbill, the MS., the picture, the "bit" of china, until he is absolutely, at this moment, in possession of one of the most interesting and valuable collections conceivable. It is impossible to name anything rare of which he has not got a specimen, and generally a very choice one. He will tell you that "he has got a few old plays," but these are sure to prove to be of the rarest sort. "Yes" —this modestly—"he had a fine copy (uncut) of Marlowe's 'Faustus,' also of the 'Rich Jew.'" He had mezzotintos in the finest states, and somehow contrived to have those which were unique, or of which only a few were in existence. He rarely contrived to pay more than a shilling or two for each.

What a contrast this to the opulent collector, who looks through his catalogues, and sends an order to his chosen dealer or broker to bid for him, and has thus to secure at the highest possible market price anything he desires to possess. There money is no object, and things thus purchased in *market overt* contrast strangely with the treasures so quietly and cheaply acquired by the collector just described. Him a strange good fortune seemed to attend. Perhaps it was that he never hesitated, but struck in time. *Frappez vite* and *frappez fort* should be the book-hunter's motto.

Perhaps the most extraordinary of book-gatherers was the famous Heber, brother of the better known Bishop. This poor delusionist carried book-collecting over the borders—into lunacy almost. No poor sot ever swilled glass after glass so greedily as this Heber devoured books. He bought libraries without seeing them, and died before he had seen all the books he possessed. But at last the end came, and the hour struck when he could see or handle books no more. No friend stood by his bedside, save the insensible quartos and folios to which he had sold his souL That great auctioneer Death had his hammer raised for the final "going, going, gone!" This was in November 1833. No one cared for the loss of this poor foolish buyer. But now the cry was "the library!" What was to become of *that?* There is an unpublished letter of the famous bibliophilist, Rev. Mr. Dyce, to another as ardent, Sir Egerton Brydges, which exhibits a melancholy picture.

Hearken to this brother collector : " Poor man !" he wrote, " he expired at Pimlico, in the midst of his rare property, *without a friend to close his eyes,* and from all I have heard I am led to believe that he died broken-hearted : he had been ailing some time, but took no care of himself, and seemed indeed to court death. Yet his ruling passion was strong to the last. The morning he died he wrote out some memoranda for Thorpe about books which he wished to be purchased for him. He was the most liberal of book-collectors : I never asked him for the loan of a volume, *which he could lay his hand on,* he did not immediately send me."

The sale of this library is one of the great "book eras" of the century ; and the prices, appearance of rarieties, &c., have all the interest that " a leading case" has for barristers. It took place in April 1834, and was extended over some years, which was natural, considering the vast number of volumes that were to be disposed of. The catalogue is itself a treatise, extending to six thick volumes, closely printed, and

containing a vast amount of bibliophilite lore. There
is a copy in the Athenæum Library—the *official* one
it may be called—which was presented to it by Messrs.
Payne & Foss, the booksellers, who prepared it ; and
at the commencement is given an exhaustive MS.
analysis of the prices, number of volumes, loss or
gain on the sale of each volume, &c. From this it
would seem that there were 119,613 volumes sold !
which it required no less than two hundred and two
days, or nearly seven months, to sell ; and the sum
realised was £56,774.

Few have a conception of what a serious thing a
well-furnished library is, until he has turned over these
marvellous pages ; or even of a single department, in
which there may be thousands of volumes whose titles
he may have never seen or heard of before. Thus
a volume was devoted to "early English" works—old
quaint things of the sixteenth century, prose and
poetry, masques, interludes, dramas, &c. Indeed "it
may be asserted that so complete an assemblage of
plays, extending from the earliest period at which they
were printed down to the closing of the theatres in
1647, were never seen." The value and rarity of which
may be conceived when it is stated that it is now
difficult to procure an "interlude" or pageant—a single
one of which may cost ten, twenty, or fifty pounds.

Book catalogues have ever a certain interest and
fascination, they contain for the fanatically curious
such an odd and heterogeneous amount of information.
The odd notes, the prices, the glowing descriptions, all
make these records pleasant reading, and form part of
the romance of the saleroom. Some collectors write
their own catalogue, as did Mr. Henry Huth, whose
five magnificent volumes printed at the Chiswick Press
" on hand-made paper and strongly bound in half

morocco, top edges gilt, Roxburghe style," form a treatise on bibliography rather than a catalogue. Ten guineas is the price of this record, and the "impression," we are told, " has been almost disposed of."

Every collection seems to reflect its owner's character ; and there is a curious interest in contrasting the different sides of character of men like George Steevens, Malone, Cole, George Daniel, and others, whose books and MSS. denote what is delicate and interesting, but whose character to the world was rough, violent, and insolent. George Steevens seemed indeed an odious person—truculent and malignant in his resentments, tortuous in his proceedings, and, as Miss Hawkins hints, reported to have died like one who had sold himself to the evil one. Yet among their books these men were all interesting. I own to a fancy for collecting the catalogues of certain famous men— actors, poets, &c., which reveal by many little touches their characters. Thus I have the one of Garrick's elegant library, in all the languages, showing the taste and accomplishments of the owner : of Topham Beauclerk's, interesting to the Johnsonian (the owner is said to have departed but once from his inflexible rule of never lending a book) ; Kemble's, the junior James Boswell, a most interesting one full of records of the Doctor, the famous Perkins, Henderson the actor, the Stowe, Duke of Sussex, &c.

Among the famous sales were Dr. Meade's, in 1754 ; Mr. Woodhull's, in 1803, "rich in *editiones principes*" (he had thus a sale in his lifetime and one after his death) ; the Lansdowne, in 1806, 31 days ; Brand in 1807, 37 days, a remarkable assemblage on typography : " hundreds of uniques, Caxtons, Wynkyns, a most covetable *tout ensemble;* this glorious sale realised £17,000 " (so sings our bookseller), Stanley's,

in 1813, "which realised over £1000 a day, being rich
in Italian and Spanish works ;" the Morley or Willet
sale, in 1813, of block-printed chronicles, vellum and
large paper copies, and other indescribable treasures ;
Borromeo (good name of an owner of volumes), in 1817,
"the rarest and most curious assemblage of early
Italian volumes ever offered ;" the Bindley, in 1818,
a truly remarkable sale of "rare, curious, and early
English literature"; the Fonthill, of 20,000 volumes,
in 1823 ; the Hibbert, in 1829, a collection formed to
illustrate the history of printing, and therefore offering
the most splendid and unique examples ; George
Chalmers, in 1841 ; Bright, in 1845 ; Upcott, in 1846,
remarkable for its works made up of "cuttings ;"
Bernal, in 1855 ; Sir M. Sykes, in 1824 ; Whiteknights,
in 1829 ; G. Daniel, in 1864 ; to say nothing of innumerable others.

It is curious that within recent times there have
been at least two casualties at auction-rooms which
have wrought havoc on famous collections. Mr George
Offers' collection was to be sold in 1865, and was one
of the richest gatherings of early Scripture editions—
Liturgies, Fathers, "Bunyaniana," Caxtons, Books of
Hours, &c. There were to be eleven days' sale of
these treasures ; but the prices are only marked down
to the end of the second day, when a conflagration
took place at Sotheby's, which destroyed almost the
whole. Many purchasers had left their books, but the
wisely cautious book-buyer always takes his purchases
away on the day he buys. The Charlemont collection
was also partially burnt, and many works irreparably
injured by water when they escaped the fire.

A great day or days at Sotheby's—not the sale days,
which are theatrical, but the quiet or viewing days,
when you can inspect and compare at leisure, for hours

2 G

if you will—furnishes a charm and instruction which
would have delighted Doctor Dibdin himself, or the
amazingly erudite author of " Mores Catholici."

The last four years have been notable for some
famous sales, and opportunities, which will not occur
again, have been offered of seeing some of the most
famous books in the world. Indeed it might be said
that all the Masterpieces of Printing have been laid
open to view in the Sunderland, Hamilton, Beckford,
and Syston Park sales.

The earlier months of the year 1881 were notable for an announcement that went forth, that the
Blenheim Library was shortly to be sold. Already the
fine collection known as the " Marlborough gems,"
which had been celebrated in a volume, had been disposed of *en bloc* to a private purchaser. The books
were now to follow, while later in the year of grace
1884 the gems of the picture-gallery—great and famous
works of Velasquez, Raphael, and Rubens—were sold
to various purchasers. Soon the halls of the great
palace will be left vacant and the walls stripped.

The news of the coming sale fluttered the book-collecting and bookselling circles all over the world, for
it was known that this Sunderland Library was among
the most famous, and stored with articles that would
have rejoiced a Frognall Dibdin to celebrate. The
sale was fixed for December 1, 1881, and occupied ten
days, during which Messrs. Puttick's historical rooms
were crowded with buyers from the chief capitals of
Europe. The books themselves astonished many who
were not curious or interested in such things, from
their magnificent character, though it was remarked
that the old calf bindings showed neglect, and were
in rather sorry condition. For some time after were
seen on the stalls many a stray volume, with the florid

arms and escutcheons of the ducal house on the sides, fallen from their high estate and palatial lodgment.

The first portion was announced as being "a remarkable collection of the Greek and Roman classical writers, in first, early, and rare editions, with a large series of early-printed Bibles, in various languages ; rare editions of the great Italian writers, notably Dante, Boccaccio, Petrarch, and Ariosto ; of chronicles in Spanish, Portuguese, English, and French; while there were many very curious tracts relating to English and French politics, with first editions of the writings of the chief French, Italian, and Spanish poets of the sixteenth and seventeenth centuries." Here were also found the first editions (*editiones principes*), nearly eighty in number, of all the Greek and Roman classics and classical writers, besides numerous other early editions in profusion, innumerable Bibles, polyglot and others. But what this collection was chiefly remarkable for was the vast number of books *printed upon vellum*, and which, it was claimed, was unrivalled in this respect by any library in Europe. There were no less than *fifty-eight* of these choice and desirable works, most of them belonging to the "*incunable,*" or "cradle" category, dating from the fifteenth century—noble, splendid works, most of them set off with illuminated borderings on the front leaf, and with initials in gold and colour at the beginning of every chapter.

Here too were sold an Anacreon on vellum, "perhaps the only copy known," for £221 ; an Ariosto for £300 ; the Romance of King Arthur, a manuscript with annotations, for £535 ; and the "fourth printed book with a date," to wit "Balbus de Janua," for £285. There were no less than 166 rare Bibles set up for sale, of which Cardinal Ximenes' famous " Polyglot " of 1514, in six volumes, brought £195. There also appeared here the famous Bible of 1462, printed on vellum, a copy of which, at the Perkins sale, astounded all by the price it brought.

But the real excitement of the sale was the sale of the two editions of Boccaccio. The first is stated to have been the "first book printed at Bruges," by Colard Manson, who is connected with our Caxton. This volume was measured scrupulously as being 14⅞ inches by 9⅞. It was sold for £960. But then the decks were cleared for *the* Boccaccio, the famous "first edition of the Decameron with a date," "*of extraordinary rarity.*" It was described with nice and minute accuracy as being "printed in Roman letters, lines without numerals, catchwords, or signatures, four leaves missing, the plain margin of columns 212, 242, 259, and 260 mended, two corners defective. It measured 12⅜ inches by 8½, being nearly an inch taller and half an inch wider than the Roxburghe copy, and made such a sensation at the beginning of the nineteenth century and realised such a sum at the sale of the library of John Ker, third Duke of Roxburghe, in 1812, as no single printed volume ever did before or since." Such was the only perfect copy known of the world-famous edition of the Decameron of Boccaccio, a small folio printed by Christopher Valdarfar, Venice, 1471, black letter, in faded yellow morocco binding, and originally published, it is believed, for *about ten shillings.* About this famous work hovers a sort of bibliographical romance. Only three copies were known—one in Lord Spencer's library at Althorp; one in the Sunderland ; and the third said to be in the National Library at Paris—but only " *a cruelly washt and cropt* " thing. The most famous is the one which produced the excitement at the great Roxburghe sale.

Dr. Dibdin, who styled this auction of the biblio-maniacal Duke "the *Waterloo of Book Sales*," gives a graphic description of it in the "Ninth Day of his Bibliographical Decameron" (vol. iii., pages 62 and 117), from which we gather that no less than three noble candidates had gathered to struggle for the prize, the Duke of Devonshire (who at the same sale gave £1060 for Caxton's "Histories of Troy"), Earl Spencer, and the Marquis of Blandford (afterwards Duke of Marlborough). The scene is described by Dr. Dibdin with bated breath. The sale was held at the Duke's house in St. James's Square, where he had expired, his bedroom adjoining his beloved library. The eagerness, the prices given, vast for those days, were extraordinary.

Mr. Evans, the auctioneer, prefaced the sale of the articles by an appropriate oration, concluding by in-forming the company of the regret and even anguish of heart expressed by a foreign connoisseur that the Imperial Library had not a copy. It was known that an agent of Bonaparte was present. "Silence followed the address," says our Doctor. "On his right hand, *leaning against the wall*, stood Earl Spencer ; a little lower down, and standing at right angles with his lord-ship, appeared the Marquis of Blandford. The Duke, I believe, was not then present ; but my Lord Althorp stood a little behind to the right of his father.

"The honour of making the first bid was due to a gentleman from Shropshire, who seemed almost elec-trified at his own temerity in offering '100 guineas.' Soon, however, the bidding rose to 500 guineas (the sum Beloe had prophesied it would fetch). At length 1000 guineas is named by the Earl Spencer, to which the Marquis of Blandford quietly added 'ten.' From this point these two worthy noblemen were the only bidders, neither evincing any desire to yield. '£2000,' says the Marquis! For a quarter of a minute the Earl hesitated, at length he boldly cries, '£2250;' nothing daunted, the Marquis as quietly adds his usual 'ten;' and after due and deliberate suspension 'in mid air,' down drops the hammer before the amazed and excited auditory at the last-named handsome figure, namely, £2260. When the Marquis bid the last £10 Lord Spencer said, 'I bow to you.' Presently, after the Marquis offered his hand to Lord Spencer, saying, 'We are good friends still,' his Lordship replied, 'Perfectly, indeed I am obliged to you.' 'So am I to you,' said the Marquis, 'so the obligation is mutual.' He declared it was his intention to have secured it at any price."

It seems the Marquis possessed another copy, but which, alas! wanted five leaves, so that, as his disappointed rival remarked, he might be said to have given that great sum for the five leaves. The book itself, the subject of this mad and ridiculous contest, was described as being certainly one of the scarcest, if not the scarcest, book that ever existed. It is known that it was a bone of contention among the collectors in the reign of the first two Georges. Lord Sunderland had seen it, and Lord Oxford cast a longing eye upon it. In 1497 the work was publicly burnt, and copies in the beginning of the fifteenth century were scarce, and this identical copy, it is thought, owed its safety to the ingenuity of a former owner, a Jesuit, who had it lettered on the back "Concilium Tridenti," and was so accidentally discovered by a bookworm. It came into the possession of an ancestor of the Duke of Roxburghe, previous to the year 1740, at the price of £100, then considered an extravagant sum. How it first reached the Duke was curiously explained to

Mr. Beloe, the " septuagenarian," by Mr. G. Nicol. It appears that this copy was in the hands of a London bookseller, who showed it to Lord Oxford and Lord Sunderland, then the great collectors of books, and competitors for rare publications, and asked 100 guineas for it, which they hesitated to give. Whilst they were deliberating, an ancestor of the Duke's saw and purchased the volume. The two noble collectors were invited to dinner, and the subject of Boccace being purposely introduced, Lord Oxford and Lord Sunderland began to talk of this particular copy. The Duke of Roxburghe told them that he thought he could show them a copy of this edition, which they defied him to exhibit. To their mortification and chagrin he produced the book in question. " I have a perfect recollection," goes on Dibdin, " of this volume in the library of the Duke. It had a faded yellow morocco binding, and was a sound rather than a fine copy." It may be said that foreign writers and book-fanciers were as much amused as astonished at this fancy price, and threw serious doubts on the rarity of the volume. They have since, however, established their claim to be as frantic and extravagant in the pursuit as the English are. So resolved was the infatuated Marquis upon the acquisition of this book that he was prepared to give £5000 to obtain it. The object of this struggle subsequently came, at the sale of the Marquis of Blandford's library in 1819, into the possession of the Earl Spencer for the sum of £918, in whose library at Althorp it now rests. The Earl had the book bound in the most superb style by Charles Lewis, having the arms of the Duke of Roxburghe within, and his own without, on dark green.*

---

* This is perhaps the only instance of an English duke devoting himself to the bibliomania. His name is honourably associated with the club that bears his name. Dr. Dibdin and

At this Roxburghe sale there were other extraordinary prices obtained for objects that seem quite beyond their value, as, for instance, that " collection of twopenny portraits of criminals," which fetched £94, and the selection of old halfpenny ballads, which would have delighted Macaulay, "pasted in three volumes," which fetched £477.

Caxton's " Recueil " was also the subject of another ridiculous contest. This was the first book printed in the English language, but it wanted the last leaf. Lord Spencer had a copy that wanted the first.   It had been sold at the Steevens' sale, and secured by the enthusiastic Earl for £200.   Sir Mark Sykes, Lord Blandford, and Mr. Ridgway, acting for the Duke of Devonshire, contested for it.   Sir Mark retired when he reached £500 ; the Marquis went to £1000.   "Let them be guineas," cried Mr. Ridgway, and the baffled Marquis making no sign, the book became the property of the Duke.   " Why," says Dibdin, pathetically, in a letter, " tear open wounds which promise in due time to be closed.   More mischief has ensued, more bibliomaniacal wretchedness has ensued, than the healing influence of an undisturbed century may be able to counterbalance.   It has been a sort of book

Joseph Hazlewood were instrumental in founding this club of noblemen and gentlemen, which was limited to forty members, called the Roxburghe Club, and inaugurated at the Old St. Alban's Tavern, London, dating from Thursday, 17th June 1812. Each member undertook to give to his brother Roxburghers, in turn, a volume printed for the special occasion. It is now, however, arranged that an annual subscription of five guineas is received, which is devoted to the publication of some unpublished MS., or the reprint of some rare and valuable work. The collected works of the club always realise high prices. At Lang's sale in 1828 thirty-nine volumes fetched £111, 6s. ; Hazlewood's, in 1834, forty-four volumes, £115 ; Sir F. Freeling, in 1834, forty-four volumes, £90 ; and at Harvard's, in 1858, sixty-one volumes (sold separately) produced £125, 2s.

earthquake." These people seem to have lost their wits.

With these traditions, one of the cherished glories of the book auction-room, it may be conceived how eagerly, after an interval of nearly seventy years, the reappearance of such a treasure with such a history was looked for. Still, after all the speculation, it brought but £585 ; a vast sum certainly, but still a sad falling off as compared with the £918 and the enormous £2260.

The second edition of the same book brought £400. Later came some astonishing prices ; a superb " St. Augustin de Civitate," printed by Jenson on vellum, produced £1000 ! Bourbet's " L'Amoroux," £640 ; and the " Voyages de Bry" (1590), in a few parts, the astonishing sum of £750. The grand competitors through the various contests were Mr. Quaritch of Piccadilly, and a foreign dealer, M. Techener, who contended with each other regardless of limit; but it was rumoured that each represented influential patrons, such as Baron Rothschild of Paris, the Duc d'Aumale, and other connoisseurs. The total cash received during these ten days was £19,373, 10s. 6d. ! No wonder the hopes of the family ran high as to the prospective gains from future sales. But these fell off considerably, and never approached that magnificent return. Many valuable books went at extraordinary low prices—for odd shillings and half-crowns ; and the skilled amateur, for months afterwards, might have seen on the various stalls innumerable "desirable" lots to be secured "for a song." Shrewd American dealers bought enormous quantities, *en gros*, as it were, of these serviceable works, and shipped them home. The total sum realised was about £73,000.

The Syston Park Library, a model for the splendid condition of its treasures, offered a curious show, from

2 H

the quality and rather monotonous tone of the binding.
What the nice connoisseur noted was the absence of
a certain *style* and character. Every work was plenti-
fully overlaid with gilding, but no volume had a character of its own, and there was often a strange lack
of appropriateness in the dress adopted for each. The
stately " Fifteeners," as they are vulgarly termed, the
grand old signors of the early years of printing, so noble
and dignified, were mostly dressed in buff coatings,
their backs squared and stiff, the lettering rather thin
and poor, and not very brilliant. Elaborate gold tooling on a pale yellow ground is not effective. How
different is the *character* imparted by the old bindings !
The rich, deep-toned crimson morocco, and the sparing
use of gold, would surely have been a more appropriate
roquelaure for these hidalgoes. This gives a sinuosity
to the sides, which bend inwards to the edges of the
leaves, while the rounding of the backs and the bold
ribs furnish detail and protection. The remarkable
feature of this library was the collection of first editions of the Classics—books almost like MS., on which
we look with admiration, reverence, and wonder. They
suggest old Venetian portraits, so stately and noble
are they, so rich and costly and elegant in their
material. As was justly said by a critic, " Those who
admire the magnificent *editiones principes* from the
famous early presses of Italy and France, when the
printer was the rival of the painter in the love and
worship of his art, will find an ample feast of delight
in reviewing a collection wonderfully fine for condition
and remarkable beyond most for completeness. Almost the only *lacunæ* are the absence of a Phædrus
and the want of one volume of the Ovid, first edition
of 1471 of three volumes, the rarest of all, and of which
only one perfect copy is known, the first book printed
at Bologna, and of which Brunet had never known a

copy sold in his time. Many are the choice editions of the Aldines and Elzevirs, several on vellum or large paper, generally in exceptionally good condition and superb bindings, from the libraries of such high historic repute as those of Lorenzo de' Medici, Marguerite de Valois, Diane de Poictiers Barbarigo, Doge of Venice, and Catharine de' Medici, Thuanus, Maioli, De Menars, Grolier, and of more modern collectors."

At the present moment the cultured *amateur*— rather the *dilettante*—flourishes to a degree that has never before been known, and to all the arts brings a taste, knowledge, and above all a purse, which has hitherto never been rivalled. "He holds the field." He is the "patron." His gifts are elegant and solid, and there is little of that ridiculous affectation and "airs" which was the stock-in-trade of the old amateur. This cultivated being stamps his own graces upon his collection to a degree that could scarcely be conceived. And it is only when we compare a gathering of the kind, to whose selection patience, time, and taste has been brought, with the larger "*omnium gatherums*," that we recognise the immeasurable superiority of the former. Open before me is an elegant monument of this elegant ease in the shape of a finely-printed catalogue, significant of the owner and his library, which is the work of Mr. Frederick Locker Lampson of Rowfant. Herein he describes his elegant and valuable collection—a dainty record—adorned with an etched portrait of the owner, and a Cruikshank sketch of his study ; while Mr. Andrew Lang, a congenial and well-skilled expert, ushers the whole in with a ballade on "the Rowfant Books :"—

> "The Rowfant books, how fair they show,
>   The quarto quaint, the Aldine tall ;
> Print, autograph, portfolio !
>   Back from the outer air they call

> The athletes from the tennis hall ;
>   The rhymer from his rod and hooks.
> Would I could sing them, one and all,
>   The Rowfant books !
>
> The Rowfant books ! These long ago
>   Were chained within some college hall ;
> These manuscripts retain the glow
>   Of many a coloured capital ;
> While yet in satires keep their gall,
>   While the *pastissier* puzzles cooks,
> There is a joy that does not pall—
>   The Rowfant books !"

The merit of this collection is that it was formed on a system steadily pursued—for the illustration of old English, modern poetry, and drama—to be accomplished by selecting only the rarest and most tasteful exemplars.   The test is that the scholar in such department would here find himself fully equipped.

There is a quaint " relish " in the owner's introduction of his cherished tomes.   " It is a good thing to read books, and it need not be a bad thing to write them; but it is a pious thing to preserve these that have been some time written : the collecting, and mending, and binding, and cataloguing of books are all means to such an end.   This is my apology for the present volume.   I had intended to annotate some of the more curious and rare volumes, for I have a decided opinion about a good many of them.   By doing so I should have given my catalogue the distinct quality that comes of ownership and affection."

First editions of poets during that dainty era, 1550–1600, abound, and forty choice Shakespeare quartos, headed by the first folio in fine condition, fill the connoisseur with envy and admiration.   While, of a later generation, the first editions of Lamb, Byron, Tennyson, Coleridge—always dainty things, and now much coveted—swell the ranks of the moderns.   The owner of Rowfant has himself laboriously appraised and collated each volume, sternly rejecting all that is not choice and perfect, and has added many a piquant note of his own, or inscription into the book itself.

It may be added here that this gathering together of old plays has always had a fascination for collectors. Those who are not inclined to anything else are drawn by the wish to accumulate these elegant little volumes, with their quaint old spelling and *tawny* paper, each, according to strict bibliograph etiquette, a volume in itself. There is, as usual, a melancholy interest in looking over such a collection. Many will be found to have three or four book-plates, showing the different owners, how it has passed from hand to hand, the owner himself having passed away ; and each is generally bound in the best style, often " by Bedford.' This cost may be set down at a guinea, while the little book itself may have been secured for five shillings. Not long since, we saw one of Mr. J. Payne Collier's little reprints, issued at 1s. 6d., coming from Mr. Ouvry's rare and valuable library—a trifle, which yet had been bound in exquisite fashion, certainly at a cost of a couple of guineas. Many collectors consider their books as *ornaments* also ; they please themselves by taking them out of the glass-enclosed bookcases— *fondling* them, as it were. This binding is a difficult question, for to see some rare little tome " done up " in ragged " *half*-binding " — that is, covered with marbled paper and cheap roan—is revoltingly inappropriate, or, as Lamb would say, heartless. At the same time, new and brilliant binding, gilt edges, &c., are equally out of keeping with the sober dignity of an Elizabethan play, though by and by, when thirty years have mellowed it, it will be fit enough.

Mr. Malone's valuable collection of "Old Plays" now

reposes in the Bodleian Library. The foundation of his dramatic collection was, he tells us, one hundred and nineteen volumes of old plays printed in quarto, containing on an average eight plays in each volume, given him by George Steevens, I believe, in 1778. To these he added forty-eight in quarto, twelve in 12mo and 8vo, besides an almost perfect collection of single plays of all the early dramatic writers. Among these were such rarities as the " Gorboduc " of 1562 ; also Lyly's plays in one volume quarto. " This," said the owner, "is one of the most curious and expensive volumes in my library. The plays were purchased for the most part at very dear rates, and are not to be had now at any price. For Midas alone (a ' Children of Paules ' play) I think I paid seven guineas and a half ! "

Another " amateur," Mr. Ruskin—one of the most interesting personalities of his time—some years ago, in protest against what he considered the grasping dealings of publishers, determined to publish his own works himself, selecting " Mr. George Allen, Sunnyside, Orpington," as his agent or deputy. This is really a unique enterprise, and one of great extent and importance from the long list of issues, reprints, &c., which the author's works now fill. But this dispensing with a middleman is only to be done by a Ruskin, and the general principle is not practicable. There is something specially appropriate in a writer like Mr. Ruskin supplying his own books ; for as the writing and matter represent his mind, so does the book—its type, shape, &c.—express the form and pressure of the author's mind. There is an elegance of grace and dignity about his grander works, such as " The Modern Painters " and the " Stones of Venice," that marks this impress in the most striking way. Even the exceptional size has a nobility. There was infinite care used in the working, hence the grace of the illustrations. A fine copy of "The Modern Painters" has been priced at £40 ! and a fine set of Ruskin is of extraordinary value. His publishing notices are characteristic, and show his own familiar touch :

"Works by Mr. Ruskin published by and to be had of George Allen, Sunnyside, Orpington, Kent (five minutes' walk west of Orpington Station, South-Eastern Railway).

"Advice by Mr. Ruskin : ' I have directed Mr. Allen, in this and all future issues of his list of my purchase-able works, to advertise none but those which he is able to despatch to order by return of post. The just estimate of decline in the energy of advancing age—the warnings, now thrice repeated, of disabling illness consequent on any unusual exertion of thought—and chiefly, the difficulty I now find in addressing a public for whom, in the course of the last few years of Revolution, old things have passed away, and all things become new, render it, in my thinking, alike irreverent and unwise to speak of any once-intended writings as " in preparation."

" ' I may perhaps pray the courtesy of my readers—and here and there, the solicitude of my friends—to refer, at the time of the monthly issue of magazines, to this circular of Mr. Allen's, in which they will always find the priced announcement of anything I have printed during the month. May I also venture to hint to friends who may at any time be anxious about me, that the only trustworthy evidences of my health are my writings ; and that it is a prettier attention to an old man to read what he wishes to say, and can say without effort, than to require him to answer vexing questions on general subjects, or to add to his day's appointed labour the burden of accidental and unnecessary correspondence.'

" Mr. Allen has positive orders to attend to no letter asking credit. All books are sent carriage paid to any place in the Postal Union on remittance (in advance) of the full prices of the volumes required. In the case of foreign countries, it is suggested that the cost of registration for the more expensive works be added to their prices, to insure safety in transit. *N.B.*—Correspondents are respectfully requested to note that the utmost despatch is used in replying to orders and letters of inquiry ; but as these are very numerous, it is not always possible to attend to them at once, especially at the time of issue of new publications. Much trouble and delay will be saved if correspondents will invariably give their full address, and, in advising change of residence, their former one also. Stamps not accepted for sums over half-a-crown. Amounts of less than five shillings not acknowledged unless a stamped envelope is enclosed."

The American amateurs now compete with the British, and some very fine and rare treasures and choice editions are being collected into libraries by opulent bibliomen with long purses. We hear of first folios and rare things of the kind finding their way across the Atlantic. In the very handsome catalogue of an American bibliophile, Mr. Farmer, the true principles of the collection were set out judiciously enough.

" Mr. Farmer's theory was large paper copies rather than small ; the *relicures* of Hayday, Riviere, &c., in preference to cheap store bindings ; limited editions on fine paper instead of unlimited on wood pulp ; unique extra illustrated copies rather than volumes manufactured by the thousand with well-worn plates and indistinct impressions ; the choicest examples of American printed books, reprinted by the Riverside Press, or of the British printing-offices, exhibited in the typographical beauties of Baskerville and Whittingham—in fact, always *editions de luxe;* uncut copies not *ravished by the binder's plough*, and above all, original editions, if with plates, but if not, then the best printed and the best edited the book market has to offer."

The late Mr. Bohn's catalogue, an enormous bulky volume, weighing many lbs., was supposed to be the biggest in the world. It seemed by actual measurement to be about a foot thick. He was in truth an extraordinary man, combining original taste in all departments of art and literature with singular knowledge. He, like many successful bibliophilists, was a German. His "Bohn's Library" was a truly magnificent enterprise, carried out with extraordinary spirit and ambition. His collection of china was vast. He had also collections of paintings, virtu, books, rarities of every kind, all selected with the same judgment, which at his death were sold at very remunerative prices. He brought to his task powers of tact and energy, and an instinct akin to the political or financial. He appeared to forecast prospective rises in value. Like many others of his countrymen he rose from being a humble assistant in a bookseller's "store."

At all periods the amateur has been eager to indulge in the luxury of a press of his own. There is much to be said for this costly fancy ; for if taste and character are present it is sure to impress itself on the works, and even on the printing. Such form and pressure of the mind reveals itself. This is particularly manifest in the work of Horace Walpole, whose books betray an *elegance* of subject, touch, and sentiment that betokens the man of congenial refinement, and makes them quite distinct from the ordinary work of eminent publishers. His own compositions—such as the pleasant apology for Richard III., and the " Royal and Noble Authors "—are admirably adapted to the mode of expression used. It is a claim on posterity to have issued Gray's Odes. There is a distinct physiognomy in these charming little books. Among them are Lord Whitworth's account of Russia in 1710, Lady Temple's poems, Henault's tragedy " Cornelie," Lord Herbert of Cherbury's Life, trifles by Sir William Jones and Hannah More, and so serious and important a work as the "Anecdotes of Painting." On an average about two hundred copies only were printed of each. Perhaps the rarest is the hieroglyphic Tales, of which only six copies are said to have been printed ; the printer's private copy sold for £16. Rarest perhaps of all are these occasional leaves of congratulatory verses which the virtuoso used to have " worked " off for some visitor of distinction. Kirkgate, his printer for a long period was, however, left by the noble owner without even the slightest mention in his will.

Another important private press was that of Lee Priory, directed by Sir E. Brydges, but not at all so attractive, though the collection is much sought, and brings in good prices. As of course the subject is large enough to be treated in a volume devoted to itself. There were also the Boswell, Philips, and other presses.

A collector of much taste and judgment was the late Mr. John Forster—"mine own fast friend"—whose handsome library at Palace Gate was richly stored with rare and interesting volumes, autographs, and prints, to say nothing of pictures and sketches. The interest of the collection is found—it can be seen at

South Kensington Museum, to which he bequeathed it—in the intimate connection of these treasures with famous men, and particularly with the famous literary personages with whom he had been associated all his life. His own admirable literary work—always of the best and most finished kind—brought him into further connection with literary memorials of every description ; and there was no greater treat than to turn over one of his well-stored portfolios. His artistic friends seemed to have delighted in recording their connection with the many social hours he furnished them, by pleasant, spirited sketches—perhaps the happiest souvenirs that could be devised. Among his books he delighted to have such as had been in the possession of famous writers, and were enriched with signatures and inscriptions. He possessed most of the correspondence of Garrick, filling many great tomes ; and his more precious volumes were bound in a solidly sumptuous style, to do honour to the subject.

There is another class of amateur not so inviting or acceptable. He is figured in the worm which feeds on books. This "prowler" scans the catalogues carefully for anything in *his* line, and there are dealers who purvey for his taste.

In certain booksellers' catalogues this department is often labelled " Facetiæ," supposed by the innocent readers to stand for books of a humorous or Rabelaisian character. In this class might be included " Macaronic " poetry. It is lamentable to relate, however, that there is a demand for books written in Latin and French, and often in very elegant Latin and French, of such a character as to forbid them the freedom of the drawing-room table. There are many such, belonging chiefly to the seventeenth century, and one, a notorious one, by a professor. There have been collectors of these odious things. Selwyn mentions a noble lord of his acquaintance who imported some thirty copies of one of Crebillon's stories, which he disposed of to his loose friends—an instance of rare good nature. There was an English earl who in 1789 " privately " reprinted the works of one Baffo, an Italian writer, styled *Le Rimeur le plus obscène et le plus sale de son temps*, to give away for presents ! It is now, we are told, very scarce. Mr. Beckford enjoyed the privilege of a copy, which was sold for £11, solely upon its claim to *saleté*.

One person not long since dead was held to possess " one of the finest collections " of these things conceivable, and which he later sent to the Continent for sale. " *Facetiæ !* " Heaven save the mark ! We should like to hear the burning tongue of Thomas Carlyle on this abomination.

As to the insect book-worm, few have an idea of the ravages caused by these deadly enemies of books. Their performances excite amazement. As when we see some huge folio—a St. Thomas or Bellarminus— bored straight through with a tiny tunnel, the material in each leaf being cut out and carried off. One such tunnel literally destroys a book. There is something painful in finding leaf after leaf unto the end thus pierced. These depredators are so tiny as to escape detection, though not so long since one was captured *flagrante delicto*, and exhibited to the curious.

§ Of the Shakespeare Folios and Quartos.

HAKESPEARE, so philosophical and occult—inexhaustible, almost, in repaying the student's labours—so overlaid with speculation and commentaries, has naturally furnished a vast contribution to the "libraries of the curious." He stands alone in this fruitfulness ; Racine, Molière, and other great classics offering their text without exciting much controversy. But we must add to this fruitfulness the strange dispensation which attends the greater genius : that sense of mystery and obscurity which prevents us ever reaching, with anything approaching assurance, to the knowledge that we have what Shakespeare really *wrote*. Depending on various and conflicting versions, we are forced to hold the *general* sense, as in the case of the oracles, but the literal and exact form escapes us. There is no authorised *canon* of Shakespeare ; and, strangest of all, the writer of these immortal pieces, unlike other authors, seems to have been least concerned with their publication and editing. He who wrote for all time seems not to have cared to bring his work before the British public, nor to have bethought him of editing, printing, or correcting for the press,

nor of any of the welcome incidents that attend on
authorship.

This curious fate has naturally had extraordinary
results. The plays given to the press by others than
the author, as they were found, picked up, or copied,
naturally reflected their disorderly origin ; each shape
being different, and often opposed to the other. The
plays were clearly printed from notes or recollections,
and rude playhouse copies. Further to complicate
the matter, the compositor did his best to add to the
disorder, and every page of the first folio " teems with
errors." In truth, it is with the works of Shakespeare
as with the Scriptures ; there is no original text, but
only the *best*, or what is thought to be the best. In the
case of the Scriptures there are the various recognised
MSS., the Vatican and others, while of Shakespeare
there are the little quartos and the four folios. None
of these can be shown to have been in relation with
the author or with his original MS. Hence no one has
more special claim to authority than its fellows.
Round the quartos and the four folios there floats
a cloud of almost romantic details. An army of
laborious commentators has given days and nights
and their whole lives, to the comparing of copies, the
counting of lines, the searching for analogous passages,
in other authors, until a flood of light has been shed
upon the question. Behind these are ranged the collectors and their searchings—the story of the rare
quarto, the restorations, and, above all, the "fear-
some" prices. These, it may be conceived, will rise
with every year, owing to the demand in America and
the Colonies.

Nothing is more mysterious than the fate that has
pursued this comparatively modern volume, the First
Folio : works a hundred and a hundred and thirty

years older have fared infinitely better, and have swept
down the rapids of time without damage or wreckage.
But this work is usually found frayed, maimed, soiled,
smeared, imperfect, leaves and sheets torn out in the
middle, the beginning, and end. Almost every copy,
save two or three that can be named, is "made up"
—that is, the defects of one are supplemented from
others.

George Steevens supplies a fair, sensible reason. "Of
all volumes," he says, "those of popular entertainment
are soonest injured.   It would be difficult to name
four folios that are oftener found in dirty, mutilated condition than this first assemblage of Shakespeare's plays,
'God's Revenge against Murder,' 'The Gentleman's
Recreation,' and Johnson's 'Lives of the Highway-
men.'   The folio Shakespeare," goes on Steevens,
"was generally found on the hall tables of mansions,
and that a multitude of his pages 'have this effect of
gravy' may be imputed to the various eatables set out
on the same boards.   I have repeatedly met with *flakes
of pie-crust between the leaves of our author.* These
unctuous fragments, remaining long in close confine-
ment, communicated their grease to several pages
deep on each side of them.   Since our breakfasts have
become less gross, our favourite authors have escaped
with fewer injuries.   I claim to be the first commentator who strove with becoming seriousness to account
for the frequent stains that disgrace the earliest folio
edition, which is now become the most expensive book
in our language.   For," asks the astonished Steevens,
"what other English volume, without plates, and
printed since the year 1600, is now *known to have sold
more than once for thirty-five pounds fourteen shillings ?*"   There is a pleasant quaintness in all this.
He tells us, moreover, that most of the first folios then

extant belonged to ancient families resident in the country.

Every possible adulteration, he tells us, has of late years (that is, sixty years since) been practised "in fitting up copies of this book for sale. When leaves are wanting, they have been reprinted *with battered* types, and foisted into vacancies. When the title has been lost, a spurious one has been fabricated, with a blank space left for the head of Shakespeare, afterwards added for the second, third, or fourth impressions. To conceal these frauds, thick vermilion lines have been usually drawn over the edges of the engravings, and discoloured with tobacco-water till it had assumed the true *jaune antique.* Sometimes leaves have been inserted from the second folio, and, in a known instance, the entire play of Cymbeline, the genuine date being altered. And this is the more easy, as the matter of both editions corresponds exactly page by page and line by line, though differing in words."

It is difficult to account for this craze, or indeed to define the element that is priced so highly. It is not the text, for that is accessible in *facsimile* reprints ; nor is it the scarcity, for there are other works far more rare, yet not so costly. It seems really a compliment to the surpassing merit of the bard himself combined with the other elements. Fine choice copies are also extraordinarily few, and bring increasing prices. It will be interesting to note the steady growth of this amiable mania.

In 1821 a pleasant writer, Mr. Davis, in his "Journey Round the Library of a Bibliomaniac," quotes the prices given for this interesting monument. In 1792 Daly's copy brought £30 ; Heathcote's (title wanting), £37 ; S. Ireland's, in 1801, £14 ; Duke of Roxburghe's,

£100 ; Sebright's, in 1807 (title wanting), £30 ; Stanley's (title also wanting), £37 ; Sir P. Thompson's, in 1815, £41 ; and in 1818, at the Sanders sale, "a fine original copy in a genuine state" brought £121. The third edition is nearly as valuable as the first ; the second is "adulterated" in every page. Droeshout's portrait served for all the four editions. "Good or first impressions of this portrait are valued by judges at about five guineas ; inferior ones are scarcely worth a guinea, as the lines have been crossed over the face to give strength to the impression."

A leading bookseller was offering some years ago a set of the four folios. He gives accurately (though incidentally) copies of the title-pages of each edition, which is interesting, and shows how damages are repaired and the book can be "made up." The third edition, it is known, did not go off briskly, and was, as it were, reissued with the seven additional plays. The prices asked were not too much. The titles are given in full, and will be found interesting ; for, with the quaint titles of the separate plays, they have been abolished by modern editors.

"SHAKESPEARE.—Mr. William Shakespeare's Comedies, Histories, and Tragedies, published according to the true original copies. London, printed by Isaac Iaggard and Ed. Blount. 1623. Folio, first edition, the title containing the portrait and verses opposite to it in *fac-simile*, so well done as to almost defy detection ; otherwise perfect and genuine throughout. Size, 12⅞ × 8¼.

"The second impression. London, printed by Tho. Cotes for Robert Allot, and are to be sold at the Signe of the Blacke Beare in Pauls Churchyard. 1632. Folio, portrait on title and verses opposite. The verses are mended, and a portion filled in, but only an experienced eye could detect it. Some of the end leaves are mended a little at the corners; otherwise perfect and genuine throughout. Size, 12⅜ × 8½.

"The third impression, and unto this impression is added seven plays, never before printed in folio, viz., Pericles, Prince of Tyre; The London Prodigal; The History of Thomas, Lord Cromwell; Sir John Oldcastle, Lord Cobham; The Puritan Widow; A Yorkshire Tragedy; The Tragedy of Locrine. London, printed for P. C., 1664. Folio, portrait, with the verses underneath opposite the title. The portrait, title, and margins of a few leaves at end are mended and filled in, and the dedication is entirely in *fac-simile*, the whole most beautifully done; otherwise perfect and genuine throughout. Size, 12⅞ × 8½.

"The fourth edition. London, printed for H. Herringman, E. Brewster, and Rd. Bentley, at the Anchor, in the New Exchange, the Crane, in St. Paul's Churchyard, and in Russel Street, Covent Garden. 1685. Folio, portrait and verses opposite the title in *fac-simile*, beautifully done. The title has the bottom corner slightly mended; otherwise perfect and genuine throughout. Size, 14¼ × 9.

"A very good set. The four volumes beautifully and uniformly bound, by Riviere, in the best French morocco, paned sides, full gilt backs, and gilt edges."

Four hundred and fifty pounds was the price! But it is clear these were ordinary things, without pedigree—"not born," as is said of an inferior German prince. "Perhaps," says Beloe, "there is no book in the English language which has risen so rapidly in value as the first editions of the works of our great national poet. I can remember a very fine copy to have been sold for five guineas. I could once have purchased a superb one for nine guineas. At the sale

of Dr. Monro's books it was purchased for thirteen
guineas ; and two years since I was present when
thirty-six guineas was demanded for a copy." But
there are notable copies of noble dimensions,
and which can be traced from owner to owner,
each having its story, its life and adventures, as it
were ; while of the owner or possessor something
curiously interesting might be detailed. George
Daniel (the predecessor of Lady Burdett Coutts in
the ownership of a famous copy) had a curious history—himself one of the strange combative bibliomaniacs ; while George Steevens's copy would suggest
the history of a learned and stormy collector. Of his
" second folio," now in the King's Library of the British
Museum, this history is given :—" This had belonged
to King Charles I., who with his own hand had written
in it these words : " Dum spiro spero, C. R." And
Sir Henry Herbert, to whom the King presented it the
night before his execution, had also written : " Ex
Dono serenissimi Regis Car. Servo suo Humiliss.—T.
Herbert."

This precious volume came into the possession of
Dr. Askew—a well-known scholar—" a fine copy " it
was called—and at his sale it was purchased by
Steevens for the sum of £5, 10s. Yet the new owner
says, " I gave this *enormous* sum." Askew had
bought it at Dr. Mead's sale for two guineas and a
half. At Steevens's sale it was bought for George III.
for eighteen guineas, thus oddly returning into royal
custody. There is another royal association connected
with this copy. Steevens had written in it that its
former owner, Sir T. Herbert, was Master of the Revels
to King Charles I., whereas it was Sir Henry Herbert who held that office. This mistake was immediately detected and ratified by George III. in his

own hand, and thus this interesting copy possesses the autographs of two sovereigns of England. Beneath the words of Mr. Steevens his Majesty has written thus : " This is a mistake, he [Sir T. Herbert] having been Groom of the Bed Chamber to King Charles I. ; but Sir Henry Herbert was Master of the Revels."

Steevens supposes that the original edition was not more than 250 copies. Before 1649 they were so scarce that King Charles, Mr. Malone says, was obliged to content himself with a copy of the second edition ; though it is likely his Majesty preferred a revised and more carefully printed edition to the old one. Ten shillings, it is supposed, was the selling price.

But now for the successive appearances of these four folios in solemn sets ; for " no gentleman's Shakespearean library should be without them." At Heber's sale in 1834 we find the four, the first receiving this handsome panegyric : " An extraordinarily fine copy, and *one of the tallest* known." This had been Lord Denbigh's, and had come to him from the Broadley sale. It fetched, however, only £57, 15s.— a huge price then. But it lacked the Ben Jonson verses, and the title and his imprint torn off, with other blemishes. The second folio brought £9, 15s., the third £26, 10s., and the fourth only £4, 4s., about £100 covering the whole.*

---

* The reader will be amused to see the jealous nicety with which the marks and tokens of this great book have been set down. The following is Mr. Frederick Locker Lampson's " collation " of his own copy :—

SHAKESPEARE, WILLIAM.—Mr. William Shakespeares Comedies, Histories, and Tragedies. Published according to the true originall copies. London, Printed by Isaac Iaggard & Ed. Blount. 1623. Colophon : Printed at the charges of W.

At the well-known sale of Mr. Dunn-Gardiner, a gentleman who admitted nothing but what was choice and as nearly perfect as possible, a set of the four folios were sold. They were thus described :—

"Shakespeare. First edition. This copy, from the libraries of Mr. Hibbert and Mr. Wilks, is one of the finest copies known, and without doubt the finest that has ever been sold by public auction. It may, though bound in russia, with border of gold, in the quiet and good taste of Montague, be called in its original state, and may be fairly stated, as far as a book can be so designated, an immaculate copy.

"Shakespeare's (Mr. William) Comedies, &c., as before. The second impression, russia, gilt edges. The leaf with the lines preceding the title is in this copy shorter than the work itself, that being unusually large.

"Shakespeare's (Mr. William) Comedies, &c., as before. Third edition.

Jaggard, Ed. Blount, J. Smithweeke, and W. Aspley, 1623. Folio. A, 8 leaves : A—Cc 2, Aa 3—6 : b—g 6 : gg 1—8 : h—i 6 : f 1—6 : t—x 6 : ¶ 1—6 : ¶¶ 6 : ¶¶¶ 1 : aa—gg 3 : gg 2—6 : hh—tt i : tt 3 : vv 6 : x 1—6 yy 1 : y 2—6 : zz—bbb 6. In sixes. Title Ai : Dedication by " John Heminge " and " Henry Condell," " To the most noble," &c., A 2 : Address " To the great variety," &c., by the same, A 3, *recto, verso* blank : verses to Shakespeare's memory by L. Digges, 1 M : Ben Jonson and Hugh Holland, 3 leaves, verses of 1st and 3d blank. " The names of the Principall Actors " and " A Catalogue " of two leaves, *versos* blank : The Comedies, pp. 303 and a blank page : Histories, pp. 232, " The Tragedy of Troylus," &c., not mentioned in the catalogue of contents, 15 leaves, the second only paged, and that incorrectly, as 79 and 80 : Tragedies, pp. 309 (misprinted 993), last page blank.

Beneath the titles and occupying two-thirds of the title-page is a portrait of Shakespeare by Martin Droeshout, facing which, upon the opposite page, are ten lines of verse on the author, addressed " to the reader," and numbered " B 1." The volume measures 13 in. × 8⅝.

"Shakespeare's (Mr. William) Comedies, &c., as before, to which is added seven plays never before printed in folio, &c. Fourth edition. The same portrait was used for this edition, after having been retouched ; it here occupies the upper part of a leaf preceding the title, having the metrical lines beneath it."

Here begin all the niceties of folio measurements, marginal width, pedigree, and the rest. This first folio measures 12⅜ × 8 inches, and could be traced to the Hibbert Collection, where it had been bought for £85, and to the Wilks ditto, where it had leaped up to £155. At the Dunn-Gardner sale it was redeemed from captivity for £250 by Mr. Huth, in whose library it now reposes. In the choice Corser Collection, sold in 1868, there was, of course, found a fine quartette of folios. The first, described as "a very desirable copy of this ever-to-be-coveted volume, was, with the exception of the letterpress of the title-page and the corners of a few leaves which have been admirably supplied in *fac-simile* by Harris as almost to defy detection, quite complete." It was tall and broad, measuring fully 12⅝ by 8¼ inches. It fetched £160. The second folio excited attention as being "a genuine *unsophisticated* copy in its original state, remarkably tall, measuring 13½ by 8⅞ inches." It had this oddity ; the imprint in this copy is different from any hitherto described, the words "at this shop" being omitted. It brought £49, while the third fetched £77, and the fourth £12 ; total, £398.

But now to introduce a more distinguished set still. In 1880 Mr. Quaritch was offering an extraordinary collection of Shakespeare editions. There were no less than three copies of the first folio, the first "*a good and sound copy*," desirable and perfect all to two leaves. It measured 12¼ by 8 inches, and its price was

£136. It came from the Brand Hollis Library. The next copy was also defective by two leaves, but was "*a very fine tall copy, of unusual size,*" measuring 13⅛ by 8¾, from a well-known library ; a difference which exactly doubled the price, which was £300. The third—but let us hear the vendor himself : "With title, portrait, verses, and all preliminary leaves in splendid original condition, untouched by the hand of any modern renovator ; a very fine and large copy (12⅝ by 8⅜ inches), red morocco extra, gilt edges, by Bedford, enclosed in a red morocco case with key. Price £880."

"To some this price for a fine copy may seem surprisingly large, but not to those who are aware that this is probably the only copy, undoctored, genuine, sound and fine, which can come into the market for probably another quarter of a century. Even if the Huth Library had been sold, as at first announced, it would merely have produced *a short and not over-desirable* first Shakespeare. Since the beginning of this century, only *four perfect and satisfactory* copies (besides the above) have been sold, and all but this are now in safe keeping, inaccessible to many eager purchasers on both sides of the Atlantic.

"Should it be considered that this first folio, besides being the first authorised edition of Shakespeare's plays, contains *editiones principes* of no less than twenty pieces, we thus learn to estimate the real value of *a fine, unmixed, unsophisticated* copy. As all the first editions in this volume amount to twenty, it may be said that a set of separate first editions of any twenty plays would cost from £500 to £4000." Note the pleasant bibliophilist phrase. There was also for sale "a fine large, genuine, *undoctored* copy" of the second impression, measuring 12⅝ by 8⅜ inches.

But there was yet another second folio, which claimed to be "*probably the finest copy in existence,*" measuring 13¼ by 8⅜ inches, and in as *pure*, clean condition as when issued from the press. The old binding is also in a fine state of preservation. Sir W. Tite's copy sold, we are told, for £45, G. Smith's for £58, and Daniel's, "*the largest ever seen,*" for £148. For this £84 was asked. There was also a third folio, "a fine and sound copy," measuring 12⅛ by 8⅜ inches, in Bedford's binding; portrait, "with the verses printed upside down above it." A hundred and sixty pounds was demanded for it. The fourth was to be had for £25. Thus we might equip ourselves here with the four fine copies complete for the modest sum of nearly £1200. But this did not exhaust the Shakespearian treasures of our bibliopole. There was a rare supplementary stock of the dainty quartos, fifteen in number, early "Hamlets," first edition of "Midsummer Night's Dream" (1600), and a "Taming of the Shrew" UNCUT—conceive it !—rare, if not unique in this state ; and for the fifteen, five hundred guineas was asked. Seventeen hundred pounds for an armful of old books !

When that eminent and noble amateur the Duke of Roxburghe determined to add a first folio to his collection, it seems to have been a nervous and serious business. He empowered his friend Mr. Nichol to bid for him at the sale, saying in his letter : "If I am not present, I desire you will be excessively bold ; and if I should be present, your courage need not fail you till you see me turn my back and walk out of the room." Which sounds something like the soldier before battle, "If I should fall," &c. He, however, attended the struggle in person. At the agitating moment of the bidding, we are told that "his Grace had retired to one end of the room, coolly to view the issue of the contest. The biddings rose quickly to twenty guineas —a great sum in former times—but the Duke was not to be daunted or defeated. A slip of paper was handed to him upon which the propriety of discontinuing the contest was suggested. His Grace took out his pencil and wrote on the same slip, " *Lay on, Macduff.*" The Duke was of course declared victor, and marched off triumphantly with the volume under his arm, having secured the precious volume for " about £35." It measured 13¼ by 8⅛ inches. This copy was sold at his sale for £100 to the Duke of Devonshire, in whose library it now is. Sir M. Sikes, we are told, would have gone to £80 for the treasure.

But at the famous Perkins sale in 1873, where everything was of the choicest and finest, there were to be seen the four folios, justly described as "*a superb set.*" All were bound in crimson morocco, with joints and gilt leaves, and by measurement were 13⅛ inches by 8¼ inches for the first, 13 inches by 9 inches for the second, 13½ inches by 8⅝ inches for the third, and 14 inches by 9 inches for the fourth. It was noted, with just pride, that the first folio was of exactly the same dimensions as that of the famous Daniel copy, while the third was "an eighth of an inch *taller!*"

This Perkins first folio ushered in the series of startling prices. It had come from the Dent Collection, and now fetched what seems the immense sum of £585.

The great actor Kemble had, of course, a copy among his dramatic treasures at his sale, which was bought by Mr. Boswell, the Shakespearian, the biographer's second son, for £112—a huge price sixty years since. But then, was it not very nicely inlaid throughout, bound in venetian morocco, enclosed in a russia bookcase?

The sale of his miscellaneous library was commenced by Mr. Evans on the 26th of January, and terminated on the 26th of February. It contained some extremely curious articles, but the rarest of his dramatic works were not brought to the hammer, having been previously selected and purchased by the Duke of Devonshire for two thousand guineas. The books fetched very good prices at the sale. He seems, indeed, to have been a most indefatigable annotator, and had compiled MS. indexes to several of his books. The total amount of the ten days' sale was £2665, 12s. The Drury Lane Playbills from 1751 to 1818, sixty-five vols. half-bound, with MS. indexes, notes by Mr. Kemble, and extracts from an unpublished diary of Hopkins, the prompter, father of Mrs. Kemble, were sold for £120, 15s. A similar one of Covent Garden, from 1758 to 1819, sixty-two vols., brought 68, 5s. These sets of bills excited much curiosity, and gave rise to much speculation as to the price they would fetch. It was a very general impression that they ought to have been deposited in the British Museum. Mr. Booth, the bookseller, was the highest bidder, and is understood to have purchased them for Sir Gregory Page Turner. His Majesty sent a commission of seventy guineas for the Drury Lane set, and the Duke of Devonshire one hundred and fifty guineas for the two sets. The room was excessively crowded.

Mr. Boswell, the younger, when he purchased his copy of the desired folio, seems to have regarded his acquisition with mixed feelings. " *Ipse miserimus* gave a much larger sum at Mr. Kemble's sale, but I could not bring myself to a cold calculation of the value of a copy which was at once a memorial of Shakespeare and of

Kemble." *Ipse miserimus!* Surely a lugubrious tone for an ardent collector, such as Mr. Boswell was. At his sale it was disposed of at a small increase, for £120.

Lord Spencer, that most fastidious of amateurs, felt that he must have a folio to make his happiness complete. But as a typographical performance he ever felt that it was not in harmony with its nobler brethren, and his librarian thus apologises for its presence :— " The knowing," he says, " need not be surprised at the price and importance of this impression ; yet a tougher question is rarely agitated amongst bibliographers than as to what constitutes a fine and genuine copy of it. After having seen a copy lately obtained by Mr. Grenville, and that yet more recently by Mr. James Boswell, and carefully examined the present, I am abundantly convinced that this is after all but a disagreeable book. As to typographical execution, every leaf of the present copy was carefully examined by the late George Steevens for his Lordship, a task requiring no ordinary skill."

Mr. Garrick was fortunate enough to pick up a copy of the second folio from "Mr. Payne of the Meusegate "—in York, I presume. "After the death of our Roscius," says Mr. Steevens, " it should have accompanied his collection of old plays to the British Museum, but had been taken out of his library, and has not been heard of since." This he secured for the small sum of £1, 16s.* It, however, was said to

* In a bookseller's catalogue I have seen the seventh volume of Warburton's small Shakespeare. It had belonged to Garrick, and his wife had written in it, "This Book *whent with us* to Althorp on Dec. the 30th 1778 : my husband never travelled without some work of Shakespeare." How interesting is this, and illustrative too !

Turning over the catalogue of Mr. Garrick's library, the com-

want the Ben Jonson verses. His beautiful collection of plays, thus generously bequeathed, formed with great assiduity during the course of his theatrical life, is uniformly bound and distinguished by his initials, and prompted that charming handbook to the English Drama, " The Specimens " of Charles Lamb, which has educated several generations in dramatic literature. The copy of the first folio, however, could scarcely be ranked in the collection of " Old Plays," which were all of the separate " little quarto " pattern, and more than forty years later it reappeared in the sale of Garrick's library, where it brought £34, 2s. 6d. In 1844 it again changed hands, and was resold to Mr. Tolley for £86.

Garrick's second folio long after was offered for sale, and seems to have been a " folio of pretension " from the description, for it was "a fine tall copy in russia extra, gilt edges, with arms stamped in gold on the sides." Thirty guineas was the price asked. " A copy of unusual interest, partly from the fact that it belonged to David Garrick and contains his bookplate, and partly because copies are rarely found with such large margins. It measures 13½ by 9 inches, and has some

position whereof was evidence of his accomplished mind, I came upon a book, " Le Jardin des Racines Grecs," with this interesting little note in Latin :—" The gift of Gilbert Walmesley of Lichfield to Garrick at the age of sixteen, on the condition that he shall every day learn a page by heart, word for word, so that he shall be always ready to repeat without book and in the same words.—3d July 1732."

The worthy Dibdin makes this reckless charge against Garrick without offering any proof. " Garrick had free access to the library at Dulwich College, founded by Alleyn, and pillaged it without scruple or remorse. He did pretty nearly the same thing with Sir Thomas Hanmer's library. No wonder, therefore, that the Garrick Collection, now deposited in the British Museum, presents at once an object of vexation, envy, and despair to the bibliomaniac." This is incredible, as such spoliation would not have been tolerated.

of the leaves with rough uncut edges, in which state
no copy is on record but that of George Daniel, which
was the largest example known, and sold for £148.
The Perkins copy, measuring half an inch less than
this, brought £44; and the Ouvry copy, which was
smaller still, sold for £46. The verse opposite the
title and a portion of the last leaf are in admirable
fac-simile, and a part of the margin of the title has
been skilfully repaired."

This "uncut edge" in so old a book is really a
rare and remarkable instance, for it proves that the
book had not been bound, and had escaped the shears.
It is a nice question whether the original sheets of so
old a book constitute the identity, and whether the
substitution of a sheet, practically the same, makes
any legal difference. The truth is, the original sheets
belong to each other, and acquire from the companionship a special cast—they are found under the same
atmosphere, the same pressure, the same sewing and
binding, the same "lie," as it were. A new intruder
is a disturber, and does not belong to the party. It is
curious, too, how this is betrayed to the skilful and
practised eye. Mr. Croker, suspecting from the text
some suppression in the second edition of Boswell's
"Tour," took the book to pieces, and discovered "a
cancel"—that is, only a portion of a sheet had been
sewn in.

Another notable copy was the Grenville one, now in
our Museum. This came from Sanders' in Fleet
Street sale in 1819, and measures 12⅞ by 8⅜ inches.
Mr. Grenville paid £121, 16s. for it. The Stowe copy
was another giant—12⅜ by 8½ inches—and was sold for
£76. There were copies sold by the Sothebys in three
successive years — 1854, 1855, 1856—the first 12¼
by 8¼ inches; the last 12⅞ by 8½, which was bought

by Lord Gosford for £164, 17s. The copy sold in 1855 was of extraordinary interest from its having "two cancelled leaves" in the play of " As You Like It."

In the Hartley sale, held in June 1885, was offered a " first folio," about which, it was rumoured, hung a curious history. It was sold at some rather obscure sale, and adroitly manipulated by the system of "knock out," being bought for £20, to be later disposed of by the fraternity among themselves for a much larger sum. This sacrifice, produced by these "shady" tactics, was illustrated by the price brought at this unlawful sale, which was no less a sum than £480, or, as another account says, £525.

But we now are arrived at the really great day for the folio—the greatest since Mr. Herringman issued his volume in 1623. This was on the occasion of the sale of Mr. George Daniel's books in 1864, after his demise. This well-known critic, writer, and collector had fixed himself at Islington, and dwelt in that curious old tower which still rises, though in sad decay, and which has ever had a series of literary tenants from Goldsmith's time. Never was there such a collection of rarities and uniques offered, and never again will collector be offered such opportunities, or be so prompt to avail himself of them. The sale occupied ten days, but "the Shakespeare day," as it was called in the *Times,* drew an eager and excited audience. There were seen abundance of the rare Shakespeare quartos, that are well-nigh *introuvable,* which the wary and enterprising Daniel had secured in lavish profusion—rare and dainty little quartos, many of them with but two and three companions in the world. But resplendent among them all were the four grand folios. The "first" had been in the possession of Daniel Moore, Esq., F.R.S., and

by him had been bequeathed to William H. Booth,
who also left it by will to John Gage Rokewode, from
whose hands it passed to Mr. Daniel. An enthusiastic critic fell into raptures over it, called it "a marvellous copy, of unrivalled beauty, unquestionably the
finest that can ever occur again for public sale. The
copy will to all future time possess a world-wide
reputation. It was cased in beautiful old russia
binding, and preserved in a russia leather case."
It was by measurement a grand specimen. After a
spirited and exciting contest, in which the price rose
and rose, the astonishingly unheard-of sum of £716, 2s.
was bid by Mr. Radcliffe, to whom it was knocked
down. When it was known that the prize had been
carried off by Miss Burdett Coutts, the room re-
sounded with acclamation. The treasure now reposes
in a stately case made out of the wood of Herne's
oak. Nor is this price excessive, for it is admitted by
experts that in all "points"—condition, dimensions,
and general proportion—it could not be matched.

In its way the "second folio" was no less meritorious, and possibly the finest of its generation.
With a quaint enthusiasm the owner thus expatiated
on its charms. It is like a little biography :—"This
genuine and beautiful copy was bought by Mr. Thorpe
at the sale of the library at Nevill Holt, Leicester-
shire, and bought of him by me this the 16th day
of September, my birthday." Adds the collector,
1848, "*I never saw its equal for soundness and
size.*" It was, moreover, the largest example
known, and brought the surprising, for a second
folio, price of £142. The third went for £46, and
the fourth for £21. Lord Charlemont's first folio
was pronounced to be one of the finest known,
measuring 12¾ by 8⁵⁄₁₆ inches, arrayed handsomely

in red morocco with tooled borders.   It fetched
£455.*

The grand copy and its price was destined to retain
its undisturbed glories for over twenty years, until the
year 1881 came round—that of the Thorold or Syston
Park sale.   This copy shows that the appreciation of
the precious volume has been carried to the highest
point of finish.   This copy was described with a tender
minuteness, as though it had been some old picture by
Raphael or Rembrandt.   First it is proudly claimed
to be "*the largest and finest copy known,*" or rather
would be, save for some trifling but sad blemishes.   The
titles and verses had been very neatly inlaid, and,
owing to some defect in the paper, it was carefully
computed that about eight or ten letters were deficient
in three of the leaves.   An expert declared that these
restorations could not be detected by ordinary ob-
servers, so skilfully were they effected ; but in looking
close it might be made out that the " Mr. William " of
the title-page had been put in in *fac-simile ;* the last five
letters of " Shakespere " are also supplied.   " Tails "
of letters in the name of the printer, Jaggard, and one
of the figures in the date, are also restorations.   Notwithstanding these blemishes—serious in bibliomaniacal eyes—the present " very large copy," was found
to be by measurement 13⅜ inches by 8½ inches, or a
quarter of an inch taller than Lady Burdett Coutts'
famous copy.   It was interesting to see that noble
lady busily scanning the proportions of the rival copy.
Another extraordinary incident connected with this
copy is that some of the leaves are " uncut," on the

* Copies have turned up in a strange, odd way.   In 1857 one
was discovered in a carpenter's shop at Maidenhead, which had
been bought for a few shillings at a country auction.   Another
turned up in Germany.

top, front, and bottom margins, which enables us to
know the exact size of the original edition as issued.
In ordinary cases the top margin is $\frac{3}{4}$ of an inch, the
front $\frac{11}{16}$ths of an inch, and the bottom $1\frac{1}{4}$ inch—precious details, that may excite a smile, but are elements
of value when dealing with hundreds of pounds. This
copy was further adorned by a fine red morocco
"jacket" from the hands of Roger Payne. It sold
for the large sum of £590.

Is the collector happy or wretched who can gaze
on the four folios—his own—in "fine condition,"
"pure copies," but representing an outlay of £1000?
He has virtually to pay £50 a year interest during
his natural life for this enjoyment. Indeed, I have
heard one bewail his folly bitterly, and wish he had
his money back again. Much comes, however, to
the collector who can watch and wait, and he need
then have no qualms of conscience. There are
the ambitious, who set their minds to the attaining
some grand post or alliance, bearing in mind their
Shakespeare declaration, that the "hatted dame" is
as attainable with daring and perseverance as the
lowly maid. In this spirit I determined to watch and
wait patiently, and secure, not only a folio, but the
four, and in less than two years success crowned me!
I began with a second folio, and found an honest,
respectable copy, lacking, of course, portrait, title,
and last two leaves, which could be "supplied in
fac-simile." For him I paid £2, 10s. Next came
a damaged fourth folio, secured for "a song," but
which, exchanged, brought a perfect one at a cost of
£7. Next followed a first folio for £12, wanting a play
at the end and the title, but having all the "prefatory
matter." Lastly came the third, for £8. The total
was under £30. These will soon be put in order. I

2 M

picked up also some fine russia bindings, discarded by the late Mr. Bedford for some folios he was treating, and had them reclothed. Now here was a modest outlay, unattended by prickings of conscience, and the quartette, as they stand, are worth a goodly sum. This little bit of bibliographical adventure is mentioned *pour encourager les autres.*

It will amuse the reader to give an instance of what minute and laborious investigation is brought to test the merits and defects of these precious tomes, and reasonably, considering the vast prices given. Here we find a particular copy thus jealously scrutinised. The Ben Jonson verses are "neatly inlaid," that is, "inset" in new paper so deftly as to escape the ordinary reader's eye. In the title-page the words " Mr. William" are supplied in *fac-simile*, and the scraps of paper on which they are displayed are neatly joined to the rest, matching in colour and texture ; while the last five letters of the name, "peare," are also reproduced, only the "Shakes" being original. This is counting after the principles of Sir John's stocking. But mark this—"the *tails* of the letter G in the name of the printer (Herringman) and of the figure 3 in the date have also been added."

We speak of the "four first folios" or of the "first four folios" (according as the grammarians shall decide), but in strict truth there are five. The third was issued in 1663, but did not "go off," so the publisher in the following year added seven spurious plays and supplied a new title. It must be noted of this first third edition that the copy has the portrait in the centre of the title-page, and the Ben Jonson verses face it on another leaf. "*In this state it is excessively rare,*" says Mr. Lilly, who protests that it is unknown to Lowndes "*in this peculiar and pristine state."* Nor does "J. Lilly" recall the sale of any copy save one, which he sold to Mr. Dunn-Gardner, and which is now in the Huth Library. The reader will admit that so far few known works offer such perplexing oddities. But there is yet another surprise. Editions may legitimately differ, but copies of the same edition do not. Yet it has now come out that there are copies of this mysterious first folio which disagree. How strange it is that its paging should be all astray and capricious! The numerals do not follow, and many are doubled ; many more are left out, as though we went, say, from 10 to 15. But, most singular of all, there are copies of the first edition itself which so vary from each other as to have different readings. Thus it is said Messrs. Longmans once had a copy in which, instead of Roderigo's speech in "Othello" (p. 333), the line ran "And Hell gnaw his bones." A Bishop Butler possessed a copy with a *proof leaf* of a page in "Hamlet," and Messrs. Arch of Cornhill had one with the date 1622 instead of 1623.

Mr. O. Halliwell Philipps has a copy of the first folio, containing misprints, which indicate the priority of the impression.* Thus, on the second column of p. 172 of the Histories, at line 13 *and* is misprinted *add*, and in the second line following, *tis* instead of *kiss*, the correct readings being found in all other copies excepting in one in the library of the Earl of Ellesmere. These variations are of course of no value in themselves. Mr. Lenox, the well-known American collector, possessed a copy which had many variations, even in the signatures, and the title-page had the date of 1622 instead of 1623 ; but

* This, we may presume, is the copy which cost him £410 in 1867.

it is suspiciously "inlaid" below this date, and the owner cautiously adds, "If by this means the last figure has been tampered with, the alteration is very successfully concealed." As to how these things are to be accounted for I can offer no suggestion except it be from carelessness. It is sad and perplexing to think that this famous volume is one of the worst printed in the world. The book might almost be said to be unique in this respect. Professor Craik made some calculations, and discovered that there were some twenty mistakes in each page, which made a total of nearly 20,000 ! It is indeed stated on the title that it was "published according to the true and original copies," but it is believed that these were burnt with the Globe Theatre ; and the mistakes in the sense and spelling, and the startling discrepancies between the folio and the previous quartos, show that the edition was fashioned exactly as we might expect, from stray and imperfect copies, recollections of actors, and such printed copies as could be got. Thus, Mr. Dyce tells us of the "Hamlet," as it appears in the edition of 1623 :—"While the editors added con-siderably to the prose dialogue in Act II., Sc. 2, inserted elsewhere lines and words which are wanting in the quartos of 1604, &c., and rectified various mistakes of those quartos, they—not to mention minor mutilations of the text, some of them accidental—omitted in the course of the play about a hundred and sixty verses (including nearly the whole of the fourth scene of Act IV.), and left out a portion of the prose dialogue in Act V., Sc. 2, besides allowing a multi-tude of errors to creep in *passim.*" Mr. Collier says : —"Any editor who should content himself with re-printing the folio, without large additions from the quartos, would present but an imperfect notion of the

drama as it came from the hand of the poet. The
text of 'Hamlet' is, in fact, only to be obtained from
a comparison of the editions in quarto and folio."

Few can have an idea of the drudgery of collation
and the conscientious enthusiasm that will carry a
book-lover through the monotonous labour of comparing two long works line by line. When the reprint of the first folio was issued, it was hailed with
delight as an aid to students, though published at five
guineas. It was soon discovered, however, that,
though a reprint of a book that teemed with errors,
it had a fresh crop of its own ! All faith being gone,
no one could rely on it, as the mistakes were unascer-
tained. To make all clear, Mr. William Upcott in
the year 1821 undertook a laborious collation of the
reprint with the folio, and with the following result :—
" Four months," he writes, " and twenty-three days
were occupied during my leisure moments, at the
suggestion of our late librarian, Professor Porson, in
reading and comparing the *pretended* reprinted *fac-
simile first* edition. With what accuracy it passed
through the press, the following pages (26 folio leaves),
noting 368 typographical errors, will show."

The booksellers, who had expended a large sum on
the reprint, when they had heard of this grew alarmed,
and made many overtures for the purchase of the MS. ;
and " Mr. Upcott was induced to part with it to Arch
& Co., from whom he expected a handsome remune-
ration ; but all he got was a single copy of the work.
This copy, however, he disposed off to Perry (of the
Chronicle) for six guineas, at whose sale it brought
twelve."

The well-known rude and coarse portrait by Droeshout has been the subject of discussion and debate,
filling books and pamphlets. Every line on it has been

scanned and appraised. It has been searched with magnifying glasses and reproduced with laborious care. It has been found that there are " states " of this print, and that the shading of the forehead was deepened for the later editions. Nearly every copy offered for sale lacks this portrait ; to find it separate is therefore hopeless ; even a damaged impression would fetch a great sum. A *fac-simile* is priced at £2, 10s. Mr. Boaden wrote a volume in which he compared all the known portraits of Shakespeare, the Chandos, &c., and others. I fancy it would pay an engraver to re-engrave it with the minutest care, line for line, and issue impressions on old fly-leaves.*

* Mr. Lenox writes that the common description of the genuine state, that the shading is expressed by single uncrossed lines is incorrect, the genuine portrait being known by observing that the cross lines do not occur on the right side of the face. The cross lines were added for the fourth edition. Among the "fifteen hundred rarities " collected by Mr. O. Halliwell Philipps to illustrate Shakespeare, and preserved at Hollingbury Copse, is a proof copy of the Droeshout portrait of 1623, and is the only likeness of Shakespeare in existence which has come down to us in an original unaltered state. " No other copy of the engraving in this reliable state has yet been discovered, the only ones in all other libraries being those taken from a retouched plate. The latter is one of the only three impressions known of the title-page of the edition of 1632 before the spelling of the word *coppies* was altered, a circumstance which, although apparently trivial, is of value as showing that it includes one of the earliest impressions from the plate after it had been used for the first folio." Of this portrait Mr. Fairholt wrote: "The portrait in this state of the engraving is remarkable for clearness of tone, the shadows being very delicately rendered, so that the light fails upon the muscles of the face with a softness not to be found in the ordinary impressions. This is particularly visible in the arch under the eye, and in the muscles of the mouth ; the expression of the latter is much altered in the later states of the plate by the enlargement of the up-turned moustache, which hides and destroys the true character of this part of the face. The whole of the shadows have been darkened by cross-hatching and coarse dotting, particularly on the chin ; this gives a coarse and undue prominence to some parts of the portrait, the forehead

The passion for these early editions, and the devouring fanatical craze led, not unnaturally, to a whole chapter of forgeries. The story of the Ireland forgeries is familiar, carried out, as it was, with such enterprise and apparent ingenuity, to the extent of imposing on a generation ; only a few competent scholars declining to accept what seemed to them a transparent imposture. Some time ago collections of these " original " efforts were being offered for sale. It seems that one such bantling was actually made a present of by the forger to a friend, as if strangely indifferent to the propriety of his gift. " These *specimens of my Shakespearian fabrication*," he wrote, " are presented to my friend Mr. Moncreiff with best regards.—W. H. Ireland." We might as well conceive the late Mr. Fauntleroy, if happily pardoned, giving a friend with best regards one of his "*imitations* " of Miss Young's signature.*

particularly. In this early state of the plate the hair is darker than any of the shadows on the head, and flows softly and naturally ; in the retouched plate the shadow is much darker than the roots of the hair, imparting a swelled look to the head and giving the hair the appearance of a raised wig. It is remarkable that no shadow falls across the collar ; this omission and the general low tone of colour in the engraving, may have induced the retouching and strengthening which has injured the true character of the likeness, which, in its original state, is far more worthy of Ben Jonson's commendatory lines."

* This *cadeau* took the shape of a 4to volume, containing a series of seventeen original fabrications by W. H. Ireland, specially collected and neatly arranged, with autograph notes describing each specimen by himself. And the contents consisted of :—1. Tracings from the authenticated signatures of Shakespeare. 2. Three fabricated signatures of Shakespeare. 3. Tracing from an authenticated signature of Queen Elizabeth. 4. Fabricated signature of the Queen. 5. Acrostic on the name of Elizabeth, signed by Shakespeare. 6. Acrostic on the name of Mary, Queen of Scots, signed by W. S. 7. Spurious signature of Lord Southampton. 8. Facetious Letter to William Cowley, the player, signed by W. S. 9. Singular Portrait of

If we take some of these things in our hand and scrutinise them, we shall be astonished to note how poor and clumsy the imitation is, how feeble and modern the characters. At the present day such could not be even attempted. The late Mr. Henry Bradshaw detected the forged "Codex Sinaiticus" simply by the smell, when separating the genuine leaves.

A much more skilful and serious attempt was that which was known as "The Corrector's Folio," introduced by the late scholar, J. Payne Collier. Its history, as told by himself, was as follows :—In the year 1847, when turning over some old books in a shop in the Seven Dials, he lighted on an old copy of the second folio, which he thought might serve for "making up" some deficiencies in his own. He paid 30s. for it. It was, as usual, "much cropped and very greasy," and did not suit his purpose. By laborious investigations he traced it to the family of Gray at Upton Court, where one Perkins, who may have been connected with the stage, was living a few years after the date on the folio. It seems extraordinary that the pages of a work such as this, covered with MS. corrections, should not at once have attracted the wary eye of our collector. But it was not until later, he said, that he noted it. It was illustrated from beginning to end with marginal notes or "corrections." These

Shakespeare, of which Ireland writes : "The above document was enclosed in the foregoing epistle, and christened by the believers in the MSS. as a witty conundrum invented by Shakespeare!" 10. Tracing from Heminge's authentic autograph. 11. Spurious signature of John Heminge. 12. The jug watermark. 13. First signature of Shakespeare produced, and affixed to the spurious deed of Michel Fraser, on vellum. 14. Signature of Fraser written with the left hand (on vellum). 15. Shakespeare's signature annexed to the Fraser deed, with the Quintin seal. 16 and 17. Spurious signatures affixed to the deeds purporting to be between Shakespeare and Lowin and Condell the players (on vellum).

became the sensation of the hour. The writing was presumed to be contemporary ; some one, probably with the original MS. copy before him, had corrected the text. The Duke of Devonshire defrayed the expenses of printing. But at the British Museum there were some shrewd and competent men, who, when the original was submitted to them, pronounced it an imposition. They found by chemical tests that the writing was not in *ink*, but in a sort of water-colour mixed to imitate old ink, while underneath the characters had been first traced in pencil and imperfectly rubbed out ! There were many other certain indications of the forgery, but that one was sufficient. An old and learned scholar like Mr. Collier is entitled to indulgence, and it would be ungracious to hold him accountable for the imposition. In any case, one would prefer to say nothing ; only it is well known that the fanatical passions of some scholars has led them to break through all restraints, much as some eminent mineralogists will not be trusted alone in the cabinets of the curious. In Mr. Collier's case it would be affectation to deny the suspicion that attaches to his attempts to appropriate discoveries brought in aid of his side of the controversy.*

We now pass from the folios to the little quarto plays, and nothing is more interesting than the study

---

* In the catalogue of his late sale there was a copy of the " Taming of the Shrew," on whose title was a " curious contemporary MS. note"—" 1607 *played by the author*," the rest being unfortunately "*cropped* by the binder," probably the name of the character he played, with more of the kind. When the rare " Hamlet " was discovered, it is significant that he declared that some ten or twelve years before he had "a large portion" of a copy of this very edition put into his hands, mysteriously formed of " fly-leaves and linings of bindings." Strange to say, he refused to buy it for the modest price of £10, saying he had the use of the Duke's copy, and there was, moreover, a reprint.

of the contending claims of the different editions and readings. The labour and cost that has been incurred, the numberless *fac-similes* of every page and word, so that the explorer should have the various editions before him for his studies, is truly extraordinary. These *fac-similes* have been several times produced, either in perfect *fac-similes* or in ordinary type, and are of great value to the student. In 1871 that spirited Shakespearian Mr. Halliwell issued *fac-similes* of the early quarto plays of Shakespeare, including every known edition of all the plays which were issued in the dramatist's lifetime. " There were forty-eight volumes, small quarto, half morocco. Only thirty-one copies were privately printed ; five or six sets have been destroyed, several broken up, and others locked up in public libraries, so that complete sets are now becoming exceedingly rare." A hundred and sixty pounds was demanded as the price of this collection ! At the present moment a fresh edition is being issued under the direction of the New Shakespeare Society, which will only cost about £10. They are exact *fac-similes*. Unfortunately, a fire at the lithographer's premises has destroyed some of the impressions. There have been repeated *fac-similes* of the folio, notably Mr. Staunton's, but the effect is not pleasant. It is curious that as the new series of quartos is being issued, almost before it is half completed the first issues are disappearing and becoming scarce.

It is in the fascinating drama of " Hamlet," however, that all devotion centres, bibliographically as well as intellectually. It is here that the quartos and folios concentrate all their interest, and the comparison of the seven or eight copies and their variations has exercised the wits of all commentators.

The first " Hamlet" quarto is thus introduced :

"The Tragicall Historie of Hamlet, Prince of Denmarke, by William Shakespeare, as it hath beene divers times acted by his Highnesse Servants in the Citie of London : as also in the two Vniversities of Cambridge and Oxford, and elsewhere. At London, printed for N. L. and John Trundell, 1603."

The second quarto :—"The tragicall historie of Hamlet, Prince of Denmark, by William Shakespeare. Newly imprinted and enlarged to about as much againe as it was, according to the true and perfect coppie. At London, printed by I. R. for N. L., and are to be sold at his shoppe under Saint Dunstan's Church in Fleet Street, 1604."

The third edition appeared in 1605, and is from the same "types and formes."

Next followed :—"Shakespeare (William) Tragedy of Hamlet Prince of Denmarke, newly imprinted and inlarged according to the true and perfect copy lastly printed. Morocco, by Bedford, edges uncut, probably the finest copy known. Printed by W. S. for John Smethwicke, and are to be sold at his shop in Saint Dunstan's Churchyard in Fleet Street, under the Diall. N.D." This undated edition is assigned to the year 1607, on the excellent authority of the Stationers' Registers.

Then came "Shakespeare (William) Tragedy of Hamlet Prince of Denmarke, newly imprinted and enlarged to almost as much againe as it was, according to the true and perfect copy. Morocco, gilt edges, by Bedford. At London, printed for John Smethwicke, and are to be sold at his shoppe in Saint Dunstan's Churchyard in Fleetstreet, under the Diall. 1611." "A perfect genuine copy, with the original fly-leaf. An edition dated 1606 is mentioned in some lists, but no copy is known. The present, of which no copy has appeared for sale for many years, is in all probability the next edition after the preceding article."

It will be seen by comparison of the titles of the two editions that the first was merely from a copy used by the players, and with which the author had nothing to do. The second claims to be "the true and perfect copy."

The singular variations between the first quarto and the second are well known to scholars, and show convincingly how the text was obtained. In the first, the old Polonius is called Corambis; and though there are many speeches in which the subject of the incident is treated in the same fashion, the words are quite different. It seems likely that this copy was, as it were, picked up from hearsay, or from the actors, altered and made effective according to their lights, in default of written copies. It has been suggested, indeed, by Mr. Aldis Wright and Mr. Halliwell, that they were taken from a vulgar stock play on the same subject which is known to have been often acted before Shakespeare took it up. But it is not probable that Shakespeare would have condescended to borrow the literal handling of a passage from such a source.

Every one of these editions of "Hamlet" is of a rarity that seems extraordinary, considering the period and the abundance of other books of the same era. Of the first edition, that of 1603, there are but two copies known. Of that of 1604 there are only three copies : one in the Duke of Devonshire's, one in Mr. Huth's, and one in the Stowe Collection. Of that of 1605 there is only one perfect copy, which is in the Capell Collection. There is another in the British Museum, but it wants the last leaf.

But a curious little romantic adventure attends the first quarto of 1603. Down to fifty years ago such a thing was unknown and unsuspected, but in the year 1825 Messrs. Payne and Foss, eminent bibliopolists in Pall Mall, brought the Duke of Devonshire a little volume containing some rare and valuable old plays by Green and others, dated before the year 1600, and among them, *mirabile dictu*, nestled this precious little quarto "Hamlet" of 1603. True, the last leaf was gone, and no one knew, or was likely to know, how the piece ended. For £100 it became the Duke's property, and was added to his "Kemble Plays" at his house in Piccadilly. The Duke immediately ordered a reprint to be made, in which, as Mr. Collier declared, for a wonder, he could only find two letters and one "stop" wrong. Thus, with the most argus-eyed and vigilant corrector, blunders will escape notice.

The noble amateur might be justly proud of his "unique," displayed, no doubt, with a pardonable elation, to the curious. Others might have their folios in better or worse condition, but the single "Hamlet," species and genus together, put to shame the National Library. Mr. Halliwell Philipps applied for leave to *fac-simile* it for his grand folio subscription "Shakespeare;" but this was refused, possibly under the Collier influence, which had then the ducal ear. But however that might be, Nemesis came speedily. The Duke was to enjoy his superiority but thirty years in all. It came to pass that in 1855 an English student went to study at Trinity College, Dublin, bringing with him a few old pamphlets as a "memento" of his old home. He took some of them to a Dublin bookseller living in Grafton Street, named Rooney. Rooney, it was said, "gave a shilling for the lot"—

such is rumour, for he does not directly tell us what he gave. On looking over his purchase, he saw there was a copy of " Hamlet," and he tells us that seeing there a character called Corambis, and not Polonius, he knew at once it was the same edition as the Duke's unique. Unfortunately, the first leaf was missing— the title, in short. Now this, no doubt, prompted the first step taken by Rooney, which was the sensible one of applying to the Duke himself, owner of the precious unique. The Rooney last leaf would have supplied the want in his copy ; he might have destroyed or pre- served the rest, and he would remain the owner of the play now made perfect. But he, unluckily, took no notice of the communication, which he no doubt for the rest of his life bitterly regretted. The next step was to apply to the eminent Shakespearian Mr. Halli- well, who at first doubted, but was convinced, we are told, by some quoted readings, though, considering there was a reprint, this was no proof. He then offered fifty guineas, but a hundred was asked, which " could be got from the Museum." Mr. Halliwell de- clined to make any advance, adding in an injudicious spirit, " that he might whistle " for his hundred from the Museum ; on which Rooney repaired to London, bringing with him the treasure. He saw the officers of the Museum, who treated him, he says, *de haut en bas,* sneering at its " cut-down " look, finally tell- ing him if he liked to leave it for some indefinite time they would see about it. This he declined. Again he offered it to Mr. Halliwell, who declined to go beyond the fifty pounds. Taking it to Mr. Boone, a well-known bookseller, he sold it to him for £70, and Mr. Boone promptly resold it to Mr. Halliwell for £160 ! This *sibylline* system is more common than is supposed in book-buying, what is too dear when the book is cheap, becoming absolutely cheap when the price is raised later on.*

It may be conceived from this little adventure what a craze there must be for securing these precious little volumes, which are really put tenderly in cases and cabinets like jewels. We take one of these little dainties in our hands, a pretty little tract of some fifty or a hundred leaves. Any editions of " Romeo and Juliet," " Much Ado," &c., late or early, fetched a goodly sum ; but the first, of which only two or three existing copies can be counted up, would be bid for in hundreds of pourds. Here again has been discovery, and increase of price by " leaps and bounds."

Dodd the actor, so graphically portrayed by Charles Lamb, had the actor's taste for gathering up old plays. " Dodd," he says, " was a man of reading, and left at his death a choice collection of old English literature," of course promptly submitted to " the hammer." He had " picked up " his plays on the stalls, probably at a few shillings a piece, and there is an astonishing contrast between the prices at his sale and at that of Mr. George Daniel in 1864. His " Midsummer Night's Dream " of 1606 brought £1, 18s. ; " Henry V." (1622), £3, 8s. ; "Richard III." (1621),£1, 13s. ; " Merchant of Venice " (1600), £3, 5s. ; " King Lear" (1608),£5, 2s.

---

* Apropos of lost leaves, it may be mentioned that a happy piece of luck once attended two eminent collectors in " making up " their defective copies. The Duke of Devonshire and Earl Spencer each possessed a copy of the grand and rare Aldine Homer, each of which, alas ! was imperfect. Fortunately a third copy, not perfect either, came into the market. The Duke and Earl joined purses, and bought it between them, each repairing their defects from its pages, and each fortunately finding the leaves he lacked. The first volume of Lord Spencer's copy is regarded with a pathetic bibliomaniacal interest, it being the last that Roger Payne bound, or rather, death surprised him in the act.

6d. ; " Romeo and Juliet" (1599), £8, 15s. ; " Troilus and Cressida" (1611), £4, 10s., and that of 1578, £7, 10s. ; while the precious " Gammer Gurton's Needle " (1575), one of the earliest and rarest of plays set by Shakespeare, but three guineas.

With these lordly prices let us now compare a well-known author's collection, sold in 1857, and the titles of the plays shall be given at length, as a pleasant contribution to the restoration of Shakespeare.*

Thus here we read of : " A pleasant conceited Historie called the Taming of a Shrew, as it was sundry times acted by the Right Honourable the Earl of Pembrooke his servants. Printed at London by Peter Short, and are to be sold by Cuthbert Budlie. 1594. This copy differs from later editions in the same fashion that the first ' Hamlet ' differs from its successors. The names of the characters being changed, &c." A curious bit of information from a catalogue. This rarity sold for £21.

"Shakespeare (William) History of Henrie the Fourth, with the battell at Shrewsburie between the King and Lord Henry Percy, surnamed Henry Hotspur of the North, with the humorous conceits of Sir John Falstaffe, newly corrected by W. Shakespeare. Second edition, fine copy, extremely rare, a few leaves inlaid, morocco

---

* Those who are accustomed to the modern editions of Shakespeare can hardly conceive how much that is *decorative* has been added. Turning to our early folios and quartos, we are surprised to find not a word about scenic locality, all being left " general " by the author, to be indicated in a broad way by the words and action of the scene itself. This much is surely gained by comparing the early editions ; for it shows us that was all indifferent to the great mind, and he by anticipation rebuked the late authors of sumptuous revivals. There is no doubt, too, that for the reader the quaint, pedantic setting out of the title would have a more old-fashioned charm than the ordinary modern abridged one.

by Bedford. At London, printed by S. S. for Andrew Wise, dwelling in Paules Churchyard at the signe of the Angell, 1599. ' The present,' says the owner, ' is probably the finest copy known of one of the most intrinsically valuable of all the early quartos. My other copy, which is *in most wretched condition*, cost me £26, 5s., so largely have these rarities risen in value. Amongst many other localities that have been searched, it may be interesting to some to know that, recollecting the occupation of Flushing by the English in the time of Shakespeare, early editions might have been carried thither, especially as English plays were performed there, I was at the expense of sending an intelligent agent through Zealand, unfortunately without any useful results. In fact, bearing in mind the expenses of searches of this kind, and the necessity of buying duplicates for the sake of securing others, I may safely say no Shakesperian quarto ever came into my hands at a reasonable rate.'" This is a melancholy confession. The copy brought £75.

" Shakespeare (William) Tragedie of King Richard the Second, as it hath been publikely acted by the Right Honourable the Lord Chamberlaine his Servantes, by William Shakespeare, a fine genuine copy. Printed by W. W. for Mathew Law, 1608. This edition is of the greatest curiosity and rarity, and must not be confused with the more common one of the same year, ' with new Additions of the Parliament Sceane.' It is, indeed, so scarce that Mr. Collier, in his edition of ' Shakespeare,' vol. iv. p. 105, describes the Duke of Devonshire's copy as unique." This brought £30.

" Shakespeare (William) First and Second Part of the troublesome Raigne of John King of England." This was sold for £17, 10s.

" Shakespeare (William) Most Excellent and Lamen-

2 O

table Tragedie of Romeo and Juliet, as it hath been sundry times publikely Acted by the Kings Majesties Servants at the Globe. Very fine copy, edges entirely uncut, morocco by Bedford, 1637. This, and another sold at the last sale, are believed to be the only *entirely uncut* copies of this edition known to exist." Uncut or not, it fetched only £5, 15s. 6d.

But now begins a crescendo in prices.

" Shakespeare (William) True Chronicle History of the Life and Death of King Lear, and his three Daughters, with the unfortunate Life of Edgar, sonne and heire to the Earle of Glocester, and his sullen and assumed humor of Tom of Bedlam, as it was plaid before the Kings Majesty at Whitehall uppon S. Stephens night in Christmas Hollidaies by his Majesties Servants playing usually at the Globe on the Banck-side. Good copy, morocco, gilt edges, by Bedford, Printed for Nathaniel Butler, 1608. The copy of this edition sold by us last year realised £22, 10s." This year it brought £20.

" Shakespeare (William) True Tragedie of Richarde Duke of Yorke, and the death of good King Henrie the sixt. The first edition, of which only one copy is known, produced £131 at Chalmer's sale. The present is the second edition, and is also of the greatest rarity when, like this copy, in an absolutely perfect state." On this occasion it brought £63.

" Shakespeare (W.) Much Adoe about Nothing, as it hath been sundrie Times publikely Acted by the right honourable the Lord Chamberlaine his Servants. Written by William Shakespeare. First edition, extremely rare, fine copy, morocco by Bedford. London, Printed by V. S. for Andrew Wise and William Aspley, 1600." £65.

" Shakespeare (William) Second Part of Henrie the

Fourth, continuing to his death, and coronation of Henrie the Fift, with the Humours of Sir John Falstaffe and swaggering Pistoll, as it hath been sundrie times publikely acted by the right honourable the Lord Chamberlaine his Servants, written by William Shakespeare. First edition, a perfect genuine uncastrated copy. Printed by V. S. for Andrew Wise, 1600. It is scarcely possible to overrate the curiosity and importance of this edition, which is almost the rarest of first editions of Shakespeare, for to the best of our knowledge, only one other copy, viz. that which sold at Heber's sale, ii. 5460, for the then liberal sum of £40, is the only other copy that has hitherto been submitted to public competition. It is almost the only first edition wanting in the Capell Collection. This edition must not be confused with the spurious one, which contains two scenes less, but has the same date, title, and imprint ; for whereas Heber's copy of the present one fetched £40, the other edition at the same sale sold for only £2, 10s. Long notes are carefully avoided in this catalogue, but it can scarcely be thought irrelevant to observe that the present is the rarest of any of Shakespeare's genuine plays that have occurred for sale during the last twenty years. ' Nothing,' says a MS. note, ' would induce me to part with it, had I not a copy largely made up with excellent *fac-simile*, which, though of slight comparative pecuniary value, is as useful to me for the purposes of collation.' " This brought £100.

"Shakespeare (William) True Chronicle History of the Life and Death of King Lear and his three Daughters, with the unfortunate Life of Edgar, sonne and heire to the Earle of Glocester, and his sullen assumed Humour of Tom of Bedlam, fine copy, printed by Jane Bell, 1655. The rarest of the latest quartos.

With the exception of a copy sold by us last year for £10, 10s., we do not trace another for many years. Lowndes notices only one copy." It fetched £11.

These prices are extraordinary enough, but it was at the Daniel sale in 1864 that the astonishing value of rare exemplars of these little tracts was revealed. The well-skilled owner had secured about a score of the very earliest of these Shakespeare plays, and these twenty little pamphlets—for they did not rise to greater dignity of shape—fetched about £3500! The play of "Richard II." was sold for £341, 5s.; another copy for £108, 3s.; "Richard III." for £351, 15s.; "Love's Labour Lost," £346, 10s.; "Henry IV.," £115, 10s.; "Romeo and Juliet," £52, 10s.; "Henry V.," £231; "Merchant of Venice," £99, 15s.; "Much Ado about Nothing," £267, 15s.; "Midsummer Night's Dream," £241, 10s.; "Merrie Wives," £346, 10s.; "King Lear," £29, 8s.; "Pericles," £84; "Troilus and Cressida," £114, 9s.; "Hamlet" (1611), £28, 7s.; and "Othello" for £155. These seem enormous prices, and are perhaps owing to the *furore* of the sale. But at the Corser sale in 1868, where about a score of these little quartos were sold, prices went so low as £2, £7, £10, and £26; while a copy of the precious "Troilus," which at the Daniel sale brought £114, 9s., here fetched only £37, but then "*the headlines were cut off a few leaves.*"

The little volumes of the Poems, Sonnets, "Venus and Adonis," "Rape of Lucrece," are equally precious. Mr. Quaritch shall usher in the "Poems: written by Wil. Shake-speare. Gent. sm. 8vo. (12mo), with the rare portrait by W. Marshall, fine copy in brown morocco super extra, gilt edges, the sides covered with gold tooling, after an old English pattern, by F. Bedford. T. Cotes, 1640. Very rare. G. Daniel's

copy sold for £44. I have since sold a defective one
for £36 ; but these prices are only a slight indication
of the tendency of the market. Good copies will in
the future continue to rise in value." This was priced
at £70.

Next for " The Rape of Lvcrece, by Mr. William
Shakespeare. Newly reuised, 12mo, blue morocco
extra, gilt edges. I. B. for Roger Iackson, 1624.
Very rare ; only one other copy has occurred for sale
during a great many years. There is none in the
Huth Collection, and there was none sold at Sir
William Tite's sale." For this £42 was the price.

But this is not the first edition, which is dated 1594.
Of this rare little tome it is said that only five perfect
copies are known, of which two are in the Bodleian
Library. Mr. Combe, we are told, could boast a
copy, but " it wanted the last leaf." The fly in the
ointment ! The fifth copy of the little book, " a fine
and perfect copy, extraordinarily rare," was sold by
auction at Baron Bolland's sale in 1840. This amateur, it seems, secured it in a rather odd way. Dibdin
rummaging other books in the Canon's Library at
Lincoln, came upon a little bundle of tracts, which he
says he hoped to tempt them to let him have for £80.
But they refused him. Later, dining with Baron
Bolland, his host showed him in triumph the bundle,
which he had secured for the very sum. A single
tract proved to be this " Rape of Lucrece," which at
the Baron's sale brought one hundred guineas. The
" Venus and Adonis " is another precious little volume
almost *introuvable*. Baron Bolland died happy in
possession of a copy, which at his sale was purchased
by Mr. Bright for £91 ; at Bright's sale, Daniel became the purchaser for £91, 10s. ; while at his sale
it brought three hundred guineas ! Last come the

"Sonnets." The Daniel copy belonged originally to Narcissus Luttrell, who paid one shilling for it ; it afterwards passed to George Steevens, and at Daniel's sale was sold for £215 ! This little book has been often reprinted line for line and in imitation of the original.

Some years ago a copy with the imprint "G. Eld, 1609," was sold by auction, and the following interesting account was added :—" The present fine and perfect copy of the Sonnets is in its *genuine original state, not made up in any way,* but is precisely in the condition in which it was found in a volume of tracts bound up about the year 1725. The original binder cut the top margins too close, and some of the headlines are cut into the print ; but although the opportunity presented itself of remedying this defect by means of another copy, *it was thought that the extreme firmness and genuineness of the state of the leaves throughout, and their sound condition, amply compensated for it,* and that it was more desirable in its original state." We can imagine the bibliophile's distraction at this crisis. The "top margins cut too close" and the headlines "cut into the print" were terrible things, and prompted the intrusion of the leaves of the supplementary copy. But then there was compensation in the "extreme firmness and genuineness" of the maimed leaves. They had "sound condition," at least, and everything, after all, is "more desirable in its original state."

This question of copies of folio and quarto editions is not so idle or barren as might be supposed, and bears in a highly important way on the poet's share in the work. Thus one of the first interesting points to ascertain is how many plays were published before Shakespeare's death, which took place in 1616. There were some fourteen that thus appeared, and it might be assumed that so many could not have been issued in succession without his knowledge and approbation. Yet this presumption wholly fails us, as we find several editions of a particular play differing in an extraordinary degree. One speculation might be that the author did not publish his pieces, but tolerated their being published, and that all he was concerned for was their being acted or published on the stage. This is shown particularly in the discrepancies between the quarto editions of "Hamlet;" and their variations, though making it a perplexing and almost hopeless task to search out the poet's mind, still add a never-failing piquancy to the pursuit, and stimulate the editorial hound. How few know that in the first folio of "Much Ado about Nothing" a scene in the fourth act is headed, "Enter Leonato and *Jacke Wilson*," this being the name of the actor, which had slipped in in place of the character. More curious still is it to find another lapse in the same play, in Dogberry's well-known scene with the watch, where nearly all his speeches to the end are headed "Kemp," being the name of the actor who played the part. Still more singular—a unique instance too—this slip is found repeated in the three successive folios, and, which is even more singular, in Rowe's edition also.*

* Were we to select a passage which would illustrate the difficulties of fixing a "canon" for Shakespeare, it would be the perplexing and much-tortured passage in the part of Henry V., where Dame Quickly describes the last moments of Falstaff, "*And 'a babbled of green fields.*" These, as is well known, are the words of Theobald, the second commentator, but they are universally accepted and even quoted as Shakespeare's, or as the nearest that could be got to Shakespeare. The original reading was the despair of all: "His nose was as sharp as a pen, *and a table of greenfields.*" The objection to Theobald's view is that in the previous sentences had been described all that Falstaff *did*, signs

These thin, not inelegant little quarto plays, the shape in which the earliest plays were published, are inviting enough from their shape and printing, and it is not surprising that their owner should have had each dressed separately in a costly "jacket." A collection of such things has a curious effect ; it is *de rigueur* not to bind them together ; and thus we see some thousand of these thin-leaved veterans ranged on the shelves.   Mr. Halliwell Philipps, the Shakespearian scholar, has, we believe, the finest known collection of the poetical drama, a different thing altogether from a dramatic collection.   The present writer has no indifferent collection, though without pretension ; as he has about a thousand plays printed before the year 1700.   A generation ago an " old play " could be got for " an old song ; " now the really old articles have disappeared, and rarely, if ever, come into the market.   Rare old Elizabethan plays bring now from ten to twenty guineas, and one is not surprised that the owners of these elegant little tracts should be inclined to lay out a couple of guineas more in clothing them in citron-coloured or olive morocco.   A well-known actor who died a few years ago, and had amused himself, as so many actors have done, with collecting old plays, had gathered a large number of rare curious ones.

of death, fumbling with the sheets, playing with flowers, smiling, &c.   Then his *looks* are described, the physical signs of death, his " nose sharp as a pen : " hence the doubtful words are likely to be either an expansion of the metaphor, or further descriptive of his looks.   Pope declares that the words were a stage direction (*a table of Greenfields*), *i.e.*, to be got ready for the actor, which seems specious.   But the point in the passage which has been quoted, is that it is simply impossible, under our present light, to come to any decision whatever.   It is a riddle which we must "give up," and give up for ever.   There is no light, and we see not whence light *can* come.

On his death, his heirs hurriedly took numbers to the nearest old bookseller's, and disposed of them for a few shillings a piece. Many of these I secured, but some of the most precious, such as Marlowe's " Rich Jew of Malta " or " Faustus," which bring now six or eight guineas, were then disposed of for three or four shillings. At this present moment, so scarce are old plays, the collector might search all the leading booksellers' stores without finding a score. Yet two or three years ago there was scarcely an auction without its department of " old plays." It is melancholy, too, to note the waste of money, the sums expended on the mere binding of these treasures, some thin attenuated little tract being enveloped, as it were, in a rich *roquelaire* or mantle of morocco and gold. It is often ludicrous to see some ill-bred " mangy tract " of, say, ten leaves, " ill-kept, ill-fed, and as bad as bad can be," eked out with many blank pages of paper to add to the thickness, and the whole bound sumptuously in green morocco, joints, and " blind tooling," or otherwise, by Bedford, Charles, Lewis, or Rivière, and put into a cabinet under glass—too precious to be read, but to be shown to friends as a triumph of " bibliopegistic skill." Alas ! at the sale the binding will count for little or nothing in the price fetched, though the cost will have been a couple of guineas or more.

The English have certainly not been slack to do honour to their great poet, and contribute all that print and illustration are capable of. Of either Racine, Molière, La Fontaine, in France there are few " editions of luxury." Cervantes owes his finest edition to an Englishman. Of Dante and Ariosto there are one or two pretentious editions. Goethe and Schiller can boast the same. But Shakespeare, during the course of two hundred and fifty years, has been illustrated in a fashion so costly and abundant as to do honour to the enterprise and idolatry of his countrymen.   The abundance of fine editions on which the publishers' capital has been lavishly expended in fine paper, print, rich illustrations, and editorial work, must be enormous.   The present book-fancier has nearly all these fine testimonials on his shelves, and will now, an' the reader list, take them down, one by one, and display them.   For the "general reader"—one who, often, is *not* general in his reading at all—is like enough never to have seen these things.

It seems strange that from the year 1685 to 1711, a period of nearly forty years, no edition of Shakespeare was called for.   The old folios, well thumbed and worn, lay about the libraries of country-houses or on the recessed windows.   James and William, and Anne and George, kings and queen, came and passed away.   The glory of being the first editor—the first to issue Shakespeare in convenient size, with a set of handsome plates, one to every play—was Rowe the poet, whose work has been styled the fifth and sixth editions.   These are grown scarce and dear.   One may congratulate oneself now if he secures a maimed, "cropped" edition, such as mine is.   Such was the favourite one of Charles Lamb.

The four great folios were issued within a period of sixty years—and it is a thing of mark, and unique, that so many editions should have been issued in that size.   It is curious that the third should not match with its fellows, being an inch or thereabouts taller and wider.   In each of these the Droeshout plate does duty, but touched up, cut, and shaped to fit the desires of the publishers.   So desirable is this small, old, poor, and stiff effigy, and so invariably wanting in all saleable copies that turn up, that ten guineas and more has often been given for an impression. This invariable want, like the "crumb flakes" between the leaves, is evidence of popularity, for the portraits in the corresponding folios of Ben Jonson, and Beaumont and Fletcher, and Davenant are usually found in their place.

It is remarkable that from this time it seemed *de rigueur* to issue Shakespeare with an abundance of illustrations : as though the poet was so suggestive and dramatic as to enforce this mode of setting out his beauties. Next followed Theobald ; and here is on the book-fancier's shelves a beautiful tempting copy, eight volumes bound in bright crimson morocco and gold, with quaint plates by Gravelot, animated, but very general. The editions of Theobald, large and small, were to be very numerous and spread over the century. There must have been seven or eight, and the editor made handsomely off his work, and was probably the only editor who did make profit thereby.

But now with becoming courtesy let us introduce the stately, solemn quartos, a massive avoirdupois business, as Mr. Carlyle might say. Those six ponderous fellows in crimson morocco, with great golden stars and thick board-like paper, large, bright, and open type, these "grand old men" are Mr. Alexander Pope's work, and expansive reading enough. It may be noted *en passant* that there is a little discomfort in reading from these large-type works. The eye does not seem to take in enough at a time : a couple of lines will detain it. This may seem *mesquinerie*, but it holds. The book-fancier recalls a pleasant remark of the late Mr. Dickens when showing him one of the placid black letters on a yellow ground, stretching to eight or ten feet in length, and which was

stretched out on the floor.   " W——," he said, " has
to go down on his knees to correct the proofs."
Pope's was succeeded by yet another fine set of
quarto "armfulls"—Sir Thomas Hanmer's, issued by
the *literati* of the University of Oxford, and which
was also adorned with large etchings by Gravelot, then
high in favour as an illustrator.   But his dainty
figures, bosquets, gardens, are all of Versailles, and are
in the school of Lancret and Boucher.   Nothing more
amusingly un-English or un-Shakespearian could be
conceived than those smirking and elegant ladies and
gentlemen in the cocked hats and "sack backs" of
Marly and Versailles performing their graceful antics.
It is strange to think how cheerfully this mode of
interpretation could be accepted by the public, though
it seems almost intelligible when we had nearly at the
same time the spectacle of Garrick playing " Othello "
in a general officer's scarlet, and "Macbeth" in a
court dress.

Anticipating a little, we come to another magnificent series of quartos—Alderman Boydell's monumental "Shakespeare," perhaps the finest and most
costly enterprise of the kind ever undertaken.   His
system was to give commissions to all the leading painters, including Sir Joshua Reynolds, at great
prices, for subjects from the plays.   These were engraved by the leading engravers of the day, and in
two sizes ; the first "atlas folio," a splendid volume
of large engravings, that sell now for about £20.   The
next size was of a large and spacious quarto to suit
the plays, printed in the finest style.   This edition is
difficult to procure perfect, the contemporary purchaser
generally finding a plate or two wanting.   The reason
is that the plays were issued in parts, with the result
that a stray plate is taken out, or lost, stolen, or

strayed, with all loose prints a likely fate. "Grand Old Samuel," when issuing his edition in 1762, a disagreeable, calf-bound thing, cumbering the second-hand booksellers' shelves, little reckoned that it would one day come to such glory.

Yet another grand quarto set is on the book-fancier's shelves, "Heath's", full of fine engravings by Smirke, then in fashion, and others ; beautiful as regards print and paper—highly "desirable" in every way. Coming to later days, there are the two large "atlas quartos," "Virtue's edition" of our time. These were proprietors of the *Art Journal*, and when they had issued innumerable plates engraved in line, after pictures by painters on Shakespearian subjects, they were duly collected, "taken off" on large paper, and put in at the proper places. Of course, there is a "hotch-potch" air about the whole from the different sizes and thicknesses, no single plate being originally intended for this function.

The last important venture on this great and daring scale was that of Mr. Halliwell Philipps, carried out literally regardless of expense,—sixteen solid folio volumes represent this labour of Hercules, the editor's design being to collect "all that was knowable" of Shakespeare. It was issued by subscription in sixteen grand folios. It was issued at the price of sixty-five guineas the set—a great price for England—and only a hundred and fifty copies, it was engaged, were to be printed, and there was set out in the proposals a signed promise of the printer, who solemnly contracted not to print a single copy more, and even to return every one of the wasted or soiled sheets.*

---

* It may be mentioned in this connection, that the neglect of this last point once led to a very serious embarrassment and litigation, connected with the early happy years of the Queen and

The amount of money represented by the 150 subscriptions was over £10,000. Mr. Halliwell proceeded manfully with his work, bringing out volume after volume until the whole was completed. Though stored with illustrations of all kinds—a folio is devoted to a full "life"—it is by no means an artistic work, neither in printing, illustration, arrangement, or shape. The text is quite overpowered in the elaborate and learned notes. For mere reading it is an uncomfortable book—" heartless " Lamb would call it : more for the antiquaries. Now, however, it is difficult to procure, and sells at about the original price.

One of the most wonderful Shakespearian monuments is now in progress, under the auspices of an American gentleman, Mr. Furniss, whose idea is to issue an edition of Shakespeare that shall contain almost everything that has been written on each passage, or that can throw light on the history, acting, or interpretation of the plays. It may be conceived that this is a scheme that requires enormous room, and must, if ever completed, fill fifty or sixty thick volumes. It is a " variorum " edition on the largest scale. The editor is said to possess the finest collection of Shakespeare's known in the States, while his editions comprise everything in all languages. His four folios cost him £500. He exhibits the poet's glove—a doubtful relic—among his treasures. Another American has happily illustrated the extremest extent of the Shakespeare craze by writing a pamphlet in

Prince Consort. The royal pair used to amuse themselves etching plates, and a number of the trial or " waste " copies thrown aside as useless were purchased by a man in Windsor, who offered them for sale and exhibited them in his windows. This led to some painful law proceedings, the Queen wishing to recover her property and also to crush libellous pamphleteering, now deservedly forgotten.

1869, in which he spells the name Shakespeare in four thousand different ways !

Another editor, Charles Knight, engaged one of the most sympathetic of artists, William Harvey, who was full of fancy and poetry.   It is impossible now to look at one of his designs without feeling a sense of being elevated above mere prose, while the illustrators of our day seem to draw us down far below the level of the authors they illustrate into the dull actualities of daily life.   Now there is no suggestion ; everything is *literal*, the artist usually drawing from some members of his family.   Harvey was at his best in this congenial office, and presents us his refined groupings, graceful figures, and thoughtful faces.   There are scenes from town and country, and a number of charming *vignettes* and *culs-de-lampe*.   All these adornments are disposed with singular grace to set off the page. The printing is of a tone and size that is not obtrusive, but makes part of the design, as it were, while the paper is fine and delicate.   It is only when we contrast this edition with the coarse ones that followed, printed anyhow and every how, on thick paper from worn blocks, that we seem to be looking at two different works.   All honour to the amiable, accomplished, and tasteful Charles Knight.

Two other English artists have ventured to illustrate Shakespeare, viz., Kenny Meadows and Sir John Gilbert.   The first is an almost ludicrous performance, from the extraordinarily unintentional grotesquerie which always intruded into this artist's drawings, and made them recognisable at once.   All his characters, the women notably, seem Londoners of the suburbs, of the pattern described by Albert Smith.   Sir John Gilbert's illustrations were supplied for the edition of a chess-player editor—Howard

Staunton. This accomplished colourist imparted a certain flowing grace and richness of effect to his figures and costumes, always of a *flamboyant* sort. But there is no idea conveyed; it is all historical and conventional. It would indeed be a most interesting speculation to consider how, and on what principle, should Shakespeare be illustrated. The answer would seem to be—the principle on which he should be acted. It is thought now, and surely erroneously, that rich glowing dresses, &c., nay, the ingeniously devising of newer pomps and shows, out of some fanciful hint let drop by the bard, must be the true mode. But this makes the poetry earthier and yet earthier. Treatment in the abstract —the central figures standing out—scenery accessories—"supers" all indistinct and far off, like shadowy figures on a tapestry—such would be the note. So with illustrations; central figures full of thought, mind, beautiful in form, but with little regard to dress and show.

It was on this principle that a spirited publisher, Bell—on many a stall we find "Bell's British Poets," or Bell's British something else—brought out his "Bell's Theatre," and " Bell's Shakespeare." The " Theatre," in over fifty pocket volumes, is a work such as we cannot conceive of now—a really *pretty* series, each volume containing some four elegant copperplates, with figures of famous actors and actresses in character; excellent likenesses on the whole, the scene spirited, and the whole engraved within an oval frame. The " Shakespeare" in twenty volumes, but on large paper, the plates, &c., on fine paper, is a truly handsome work, desirable in every way, and worthy of him that buys as of him that sells. A "large paper" " Bell's Theatre " and accompanying Shakespeare, bound, say, in his best chocolate livery by Calverley, such " a set " might be coveted by a fancier, and do honour to his shelves. It is well known that at the time of his death Gustave Doré was engaged on what he hoped should be his most signal achievement—Shakespeare's plays illustrated throughout on the scale of his Bible. He had made, it is said, some progress in the work. But it seems certain the result would have been failure. No Frenchman seems to understand Shakespeare, and we should, to a certainty, have had put before us a series of melodramatic, if not violent scenes, conceived in the Porte St. Martin spirit. Hamlet, Macbeth, and other heroes would have been shown as Frenchmen, just as like views of London by the same artist are unrecognisable, and seem bits of Paris.

There are other illustrated Shakespeares of less pretension, but marked by much artistic merit. Such are the small editions of Whittingham and Tilt, full of spirited and expressive little woodcuts ; an edition issued by Scholey, remarkable for a curious series of woodcuts in a free and open style ; and a little known edition, with some graceful plates by Stothard and others of his school. These are in that refined and delicately finished if not sentimental manner, which is at least in a spirit of respect suited to the great poet. Of minor editions there is almost no end. In short, the lavish extent to which the great master has been illustrated may be conceived from a startling and daring act of Grangerism. A Mr. Wilson in 1824 attracted attention by having devoted a portion of his life to the illustration of Shakespeare. He had set himself diligently to the work of stripping and spoliating every book of plates that were on the subject, ruthlessly cutting out every plate from each illustrated edition, and incorporating them into his own, with a thousand processes of "insetting," "laying down ;" the result of which promiscuous slaughter was a collection of many thousands, which was thought so important that either he or another foolish person printed a list of the prints, "with a view," said the preface to the volume, "to furnish the collector with a catalogue from which he may select the *more attainable materials* for the *illustration* of our great bard," *i.e.*, cut out and paste down every suitable print, maim and maul every Shakespearian volume.

But a more elaborate tribute to Shakespeare is preserved in the library at Althorp. Lady Lucan, mother of the bibliophilist Lord Spencer, and Dr. Johnson's friend, devoted herself from the fiftieth to her sixty-sixth year to the duty of illustrating the historical plays with pencil and brush. With laborious care she copied portraits, arms, devices, illuminations, scenes representing towns and palaces, the result being five magnificent and richly decorated volumes, Boydell's edition being selected as the foundation to work on. These sumptuous tomes were "clothed" in green velvet with silver gilt edges.

There are actually two wholly Shakespearian libraries existing ; one in England at Birmingham, the other in America, known as "the Barton," each devoted to the collection of editions of Shakespeare, books on Shakespeare, or books that deal indirectly with Shakespeare. A vast number of volumes are here collected ; in each some thousand works.

§ L'Envoi.

F the courteous and sympathetic reader shall have attended me so far, he may have enjoyed a tranquil stroll through the prim, quaintly laid-out gardens and agreeable *plaisaunces*, where all the old conceits, trimmed yews, &c., of letters and bibliomaniac lore live and flourish. So do we read in the old dramatist—

> " That place that does contain
> My books, the best companions, is to me
> A glorious court, where hourly I converse
> With the old sages and philosophers."

Or, as another enthusiast hath it, "A man loveth his books as a lover loves the portrait of his mistress ; and, like the lover, he loves to adorn that which he loves. He scrupulously takes care of the precious volume which has filled his heart with keen sensations of delight or sorrow, and clothes it in all the glories of gilded cloths and moroccos. His library is as resplendent with golden laces as the toilet of a favourite ; and by their exterior appearance itself his books are worthy of the regards of consuls, as Virgil wished his own to be." For there may be plenty who love the garden, yet know nothing of the flowers and their botanical names ; and there have been many passionate collectors of fiddles who could not and did not care for playing. That there has ever been this interest in what is a mere book, its covers, associations, owners, &c., has been shown in the foregoing pages, where the abundance of goodwill may be accepted to supply other shortcomings. And so to bibliophile, biblionoste, and bipliopegist, and above all to the "courteous general reader," I commend this little volume.

INDEX.

Printed by BALLANTYNE, HANSON & CO.
Edinburgh and London